Music
in
American
Education
Past
and
Present

Music
in
American
Education
Past
and
Present

A. THEODORE TELLSTROM
Chief
Bureau of Music Education
THE STATE OF NEW YORK

HOLT, RINEHART AND WINSTON, INC.
New York   Chicago   San Francisco   Atlanta   Dallas
Montreal   Toronto   London   Sydney

Cover: *Cycladic figurine of a harp player.* c. 2500 B.C. White marble, 6½ inches high. Andre Emmerich Gallery, Inc., New York.

Affectionately Dedicated
to My Wife
Ann Cauvet Tellstrom
in deepest gratitude
for her help in editing the original manuscript
and for her
encouragement and understanding

Preface

Each generation has needs and aspirations which may differ from those of the one before it. To be relevant, education must reflect the civilization it represents. Over the years various schools of educational philosophy and psychology have defined the purposes and procedures of education. Each legitimate platform, therefore, emerges to cope with the needs and requirements of those who are most affected by it. It can be expected, if music properly belongs to the family of subjects in the curriculum, that the principles and practices of each period must have a profound effect upon the development of music education programs in the United States.

An understanding of what has been done in the past can set the stage for what must still be accomplished in the future. Knowing why things have been done and how they have been accomplished prepares music educators to determine with reason those principles which should be maintained, modified, or cast aside. In this way the structure of future educational policies will more likely reflect the conditions and environment of the times.

Music in American Education: Past and Present can help music educators recognize that in their training *music* is the adjective, *education* the noun. Thus, while thorough preparation in music is essential, this preparation can be of relatively small value if not accompanied by a commensurate amount of study in the field of education.

An important part of the training or growth of the music educator with which this book deals, is the gaining of an ability to recognize the place of innovation. New methods always appear and many have a distinct service to perform. However, to the unpracticed, rather than being recognized as devices which can have a function *within* the larger educational strategy, they often appear as, and are accepted or rejected as, definitive formulas in themselves. As a result the new teacher becomes method-conscious rather than attuned to the relevance of major principles. Nevertheless, music educators and students in teacher training institutions must recognize the need for and cultivate an awareness of new educational policies which are constantly being developed and which have enormous power in the construction of any sound program. Each subject area must play its part in the total effectiveness of the curriculum. The constant evolution of new principles render necessary the frequent modification of procedures and techniques in order that the curriculum achieve its greatest potential. Deviation from established patterns is inevitable, and if supported by knowledge and understanding, new principles and procedures can eventually lead closer and closer to greater teaching effectiveness.

The general plan of this book has been to assign the first chapter of each section to the evolution and establishment of a major educational movement. The following chapter or chapters demonstrate how the principles involved were transposed into action in the area of music education.

It should be pointed out that so far as possible the material used in the succeeding pages was derived from primary sources. Available music textbooks published during the last two centuries for public school use were given careful attention and consideration. Valuable information was sifted from their contents in support of the philosophical and psychological thinking of the respective authors. Many of these texts have disappeared from most library shelves during the course of these many years. The author gratefully acknowledges the courtesies extended him by many of the major publishing houses for making available material contained in their own private libraries.

An expression of gratitude is also due Dr. Jack Lemons of Boston University, School of Fine and Applied Arts, and Dr. Eileen McMillan for reading portions of the manuscript and offering valuable suggestions in the implementation of the general plan of the book. The author also wishes to acknowledge his appreciation to the staff of the Mt. Pleasant Public Library, Pleasantville, New York, for their cooperation in locating many needed books and materials.

A. Theodore Tellstrom

Delmar, New York
January 1971

Contents

PART
II
The Industrial Age

PART
III
Seeds of Progressivism

PART
IV
A Period of
Protest and Reaction

PART
V
The Age of
Experience and Experiment

PART
I

Humanism
and
the
Enlightenment

CHAPTER

1
The
Tradition
of
Humanism

MOST AUTHORITIES AGREE that modern education began with the Renaissance. With a new assertion of the rights of the individual, there were those who questioned the authority of religious institutions over secular matters within the state. Other voices demanded that the ruler must have a greater obligation toward his subjects and that the governed should have a voice in government.

As humanity became free of the restrictive influences of medieval days, man had to prepare himself for the responsibilities of his newly won liberty. During the Renaissance three theories of knowledge competed for supremacy: scholasticism, which embraced theology as well as the philosophy of Aristotle; the beginnings of realism, which looked to science and naturalism; and humanism, based on the knowledge revived from the works of the Greek and Roman masters.

As the focus shifted intellectually from that of a purely

3

religious nature to one that began to recognize *human* nature, scholasticism was forced to step down from its heretofore unchallenged position. Realism, representing as it did a reaction against religion, was unacceptable to the majority of the intellectuals. While many criticized certain apparent abuses within religious institutions, they had no desire to destroy the theological foundations of Western civilization. A philosophy had to be found which would offer new freedom and yet remain within the bounds of Christianity. The most hopeful of those possibilities was humanism.

The Educational Philosophy of Humanism

There was little apparent deviation from the medieval concept of a dualism between the supernatural and the natural worlds. Man himself represented a duality: he was body and soul, matter and spirit. Spirit—the inner man—was of greater importance than the outer man. Under proper conditions the innate God-given talents of the inner man would unfold and develop.

Just as there are important distinctions between the early Renaissance in Italy and the later Renaissance in northern Europe, there are significant differences in the educational theories of humanism that flourished in the two areas. The humanism of Italy stressed the individual; the humanism of northern Europe emphasized man in the social context.

INDIVIDUAL HUMANISM

In the south the humanist movement became apparent as early as the fourteenth century, with a revival in the interest of the Latin classics. The fifteenth century saw an even broader fascination with ancient learning which included Greek as well.

Petrarch and Boccaccio are representative of the educational theories of Italy. They attacked Aristotelian philosophy, inspiring the reading of Greek literature in order to revive the Greek spirit. Fundamental to the whole movement were self-expression, freedom of thought, and creative activity. Education was not vocational but focused upon literature and esthetics. Emphasis was placed upon the development of the individual. Equipped with a full understanding of the knowledge of the past, he was expected to cope with all the problems of the present. It would appear that the humanists expected all intellectual, moral, and esthetic development to come from that one body of study, namely, the classics.

SOCIAL HUMANISM

Northern Europeans went to Italy to acquaint themselves with the new philosophy. Although there were many desirable aspects of the movement, there were two probable reasons why these scholars made no effort to transport the new thought *in toto* to northern Europe.

First: the northern concept of humanism mixed the idea of the new freedom with a reformed theology. As a result, the study of Greek and Latin served the purpose not only of initiating the individual into the good life but also of leading the student to the study of the Bible from the languages into which it had originally been translated. Therefore, it may be inferred that a knowledge of Hebrew was a desirable accomplishment even beyond that of Latin and Greek.

Second: while the purpose of education in Italy was to train the aristocrat, education in northern Europe was directed toward the masses as well. This was to have a profound effect upon the schools in the American colonies. Education in northern Europe is, therefore, particularly relevant to this study.

The Humanist Curriculum of Northern Europe

The education represented by humanism in Italy was originally formulated for the benefit of the upper class. The middle classes of the north, seeking to emulate the aristocrats, endeavored to avail themselves of a similar education, when possible. There were even demands for common schools for those of lower economic status, demands that did not go unheeded.

This is not to say that a completely democratic type of education was conceived. The advance, insofar as universal education was concerned, was marked by the recognition that all men deserved the opportunity to become educated. The kind of education, however, was determined by social class. The upper classes benefited from a curriculum designed as advantageous for them, while the lower classes found another type suitable to their particular needs.

Protestants and Catholics alike insisted that the basic aim of

School for children of the Burgher class in America. From *Historic New York*, The City History Club of New York, n.d.

education be religious. The Protestant reformers, however, maintained that a curriculum could not satisfy its proper purpose without also tending to the needs of the state. Comenius, Calvin, and Martin Luther were in agreement on this view. This, coupled with economic and political factors, resulted in the schools of the north adopting a much broader educational concept. The secular, or common schools offered religious and vocational education, and the schools of the upper classes not only gave instruction in religion but also in the classics of Greece and Rome. Even science found a place in these institutions.

Influenced by the Reformation, the common schools included in their basic curriculum reading, writing, arithmetic, and religion. Most of them offered music, and some offered physical education and history as well.

The focus of the curriculum centered around religion, with the Bible as the major text. The course began with the hornbook, a thin board on which was pasted a copy of the alphabet and the Lord's Prayer. The child then moved to the primer, an ABC book containing the alphabet, with a little verse below each letter. Next, the child passed to the Catechism, the Psalter, and the Bible. Thus, the curriculum for the common people was established.

The place given to music in these new common schools varied according to the stress it received from the religious leaders and in the church services of the different Reformation countries.

Instruction in singing did not have the same degree of educational importance throughout northern Europe.

Upper-class education was marked by a strictly classical curriculum in the secondary schools. There were some who saw possibilities in an emphasis upon the vernacular languages and science, but a classical education was the more universal ideal.

Attitudes of the Reformers Toward Music in Education

Martin Luther's love for music is evident from his writings. He considered the chorale one of the most important pillars of his reform. Through singing, his congregations not only became more receptive to the Gospel but more thoroughly imbued with music as well. No one since Plato appreciated the educational values of music as much as Luther. Musical instruction in his schools probably surpassed anything offered in schools today. Boys were instructed in solmization and in the singing of simple songs. Eventually, they achieved a technique sufficient to perform four- and eight-part choral works. In Luther's school music was compulsory.

About 1524 Johann Walther placed choral melodies in three- to six-voiced polyphonic settings. This excluded congregational singing, which, until then, had been so important. Now choirs were necessary if the hymns were to continue being sung. Not until the latter part of the sixteenth century did the chorale regain a form close to Luther's original idea. At that time Lucas Osiander put the melody in the soprano and composed a chordal accompaniment beneath.

Music found little place in the schools of the countries that embraced the doctrines of Calvinism (Scotland, parts of Switzerland, and Holland). Whether or not music was found in the curriculums of that period, the influence of the Protestant schools was outstanding. Whether Lutheran or Calvinist, they remained the general models of educational institutions in both northern Europe and America.

Humanism in Early American Common Schools

Looking back upon the colonial days of the United States, it is difficult to understand how the humanist influence ever gained a foothold in this country. In a colony made up of a host of different classes, ethnic groups, and religious sects, in a land with no long-established culture, it would seem impossible that any one philosophy could serve as a potent educational force. Nevertheless, the establishment of a strong Christian tradition prepared the way for humanism in America.

In spite of the differences in creed among the many denominations, they all were agreed on the origin and destiny of man and on the Christian conception of human nature and knowledge. Although the Jews maintained their non-Christian faith, they shared the Old Testament, which at that time received particular emphasis in the Christian Church as well.

The powerful religious forces at work in those days made it possible for the humanist influence to appear on the scene very early. According to the educational traditions of Europe and those maintained in America through the clergy, a classical education was essential to the professions. In order to train clergymen, lawyers, and physicians for service in the new land, schools and colleges had to be founded. Since the curriculum had been determined in Europe, it followed that the young aspirants to the professions in this country had to receive instruction in Latin and Greek.

Aside from professional study, another tradition passed from

The Young Rebel, a drawing of a Dame school, *Parley's Magazine*, 1841. Picture Collection, New York Public Library.

14 TOMMY THUMB's

Buzz, Buzz, Buzz.

Coo, Coo, Coo.

Mag,

TOMMY   THUMB's

SONG BOOK,

FOR ALL LITTLE

MASTERS and MISSES,

To be Sung to them by their Nurfes,
until they can fing themfelves.

By NURSE LOVECHILD.

TO WHICH IS ADDED,

A Letter from a Lady on Nurfing.

THE FIRST *WORCESTER* EDITION.

PRINTED at WORCESTER, *Maffachufetts,*
BY ISAIAH THOMAS.
Sold at his BOOKSTORE.   MDCCLXXXVIII.

A 1788 song book. Facsimile reproduction. Frederic G. Melcher, New York, 1956.

Europe to America. A classical education gave status. Americans, desirous of obtaining the position such training bestowed, were anxious to pursue a classical curriculum.

Practically all of those who came to settle in America sought religious freedom and escape from the hardship and persecution subsequent to the Great Schism. It followed, then, that the first schools in America were decidedly a result of Reformation activities. Since personal salvation could come through a knowledge of the Gospels, it was essential that every child should read.

Although the Dutch, Swedes, and Germans brought with them the Lutheran parish school, it was Calvinism which most profoundly affected the early development of education in the United States. The particular educational thinking that came from Scotland was noticeable in America by about 1714. Although it is impossible to point to any distinct pedagogical contribution by this group, its ministers were active in pressing for the establishment of common schools. They also deemed it essential that these institutions be supported by the civil government.

The English Puritans proved to be great contributors to the educational system of this country. Beyond establishing Harvard College, the Puritan Colony, in 1647, made it law that any town of fifty families had to establish and support an elementary school and that every town of a hundred families had to provide a Latin school. New England, through the labors of its Puritan fathers,

The first building of the Boston Latin School as drawn by Ernest W. Watson from contemporary descriptions. *New York Herald Tribune*, January 6, 1935.

became one of the outstanding sections in educational leadership in the country.

Of the many types of schools that were established in the United States, there are three that demand particular attention: the Dame Schools, the District Schools, and the Latin Grammar Schools.

The Dame Schools flourished during the eighteenth century in this country. They were generally presided over by a woman who shared her little knowledge with very young children in a room of her own house. The curriculum included reading, spelling, and the Catechism. Writing and counting were occasionally taught, and in some instances, sewing and knitting.

From the Dame School children were sent to the equivalent of an elementary school. These were referred to by several different names such as neighborhood, district, or even writing schools. While they were somewhat more advanced in nature, the basic curriculum was devoted primarily to spelling, writing, reading, arithmetic, and religion.

The Latin Grammar School, though probably the least practical institution of early colonial days, received strong support. It was considered to be the appropriate institution for those ready for more advanced study. Here students were prepared for college and, hence, for the professions, through instruction in Latin and in elementary Greek. Other subjects were apparently neglected.

The most prominent characteristic of all the early schooling in this country was the dominance of religious instruction. To read the Bible or the Catechism was the primary reason for learning to read. It was probably the basic reason for bothering with schools at all.

Formal Discipline

As a philosophy of education, humanism has often been incorrectly accused of advocating a narrow curriculum and unimaginative teaching methods. This misconception resulted from a movement that may have grown out of humanism after 1500 known as Ciceronianism.

After the humanist principles were well established, educators gradually became so involved with the importance of grammar and rhetoric as to lose their perspective of the classical ideal. The old scholasticism of Aristotle returned in a new guise. This time Cicero was the source, linguistics represented the content, and excessive formalism marked the method. Although *understanding* was recognized as a possible value, memory seems to have been of prime import. While earlier an appeal to the pride and ambition of the pupil was suggested as a means toward motivation, Ciceronianism recalled the older method of corporal punishment. Discipline was harsh and cruel, and methods of teaching became exceedingly formal. The life of the school became completely disassociated from the rest of the world.

Ciceronianism found its way to the American colonies. Included in this movement was the doctrine of formal discipline. This disciplinary concept, which established itself in Harvard about 1742, succeeded in dominating American education well into the nineteenth century.

The doctrine of formal discipline recalled the old principles of faculty psychology. The mind was conceived as consisting of separate, independent, and ready-made faculties, such as memory, judgment, and reason. These were considered as potential powers of the mind, which could be realized only by practice and training. The exercise of one capacity was thought to transfer beneficially to another. Form was infinitely more important than content. As a result, subjects that were by no means practical could be defended by the doctrine of faculty psychology. In this way traditionally prescribed studies held secure positions, and a narrow curriculum generally resulted. Formal drill and memorization became the rule in this country, and the force of authority was strenuously exerted.

According to Burton, school hours were long, and teaching methods wasteful and time-consuming. A child could attend school for years and receive only a start in reading and writing. Discipline in all classes was most severe.

Music Education in Early American Schools

Music in the curriculum of the colonial school fared less well than in Europe. In the Lutheran parochial schools of Pennsylvania and Delaware it is unlikely that music received the emphasis it enjoyed in the Protestant gymnasia and parochial schools of Germany. The middle colonies, where these schools were primarily located, were under church control. The clergymen were usually the teachers, and it may be fair to assume that generally these men were not as well prepared musically as the cantors employed in the educational institutions of Germany.

In the Calvinistic atmosphere of New England, music in the schools was practically unknown. In general, Calvinists distrusted music as a distraction from the sacred texts. Only psalms direct from the Scriptures could be used, and these were sung without accompaniment.

Congregational singing deteriorated toward the end of the seventeenth and early eighteenth centuries. Hardly more than a half-dozen hymn tunes were used for all the psalms. Even these were either half-forgotten or so decorated by the more ambitious singers of the congregation that they were hardly recognizable.

Deaconing, or *lining out*, was instituted at first as a possible means of overcoming the difficulties. This device called for a leader to sing one line of the psalm at a time, with the congregation repeating the line after him. This idea enjoyed a very limited success.

Inaccuracy was apparently only one difficulty that had to be

Drawing of Ludwig Miller teaching at the Old Lutheran Schoolhouse, 1805. From *The American-German Review*, March, 1938.

surmounted; the congregation dragged the psalms to a point impossible to imagine. A Puritan preacher once said, "I myself have twice in one note paused to take breath." Cotton Mather, in 1718, described congregational singing as "an odd noise."

A decision to improve was finally made. If singing was to be given some attention, a way of offering this instruction had to be found. It was the singing school that answered the need; so well did it serve the purpose for which it was designed, that it remained a powerful cultural force in this country for well over a century.

Introduction to the Singing of Psalm Tunes by John Tufts was the first of a long list of psalm collections that flooded the market. The *Fasola* system was used in teaching the classes to read. This method of reading music had been brought to this country from England by the early settlers and preceded the *do-re-mi* method in the United States by many years. This was a four-syllable solmization of the scale—*fa, sol, la, fa, sol, la, mi.* About 1800 the European system was adopted, particularly in the northeast. The older method did not immediately disappear, however.

In the West and in the South, people accepted the traditional fasola system, preferring it to the new method of *do-re-mi.* The singing school became very popular in these areas early in the nineteenth century. As a matter of fact, the *Fasola* underwent an interesting change through the ingenuity of two singing-school teachers. William Smith and William Little, in their book *The Easy Instructor,* introduced the shaped-note system.

All pitches were appropriately represented on the staff except for the fact that *fa* was indicated in the shape of a right-angled triangle, *sol* as a round note, *la* as a square, and *mi* as a diamond shape.

Shaped notes, patent or buckwheat notes, as they were sometimes called, became extremely popular and maintained a strong influence in the South and West through most of the nineteenth century. A further development of the shaped-note system was later devised by Marcus L. Swan. According to his method of notation, there were seven shapes, one for each of the seven notes of the scale.

The Shakers, who had established themselves in flourishing communities from Maine to Kentucky, had still another system of music notation. This method used letters instead of notes. Scale tones were named according to the first seven letters of the alphabet. The pitch of C was indicated by "a," and so on. Time values were represented by the kinds of letters used. For example, roman letters would indicate quarter notes, and italics would represent eighth notes.

As more and more of the people became proficient in singing and in reading music, the choir developed. Lining out, or deaconing, died a natural death.

The singing school became a national institution. Its teachers were not professional but rather self-styled musicians. Among the more famous leaders was William Billings, a tanner by trade. He was not only one of the more capable teachers and composers but was also noted for his introduction of the pitch pipe and cello into New England churches. A carpenter, Oliver Holden, spent his spare time teaching in the singing schools as well as composing hymns, the most famous being "All Hail the Power of Jesus' Name."

The classes of these two men, and of others like them, were organized and directed by the teacher, and generally held in the evening. Because it was a popular belief at the time that some people had a musical ear and others did not, those who attended had reason to believe they had a talent for music. Among the students there was a majority of women. Music was considered chiefly a feminine pursuit. However, since instruction was confined to church music, not for its own sake but to render the Sunday service more meaningful and perfect, men of various ages considered their attendance at singing schools legitimate and defensible. Undoubtedly, young adults were included. Whether or not their interest was musical may be a question for argument. From the writings of the times, it can be derived that the singing school presented opportunities for socializing.

In summary, the singing school had a clearly defined aim: to improve the quality of congregational singing. The teachers were neither skilled musicians nor trained in a culture foreign to their constituents. They were products of the same background. Therefore, instead of endeavoring to develop the taste of their students to the music heard in the drawing rooms of the wealthy, they busied themselves with improving the performance ability of their constituents through the medium of the chorale.

The End of an Era

By 1750 humanism no longer fitted the American scene as it had in the past. There was a tendency to look for educational principles more in keeping with the times. Change was slow to come about, since it was not really until after the War of 1812 that there was any real belief in the stability of the new nation. Only then could educators hope for a serious hearing.

There were other reasons too why education did not progress more rapidly. Until approximately 1820, little education was considered necessary for the masses because the business of the day was carried on in a simple way. As long as a person could read, write, and understand very simple arithmetic, he had a sufficient education according to the conditions and attitudes of the day.

Until 1820 there was little noticeable change in public education in this country from that of the common schools of the eighteenth century. The curriculum reflected more of the thinking of the humanist and Protestant educators of the sixteenth century than of the movements stirring throughout Europe during the next two hundred years. These religious and humanistic aims of education survived strongly in the United States until almost the turn of the nineteenth century. Not until then did the influence of some of the leaders of the European Enlightenment seep into American educational thought as it bore directly upon the public school.

2
The
Advent
of
The Enlightenment

Implications of the Empirical View in Europe

THE EMPIRICAL PHILOSOPHY that began to find its way through Europe, and later to this country, had its beginnings in the new knowledge of the world that became manifest in the sixteenth and seventeenth centuries. The new scientific findings of such men as Nicolaus Copernicus, Johann Kepler, and Galilei Galileo, preciptated a strong reaction against traditional idealistic views. Led by such thinkers as Thomas Hobbes and Pierre Gassendi, a new philosophy of materialism was born which held that all the phenomena of the universe could be explained in terms of mechanical laws. Mind was to be considered as matter in the same way as other elements of the universe.

In spite of the substantial claims to the contrary set forth by science, the traditional view continued its supremacy for some time. Protestants and Catholics alike were agreed on one principle, at least: the dualism of man's nature. According to both churches, the spiritual element of man was by far uppermost in importance, his material body being of only secondary consequence. Man was born with the taint of original sin from the days of Adam and with certain innate talents bequeathed by God. It became the business of education to direct the individual's attention from the material to the spiritual and to help him to unfold that which was God given.

Both religious bodies opposed science on the grounds that it relied entirely upon *sense experience*, limiting knowledge to the physical sphere alone. According to the rationalist view, truth could only be achieved through *reason*, a higher form of knowledge than that provided by everyday experience. However, the churchmen held that even reason must be subordinate to religious faith.

This controversy between science and religion tended to place education in a difficult situation. It would have to choose between rationalism or empiricism. At that time René Descartes offered a temporary compromise. The French philosopher was able to incorporate the two opposing schools of thought in such a way that neither side was necessarily antagonized.

He reasoned that a dualism existed between mind and matter. Defining mind as a substance belonging to the spiritual realm, it could be considered completely free of matter, and, hence assigned to the sphere of theology. Conversely, matter was considered a material substance, subject to certain physical laws. Anything assigned to this category belonged to the realm of science. In spite of Descartes' compromise, however, the empirical view continued to grow in strength.

It was the philosopher Francis Bacon who sowed the seeds of the new education. Attacking the universities as being smothered in scholastic tradition, he pointed the way toward realistic studies. The truth founded on the study of facts was the new desideratum.

The seventeenth century saw the beginning of educational reforms that were to change both the method and substance of teaching. Instruction was gradually founded upon observation. Attempts were made to discover the laws governing the learning process, which paved the way for educational psychology. Men such as John Amos Comenius, Wolfgang von Ratke, and John Milton stood for a broader and more practical curriculum than had heretofore been conceived. They were ahead of their time in their conception of discipline, in the organization of textbooks, and in the demand that knowledge be passed on through the native language rather than through Latin.

John Locke supported the scientific view, which held that human nature was not determined completely at birth, that environment was responsible for much of a person's development. Knowledge reached man through his senses as a result of his encounters with the world outside himself. Locke endeavored to root out the traditional curriculum of the times, recommending such innovations as the use of the English vernacular in the schools, the study of French and Latin through conversation, and the addition to the curriculum of dancing, history, fine arts, geography, and practical arts.

Locke's views struck a blow to the traditional concept that man was born in sin. Locke proposed that the individual was born with a certain potentiality to be realized through experience. This concept brought education nearer to the doctrines of Jean Jacques Rousseau.

This French humanitarian maintained that human nature in and of itself was good, that what made him bad was the effect of the environment and the institutions that surrounded him. Rousseau's philosophy of naturalism attracted considerable attention in eighteenth-century Europe.

The crux of the naturalistic movement was to free society from the artificial life that dominated the upper classes. Rousseau's concept of naturalism as expressed in *Émile*, was a return of man to the state of nature. By advocating the overthrow of civilization in order that a free and simple life could be attained by each individual, Rousseau attacked the family, the Church, society, and the state. However radical some of his theories were, educational reformers were later able to refine them, and give impetus to Rousseau's principle that man must be permitted to follow the natural stages of his development. Each of these stages has very specific characteristics upon which educational methods can be founded.

Of those who strove to put some of Rousseau's ideas into practice, Johann Heinrich Pestalozzi (1746–1827) deserves particular consideration for his contributions to common school education. Greatly influenced by Rousseau's naturalism and Locke's empiricism, and yet not entirely removed from the influence of religion, Pestalozzi developed educational principles for the improvement of education for the common people. His influence upon American public school education in the nineteenth century

Johann Heinrich Pestalozzi. From Johannes Scherr: *Germania, Zwei Jahrtausende deutschen Lebens*. Stuttgart: Spemmann, 1883–1884.

was of great importance. His theories and achievements are dealt with in detail on pages 23 to 33.

The Enlightenment Migrates to America

At the close of the eighteenth century, the United States had barely established its sovereignty as a nation. While politically detached from the continent of Europe after the Revolution, the religious beliefs brought to this country by the early settlers became a cornerstone of American intellectual life. However improbable it was, under such circumstances, for the new nation to accept the elements of the Enlightenment, which was based on secularism and science, the United States eventually turned its attention to the movement and gave it its support.

RELIGION AND THE ENLIGHTENMENT

Many New England Puritans agreed with Petrus Ramus, the great French Protestant thinker, that man was capable of understanding the rational universe by virtue of pure reason. Anglicans, too, were receptive to a somewhat unorthodox view of rationalism, which looked to the Bible as a guide rather than as a set of indisputable laws. By 1740 not only rationalistic theology but also deism won noticeable recognition among the upper classes through books, periodicals, and newspapers and was widely discussed.

Those representing the more highly educated class of the Colonies did not, however, accept rationalism or deism to the point where they might be considered atheistic. It would seem that their position marked a rather comfortable equilibrium between reason, on the one hand, and revelation, on the other.

The greater portion of the population read very little. It is of little wonder, then, that those of moderate-to-poor circumstance were slow to become acquainted with progressive thought. However, as the eighteenth century reached maturity, there were clues to indicate that even the least educated were inclined to permit rationalism and deism a certain headway.

Whatever progress the new thought made, it was checked at first by at least two conditions. First, rationalist and deist thought became associated by many with the upper classes; and since a position of privilege was unpopular with the masses, it hardly behooved those in moderate-to-poor circumstance to emulate views held by men of position. Secondly, the Great Awakening, that period when Protestant evangelists directed their followers through hell-fire and brimstone sermons, tended to implement the more orthodox doctrine of repentance. However, as the Revolution drew near and the masses began to realize how deism and rationalism could serve their purposes in throwing off the yoke of authority of both church and class, the seeds of the Enlightenment began to grow rapidly.

EDUCATION AND THE ENLIGHTENMENT

Schools in America had stubbornly clung to the religious and humanistic philosophies. This placed American educational thought about two hundred years behind that of Europe. However, by the year 1750 the influence of the progressives of the seventeenth century, John Locke, Francis Bacon, and John Amos Comenius, began to seep into the educational thinking of this country.

The Latin Grammar Schools, though well established in New England, were feeling a certain pressure for more practical studies. Beginning, perhaps, with the Grammar School of the City of New York (1732), a broader and more varied curriculum was offered. Latin was retained, but mathematics, geometry, algebra, geography, and bookkeeping also became essential studies. This new type of curriculum developed in the middle colonies became known as the English School.

The New England Academy, an adaptation of Milton's educational ideas, placed great emphasis on the actual preparation for life. All teaching was done in the vernacular; Latin and Greek were continued in the curriculum along with history, mathematics, geography, and natural philosophy.

These American adaptations served both girls and boys and were established to prepare children for the activities of life rather than for college. Until normal schools were founded, these institutions prepared elementary school teachers. After 1821, with the advance of public high schools, the academies turned their attention to college preparation.

Pestalozzianism began to appear in the United States as early as the first decade of the nineteenth century. In connection with this, a few names must be mentioned. In 1805 William McLure visited the orphanage at Paris which was under the direction of Joseph Neef, a Pestalozzian disciple. Through McLure's writings the new principles reached the United States. Perhaps because of McLure, Neef came to America in 1806 and introduced Pestalozzianism in an institution at Philadelphia and, later, in another in Kentucky. In 1823 McLure and Robert Owen attempted to initiate the new principles in New Harmony, Indiana, through the establishment of infant schools. In 1818 the first appropriation was made in Boston for the introduction of primary schools. Such a step suggests that the new philosophy may have reached that city by the second decade of the nineteenth century. Confirmation of this is found in the amount and variety of literature given to the new ideas appearing in the American education journals from 1820–1860. This material not only described the new education but translated the accounts of Daniel Chavannes, Marc Jullien, Victor Cousin, and a number of the German educators. The *American Journal of Education*, edited by William Russell, 1826–1831, and its successor, *The American Annals of Education*, edited by William C. Woodbridge, 1831–1839, were especially active in giving descriptions and personal observations of the Pestalozzian schools in Europe.

Principles of Pestalozzian Thought

There exists no clearly defined exposition of Pestalozzi's educational thought. In comparison with other educational philosophers, he was more concerned with specific principles of teaching than with the development of a complete theory of knowledge. This does not diminish his greatness or render his contributions any less deserving of attention.

By his own confession, Pestalozzi found in Rousseau's *Émile* the inspiration that directed him into the service of mankind through the avenue of education. His *Inquiry into the Course of Nature in the Development of the Human Race* indicated that he was also acquainted with the ideas of Locke and Hobbes.

With such a background it is not surprising to find that he believed the poor deserved to have their lot improved and that it was up to the institutions of government to accept a definite responsibility on their behalf. The surest way of helping man, according to Pestalozzi, was through a system of universal education by which the individual could be taught how to help himself as well as to contribute more effectively to society.

Pestalozzi did not intend that the schools established for the upper classes should be augmented to enroll those of less fortunate circumstance. In fact, he asserted that the educational institutions were so far removed from the experiences of life that the poor probably received a better education at home than did those who attended school.

Instead, he maintained that reform was necessary in order to bring the process of educating more within the realm of life activities. It became the business of education to be practical.

The individual had to be trained according to that station in life which he occupied. In that way he would become prepared to participate in and enjoy whatever services and activities he would most likely find available to him. The education would at first be general; not directed toward particular skills but rather toward citizenship and morality. After the practical would come the theoretical for those interested in special or professional work. How this reformation was to be carried out can be understood through some of his principles of education.

AIMS

Pestalozzi considered education as a preparation for manhood itself rather than for any particular skill. The end could be achieved by the harmonious development of the three major capacities that made up the whole man; namely, the moral, physical, and mental elements or faculties. Of these, Pestalozzi considered morality of first importance.

The Moral Element

To become a useful member of society, a man must be independent. The success of this independence rests in his moral character, according to Pestalozzi, secured by the development of the will through the exercise of his powers of love and faith. The will must be aroused by feelings rather than explanation.

Pestalozzi tried to awaken the moral sense in the souls of the children with whom he dealt, insisting that the child must be moral even before he could be religious. He first endeavored to instill in his wards the right feelings of love toward men, presuming that the individual could hardly offer gratitude and confidence toward an unseen God if he could not first realize such feelings about men.

Accordingly, he expended every effort to make his pupils

conscious of their own moral powers. To accomplish this he appealed to the hearts of his children, rather than force upon them verbal precepts. He felt that this would change the condition of their moral character.

Corroboration of this foremost principle may be found in Pestalozzi's work at Stanz. He had about eighty children of varying backgrounds. Pestalozzi fed them and clothed them. His attention to the children demanded almost around-the-clock duty, but he was convinced that only love could animate his wards and melt their animosity. He placed his own personal health in danger in order to succeed in his purpose. Words could not teach feelings of love, the condition of morality; understanding could.

Pestalozzi considered music a prime contributor in effecting the moral aim in education. It was not the formal study of the subject or the appreciation of concert music that interested him. Rather, it was the singing of national melodies which in themselves recalled memories of the finest hours of history and the richest moments of domestic life. According to Pestalozzi, it was not nationalism that music developed so much as it was the cultivation

Pestalozzi at Stanz. From Ellwood P. Cubberley, *Public Education in the United States*. Boston: Houghton Mifflin, © 1919.

of the right spirit which could override emotions unworthy of men. Supporting his view, Pestalozzi quoted the words of Luther:

> . . . in its solemn and impressive simplicity [music] is one of the most efficient means of elevating and purifying genuine feelings of devotion.[1]

The Physical Element

So that the capacities of the individual might be harmoniously developed, physical education was emphasized. Pestalozzi saw in exercise an effective means not only of safeguarding the health of the body but of correcting certain physical defects. In a letter to Greaves, he indicated that through consultation with physicians he had learned that certain gymnastics had a beneficial result to those suffering from lung disease.

He further indicated that physical education had a value beyond that of gymnastics. Pestalozzi relied upon the senses as the pathways through which the outer world could be transmitted to the mind of man. Exercise would sharpen the senses. He emphasized, again in a letter to Greaves, that exercises in judging distance, the size of objects, the shades of colors, and variations of sound would prove of extreme value educationally.

According to Pestalozzi, gymnastics also served the development of certain more intangible values, such as courage, industry, and a spirit of togetherness among children.

Not only could it promote the normal development of the young, but it might correct defective development, training the muscles as well as the senses, even curing disease in some cases.

The Mental Element

Pestalozzi maintained that, as the conscience was cultivated with a view toward independent action, the intellect had to be trained in order to impose limits on the independence achieved through the moral side of the educational process. Intellectual and moral education were to proceed together. Education was the process by which the individual was to be guided toward a realization of himself and a knowledge of the world about him. Through the acquisition of knowledge, the individual exercised his active powers

---

[1] H. Holman. *Pestalozzi.* London: Longmans, Green & Company, 1908, p. 162.

by the mental effort he had to expend. His capacity to make more accurate judgments pertaining to moral questions was thereby strengthened.

Pestalozzi was not concerned with a narrow vocational education. Rather, he was interested in setting the machinery of the faculties in motion. He had little interest in specific facts or subject matter.

One of his prime principles was that life itself educated. He held that from the moment of birth, instruction began. Nature became the first teacher just as soon as the child's senses were alive to things of the outside world. Where moral education was developed through man's inner nature, intellectual growth was achieved from the impact of the outer world upon man through his senses.

All knowledge of the outer world, according to Pestalozzi, came to man through his senses. This was the starting point of the education of the intellect. An idea was the result of the action and reaction between the mind and the impression. If the idea proved valid, the perception must have been valid. It behooved the educator, then, to train the individual in more and more accurate perception, for only when a percept was complete and mature, could the child know an object in detail. Intellect, to Pestalozzi, implied the power to know; therefore, how to impart knowledge to the individual was of utmost consequence.

PSYCHOLOGY

Out of Rousseau's convictions about the virtues of the natural man had come developmentalism. This psychology endeavored to guide the child in his natural process of growth, to aid him in the unfolding of inherent capacities. This natural growth could be helped or hindered by the psychological methods used in the treatment of the natural capacities. In developmentalism the emphasis was upon the development of the child from within, which was the reverse of the concept which had hitherto been predominant. The early developmentalists, of whom Pestalozzi was one, seemed to sense that the workings of the mind demanded a great deal more explanation than the traditional faculty psychology had offered.

The term *faculty*, however, was frequently mentioned in the writings of Pestalozzi. Dismissing the popular notion of the various capacities of the mind, such as remembering, reasoning, and volition, Pestalozzi dealt with the *whole man*. He considered the entire human organism a compound of three faculties: mind, body, and soul. These areas included every portion of man rather than just those regions of the mind to which the faculty psychologists attended in their educational practices. Only insofar as the exposition of elementary education was concerned would these three parts be treated separately. In life, man had to be considered a unity.

Developmentalism

Pestalozzi seemed to have recognized that life is an evolutionary process and that education must adopt a genetic view. Education could only assist nature in the development of the child. His opinion seems to have anticipated much of the thinking from the mid-nineteenth century onward. A development of this point of view will consider three pertinent topics: the pattern of nature; self-activity; interest.

The Pattern of Nature   Education represented a continual process, with an active mind the only major ingredient. The theory forbade treating one student the same way as another and condemned any condition which sought to extract the same body of material from every individual of any particular classroom.

Influenced as he was by the opinion that the individual unfolded in a way corresponding to that in which the race itself developed, Pestalozzi theorized that knowledge and skill enjoyed a growth through the centuries from the simplest beginnings to the greatest complexity. In seeking the most natural way of educating children, he found that by following the pattern suggested by nature, the best results were obtained.

Pestalozzi wished to psychologize education. He was determined that a system could be so devised that a teacher or parent could perfectly instruct a child whether or not he knew very much about the subject. His purpose was to mechanize instruction according to those principles suggested by nature.

Self-Activity   Pestalozzi was basically concerned with what the individual achieved through his interaction with external stimuli rather than with the memorization of facts. It followed that the principle of self-activity became a vital ingredient in Pestalozzian practice.

According to the Swiss educator, man had an instinct for

activity. This was the gift of nature to the learning process. It was through this desire to react to things that the individual could achieve a knowledge of life. From the standpoint of education, it became clear that facts could not be poured into the child's mind. Rather, the individual could only be assisted as he, through self-activity, strove toward his own growth and development. Knowing and doing were very closely connected, and if one ceased, so would the other.

Interest   According to the more traditional approach, severe discipline became the motivating factor. In opposition to this, Pestalozzi proposed *interest* as the prime stimulant. He was convinced that any child's readiness for action proceeded from a desire sparked by interest. This is not to suggest that Pestalozzi endorsed amusement to the exclusion of effort in the learning process. He firmly believed that lengthy explanation should be abandoned. The child's interest was to be aroused through questions and frequent illustrations. Material was to be presented attractively. From such motivation the mind could be set into motion. Pestalozzi noted "a most remarkable reciprocal action between the interest which the teacher takes and that which he communicates to his pupils."[2]

The Learning Process

Pestalozzi was concerned with the development of each individual according to the laws of nature. However, he did not believe that random influences of nature should be the only teacher. Man had to intercede with some intelligent control. The method with which he proposed to assist nature in the learning process was the *scientific* or *inductive* method. This system had already achieved some renown through the writings of Bacon in his *Novum Organum*.

Pestalozzi referred to this method by a rather free translation of the term *Anschauung*, observation or perception. Anschauung was the basis of all knowledge because it consisted of impressions from the outer world upon the senses. By this means the learner created from his own activities a certain knowledge of life. It was the acknowledgment of this interaction between man and the world that led Pestalozzi to the assumption that life itself educated.

Education had to assist the learning process because this

[2] Lewis Flint Anderson. *Pestalozzi*. New York: McGraw-Hill Book Company, Inc., 1931, p. 203.

interaction could not always be relied upon to offer a desirable educative experience by itself. It became the concern of the educator to arrange experiences that would always provide the best conditions for growth.

The very heart of Pestalozzi's theory of learning rested upon this broad interpretation of *observation*. According to him, man most naturally distinguished an object new to him through a process involving three different stages: "(1) how many and what kinds of object before him; (2) their appearance, form, or outline; (3) their names."[3] The procedure accounted for his frequent allusions to the terms "*number, form* and *language.*" For further clarification of the inductive method, these three elements will be considered individually.

Number   In opposition to the older concepts of education, Pestalozzi maintained that true knowledge could never result from the mere memorization of facts. The child had to be taught by things instead of by words. When objects themselves were not readily at the teacher's disposal, Pestalozzi emphasized the need for the use of pictures.

Concepts based upon verbal instruction, without the aid of elements that could be seen, heard, touched, and so on, could hardly be expected to offer meaning to the child. Objects had to be presented whole so that the learner might determine the number and kind of thing under consideration. This was the first step.

Only after the child was brought to recognize the whole object in its unity, was the name given. The *thing* was always offered before the *sign*. Attention was more readily fixed by objects than by words.

He arranged subject matter from its simplest to its most complex elements. The child began with the *known*, or those things which were within his grasp, and then proceeded to those things *unknown*. Through his simplification of methods, he endeavored to adapt to the nascent faculties of the child every branch of instruction that was included in the curriculum of the day. In geography, for example, the subject matter began with the schoolhouse and the village, rather than transporting the children through vague discussions and readings about far-away

[3] Lewis Flint Anderson. *Pestalozzi.* New York: McGraw-Hill Book Company, Inc., 1931, p. 8.

places. Arithmetic began by counting peas and apples instead of with abstract numbers. To gain from personal experience, and by things rather than concepts, was the first essential. After the individual child had proved through his own initiative that he was ready he was guided into the unknown and abstract.

Form When the first step in the learning process had been satisfactorily completed, it became necessary to discover the parts and properties of the objects for a still greater understanding of the whole. The object was analyzed into its separate elements. After the integrant parts were observed and the forms carefully perceived, they were also named.

Language For the last step, generalization, the individual was called upon to deal with the abstract idea. He had observed the object and analyzed it for deeper understanding. Now he was called upon to offer a definition that would indicate his understanding of the idea he had attained as a consequence of the experience in which he had been involved. The entire procedure might be summarized as the method of *whole to part to whole*.

Pestalozzi and Music Education

We have already seen that music played a part in the educational philosophy of Pestalozzi. It remains to determine to what degree music was provided in those schools and the manner in which the instruction was given.

According to Johannes Ramsauer, one of the greatest pleasures in the school at Burgdorf was singing. The children, taught by Johann Buss, were urged to sing as they walked between the school and the old castle that served as their living quarters. They sang as they went through the corridors of the school, on their walks, and in the courtyard of the castle in the evening. From the report, such musical exercise contributed greatly to the general good feeling that was always apparent among the students.

From the school at Yverdon, Roger de Guimps gave a glowing account of the musical activity. There always seemed to be singing in Pestalozzi's institute. The children were taught simple Alpine melodies, which they sang with great pleasure as they walked through the mountains that had inspired the songs they sang.

Christmas Eve was made all the more pleasurable by the musical part of the holiday festivities.

Although Pestalozzi could not sing, he must have given ample time for its exercise. Edward Biber reported that the children sang appropriate hymns for sacred holidays and that they sang in a salute to the morning sun and the coming of spring.

But there was a formal side of instruction as well. Two men, Michael Traugott Pfeiffer and Hans George Naegeli, who already had published collections of children's songs, composed a treatise according to Pestalozzian principles entitled *Gesangbildungslehre Nach Pestalozzischen Grundsaetzen*. It was published in Zürich in 1810. This was the instrument by which Pestalozzian methods in music could be taught in a systematic way.

In brief, the book was divided into several sections with the greatest emphasis given to theory. This portion of the treatise was subdivided into rhythm, melody, dynamics, and a combination of all three areas. Rhythm was first studied, and not until work in this area was well on its way, was the student permitted to progress to the next step, melody. This second section included no rhythmic work at all; the child could thus focus all his attention upon pitch. The movable *Do* system was used. When this portion of the treatise had been worked out, the child then moved to the third and last topic, dynamics. Here, attention was directed specifically to the business at hand, with no attempts to include that body of material already presented in rhythm and melody. When all three areas were mastered, another section offered studies that emphasized the development of all three aspects of the study in combination.

Pestalozzi praised Naegeli for his efforts in designing this method of music study. In a letter to James Greaves, he expressed great satisfaction with the way in which the authors had reduced the problems of music to the simplest elements. The text, he noted, permitted his children to achieve proficiency in music by the most direct means.

A report from Yverdon would indicate, however, that formal music instruction was not enjoying the success that had been reported earlier for the spontaneous singing. From Henry Barnard the following extract is offered:

Another twitch of the bell announced that the hour for playing at triangles (the geometry lesson) had expired. In five minutes the slate was covered with bars of minims and crotchets, and the music lesson begun. This . . . bore a striking resemblance to the geographical one of two hours before; the one difference being that "ut re me," had succeeded to names of certain cities, and "fa so la" to the number of their inhabitants.[4]

Eventually, Pestalozzi realized that such formal study had failed to produce the desired result. Referring again to the Greaves letter, he observed that proficiency in the art was not the intended service of music in education. It was its influence on the feelings of the individual that recommended it to the curriculum. The primary goal of education was that expressed through the moral element rather than by specific knowledge. Therefore, in his view, only as music spoke to the heart of the individual did it provide any educational benefit.

It would appear appropriate to conclude that the textbook, which had the qualified approval of Pestalozzi, was in no way completely satisfactory. Since it is not the purpose of this work to develop a case for or against the textbook by Naegeli and Pfeiffer, this suggested collision between principle and practice is hurriedly passed over. However, it remains a problem in the following pages to determine whether or not a system of music instruction could be satisfactorily devised in this country which would maintain the true spirit of Pestalozzi's principles.

[4] Henry Barnard (ed.) "Lowell Mason," *American Journal of Education.* Vol IV (1857), p. 142.

3

Music
Education
and the
Enlightenment

Beginnings of Music Education in America

THE SCHOOL MUSIC MOVEMENT in the United States began
with some experimental attempts in Hartford as early as 1830 and
in Boston about 1832. The next large city to include the teaching of
music in its public schools was Chicago in 1841, with N. Gilbert
in charge. He was succeeded in that post by such men as Frank
Lombard, Nathan Dye, and Orlando Blackman.

Cincinnati was another of the large cities that chose to in-
clude the subject of music in its public school curriculum. Professor
Stowe, who later married the famous Harriet Beecher, was sent to
Europe to study the educational systems of France, England, and
Germany. His report in 1836 led to the adoption of music education
in the public schools of Cincinnati ten years later, with the elder
Mr. Aiken a moving force.

"A rural schoolhouse c. 1855." Found in Andover, Massachusetts. Reproduced with permission from a 1946 catalogue of the Parke-Bernet Galleries.

Other Ohio cities followed, with Cleveland of particular note because of the work of N. Coe Stewart. After the publication of a report of the success of music education in Boston, St. Louis introduced the subject into its schools in 1854, with William Hodgdon the first supervisor of music. Perhaps the last of the larger cities of the United States to establish a music program in the public schools was New York City. It was not until 1897, when Frank Damrosch was appointed, that the responsibility was centered under the direction of one supervisor.

THE BOSTON EXPERIMENT

Lowell Mason is acknowledged the prime force and influence in installing music in the Boston public school curriculum. Mason was an excellent teacher, with many years of experience and an enviable reputation in the field of music in America.

In the 1820s the influence of the Enlightenment had begun to seep into the educational thought of the United States. Through William Channing Woodbridge, an educator whose work figured prominently in the history of education in this country, Mason was introduced to Pestalozzian principles.

In July, 1828, Woodbridge traveled to Switzerland to spend

three months instructing at Phillip Emmanuel von Fellenberg's Institute at Hofwyl. Visiting Pestalozzi's school at Yverdon, which was located not far from Hofwyl, Woodbridge noted the influence music had upon the children enrolled there. Among the teachers and musicians especially active at Yverdon were Naegeli, Krus, Pfeiffer, and Gersach; Pestalozzi had died in 1827.

Impressed by what he saw, Woodbridge procured as much of the music materials used at Yverdon as possible. These included the *Treatise* by Pfeiffer and Naegeli, the beautiful songs composed by Naegeli, and a number of the best textbooks for voice culture and general musical instruction. Woodbridge translated the material and sent it to Mason.

Perhaps through the enthusiasm that Woodbridge projected, Mason agreed to experiment with the new educational principles. A class of two hundred men and women was assembled. The lessons were at first prepared by Woodbridge and Mason together, with the latter presenting the lessons to the student body. The results achieved in this first class through the use of Pestalozzian principles far exceeded expectations. As a result Mason was com-

Lowell Mason. From Edward Bailey Birge, *History of Public School Music in the United States.* Published by the Music Educators National Conference.

pletely won over to the new system. He adapted it immediately to his juvenile classes, which grew to a sizable number of pupils. Some divisions included as many as four hundred students.

Mason's classes for children sparked a more active public interest in musical instruction for the many. People came to recognize that music was a subject in which everyone, instead of only a selected few, could participate and from which everyone could benefit. This new interest did a great deal to pave the way for the eventual introduction of music into the public schools.

William Fowle wrote in *The American Annals of Education* that, contrary to current opinion, the capacity for music could doubtless be developed in every individual. He noted that the degree of ability would certainly vary from one person to another, but that, in the final analysis, musical attainment was in some measure within the reach of all.

In 1830, after Mason had employed his new system for a short time, Woodbridge gave a lecture on *Vocal Music as a Branch of Education* before the American Institute of Instruction in the State House at Boston. Illustrations for the lecture were provided by Mason's pupils. The program was in some measure responsible for the resolution contained in the Snelling report, that one school be selected from each district for the introduction of regular vocal music instruction.

Despite opposition the report was accepted on January 17, 1832. An experiment was begun, which was never completely carried through. Mason, enthusiastic over this small beginning, endeavored to solicit greater interest in the cause of music study in the public schools.

George J. Webb joined Mason in the effort, and together the men met with considerable success. Through their combined efforts the Boston Academy of Music was organized in 1833. This institution promoted a number of measures for the improvement of music teaching. It also provided an impetus for the introduction of music in the public schools. According to Dwight's *Journal of Music*, the Snelling resolution was viewed with renewed interest as a result of the success achieved by the Boston Academy of Music.

In 1837 Mason traveled abroad to study the outstanding systems of music teaching in Europe. Although Naegeli had died, Mason met von Fellenberg and Gersach. It is said that he became so familiar with the new philosophy that upon his return he carried it out more exactly than did the schools abroad.

Meanwhile, in August, 1836, the Boston School Committee received a memorial from the Boston Academy of Music, accompanied by petitions from the citizenry asking that music be introduced into the public schools. This pressure bore results. A resolution was passed at once by the School Committee calling for an experiment to be carried out in four grammar schools under the direction of the Boston Academy. But because there were no appropriations for such an endeavor, the project was stalemated until Mason offered to teach in the Hawes School for the 1837–1838 season without salary.

At a public concert in the spring of 1838, all the children in Mason's classes sang in unison, beginning with "Flowers, Wild Wood Flowers." This song, according to A. W. Brayley, became "the first ever sung in unison by the pupils of a public school in Boston, and probably in this country."[1] The concert sold the School Committee on Mason's system of teaching, and music became a part of the curriculum.

It must not be assumed, however, that all children were immediately given the opportunity to participate. Horace Mann indicated that such was not the case. The study of music was confined to the upper grades of the grammar school. Nevertheless, many children, instead of a talented few, were taught to sing, and new and promising principles of education were employed.

A Philosophy of Music Education

Pestalozzi's principles were discussed in the last chapter. These shall now be reconsidered as they apply to music education in the United States.

AIMS

Pestalozzi urged that education be directed toward the development of the whole man. His efforts were essentially directed toward three elements, or faculties; head, heart, and hand—the intellectual, moral and physical capacities. With Pestalozzi, Mason concluded that it was the expansion of the human powers *through*

---

[1] A. W. Brayley, "The Inception of Public School Music in America," *The Musician*, Vol. X, (November 1905), p. 484.

Wild-Wood Flowers

Lively   Dr. Lowell Mason

1. Flow - ers, wild - wood flow - ers, In a shel - ter'd dell __ they grew. __

Flow - ers wild - wood flow - ers. In a shel - ter'd dell __ they grew, __ I

hur - ried a - long and I chanc'd to spy this small star-flow'r with its

sil - v'ry eye; Then this blue dai - sy peep'd up its head, __

Sweet - ly this pur - ple or - chis spread. __ We

gath - er'd them all __ fo you, __ we gath- er'd them all __ for

you; All these wild - wood flow - ers, sweet wild - wood

flow'rs, All these wild - wood flow - ers, sweet wild - wood flow'rs. __

This song, according to Brayley, became "the first ever sung in unison by the pupils of a public school in Boston, and probably in this country." A. W. Brayley, "The Inception of Public School Music in America," *The Musician*, Vol. X, Nov. 1905, p. 484. "Wild-Wood Flowers" by Dr. Lowell Mason. From Luther W. Mason, *The New Second National Music Reader*. Boston: Ginn and Company, 1887, pp. 92–93.

the acquisition of knowledge that was relevant rather than the knowledge itself.

Mason considered music one means through which the *whole man* could be developed. He was never primarily concerned with training musicians.

Mason's *Manual of the Boston Academy of Music for Instruction in the Elements of Vocal Music on the System of Pestalozzi* embodied the principles of the great Swiss educator and adapted them to the study of music. In 1834, at the time of the *Manual's* publication, it was probably the only text of its kind in this country. The *Manual* refers to the moral, physical as well as intellectual benefits to be derived from music.

Music Education and the Moral Element

A careful study of Mason's writings discloses an abundance of material in support of the theory that the basic function of music was to develop the moral nature of man. According to the *Manual*, the art of music should be cultivated because it represented the means through which the whole man could be ennobled, purified, and elevated. From *The Song-Book of the School-Room* it is found that song material should be of such kind as to purify the thoughts and feelings of the young. Music's greatest contribution was its moral influence.

Pestalozzi had endeavored to awaken the moral sense in the children whom he taught. Attempts to teach children to be good, noble, and moral through drill alone must prove futile. Rather than forcing upon them verbal precepts, Pestalozzi appealed to the hearts of his children.

Mason shared Pestalozzi's idea that character could not be taught by mere explication of principle. He proposed that it was through song that the character of the child could best be elevated. Because music drew out the feelings of the individual, lessons in all aspects of morality could be imparted to him through music. Music education during Mason's tenure evaluated its success in terms of moral values rather than musical skills.

Music Education and the Physical Element

Pestalozzi had projected a number of reasons why the physical element was indispensable to the education of the whole man. The training provided a safeguard to bodily health; it corrected certain physical defects; the exercise promoted, among other things, a spirit of togetherness; and it provided for a sharpening of the senses.

Mason recognized that music could make a direct contribution to physical development. He saw training in vocal music as conducive to good health, as it expanded the chest and stimulated the activity of the vital organs. He reasoned that voice training was good for the lungs and could be a factor in the prevention of consumption.

Pestalozzi maintained that physical training sharpened the senses. Music provided exercise in aural discrimination, teaching the ear to distinguish pitch differences as well as changes in duration.

Contrary to the general opinion, Mason maintained that it was possible to teach all children to sing. A child was not necessarily born with a musical ear; his musical ability depended upon training.

Music Education and the Intellectual Element

Subject matter as such, according to Pestalozzi, was the least important aspect of education. The educator's responsibility lay in developing or disciplining the intellect to the extent of imposing certain limits upon the individual's independence in the interests of education's moral dimension.

Mason's writings indicate that he supported this principle. Although his textbooks imparted information that would lead the child to an understanding of the musical score, the process of learning was elevated to a position of greater import than the facts themselves. According to Mason, the teacher had to set the child's mind in motion by leading him to the information, exciting his curiosity, and directing his attention. Success was measured by the individual's ability to cope with the learning situation itself. The *Manual* stressed that the primary intellectual aim was discipline acquired rather than knowledge attained. "That person is not the best educated, who has learned the most, but he who knows best how to learn."[2]

Mason maintained that it was not the student's proficiency in music that measured his progress; this was of real value only to a music theorist: the true measure was the power the student gained *through* the learning situation to recognize *real* value,

[2] Lowell Mason. *Manual of the Boston Academy of Music.* Boston: Carter, Hindee and Company, 1836, p. 26.

represented at all times by the moral influence. The intellectual aspect, though important, was decidedly secondary to education in the broader sense. Nevertheless, a discipline of the intellect had to be developed and was best achieved through certain psychological principles.

PSYCHOLOGY

The discussion pertaining to Mason's psychological foundations will be considered in two parts as follows: (1) The general view, as suggested through developmentalism; (2) the more specific view, which dealt with methods appropriate to the learning process.

Music Education and Developmentalism

The developmentalists urged that education be based upon principles suggested by nature. The powers of the individual child could not be anticipated but would unfold when he arrived at a point of readiness. The topics of the last chapter will now be reconsidered in connection with Mason's work, namely: (a) the pattern of nature; (b) self-activity; (c) interest.

The Pattern of Nature   In his teaching Mason stressed that attention be focused on the *individual* rather than on society as a whole. Each class—and more specifically each individual member of the class—learned at a different pace from any other. Much of Mason's writing seemed to support this observation. An extract from the *Manual* may serve as an example: "So various indeed are the circumstances of different classes that it is impossible to give any other than very general directions."[3] Learning had to be adapted to the capacity of the pupils and the general requirements of the class.

Mason recognized that the child's capacity determined the subject matter that should be presented to him. The child had to progress at his own rate of speed, to observe and discover according to his own particular power and growth sequence, and to derive from each subject what would be most beneficial to his own needs. This, he maintained, echoing Pestalozzi, was "Nature's method."

Self-Activity   The entire process of learning, according to Pestalozzi, revolved around the principle of self-activity. Learning was

[3] Lowell Mason. *Manual of the Boston Academy of Music*. Boston: Carter, Hindee and Company, 1834, p. 27.

the result of the interaction of the child with external stimuli. Education relied completely upon those activities with which the individual became thoroughly engaged.

Mason acknowledged this idea of *learning to do by doing* throughout his work. The child was rarely *told*, but rather was made to experience first those things about which he might learn. Learning was not a process wherein precepts were poured into the mind from outside, but rather one of discovery on the part of the learner through his own effort. In every instance the individual became an active participant.

Earlier it was remarked that moral education was one of Mason's uppermost aims. Values were not taught through memoriter work; values had to be *felt*. Children could learn to feel moral value by singing, deriving the lesson from the thoughts of the text and through the melodies and harmonies. By singing, too, children were taught the technical accuracies of time and tune. Mason maintained that children could grasp an idea of certain technical aspects purely by rote experience, even though the activity might be ostensibly recreational. Only a fraction of the whole teaching experience lay in the *telling*; the real meat of the learning process was the *doing*.

Interest   Pestalozzi considered the teacher's function to be that of a stimulator. Success rested on the degree to which the instructor motivated the child in the path of discovery, a condition to which *interest* was fundamental. The principle was reflected in Mason's writings sufficiently to serve as evidence that he had put this precept into action. From his travels abroad Mason wrote of the qualities of a particular teacher by saying that the method used was distinctly Pestalozzian, always interesting and filled with many kinds of illustrations.

Mason never interpreted the principle of interest as license to follow any whim to which the child might momentarily be inclined. The subject was never permitted to be degraded into an activity whose goal was merely "play, or pastime, or even so low as merrymaking or buffoonery quite unbecoming a school-room."[4] Distinct values had always to be derived from the music activities. The lessons were to be made pleasant, and the child's span of attention had always to be considered. Lessons that were too long or activities

[4] Lowell Mason. *The Song Garden Series, Book II*. Boston: Oliver Ditson and Company, 1864, p. 3.

that failed to call forth a favorable response from the children were avoided.

Once motivation had been established, the child was led to eventual self-development. This was the ultimate aim of education as both Pestalozzi and Mason understood it.

Music Education and the Learning Process

Though Nature's way was the best way, Pestalozzi conceded that education must provide certain controls and methods. The focus of this portion of Pestalozzi's theory of learning was in the scientific, or inductive method, in which *anschauung*, or *observation*, was most important. For purposes of teaching, Pestalozzi broke observation down into three major steps: (1) *number*, (2) *form*, and (3) *language*. As an exponent of Pestalozzi's theories, how did Mason apply this principle in the field of music education?

According to Mason, *observation* referred directly to learning through sense perception. Any phenomena studied were placed under the observation of the class. Touch, sight, hearing, smell, or taste conveyed an acquaintanceship with the characteristic properties of the object. The *thing* became more important to the learner than did its representative *sign*.

Material gleaned from the writings of Mason permits a predication that the inductive, or scientific, method was of primary importance to the system he evolved. From Mason's *Pestalozzian Music Teacher* the inductive method is shown to be the best system of teaching because it coincided with the principles of nature. From still another of his books he emphasized that the elements of music were explained in such a gradual way as to manifest use of the inductive method.

While there is evidence that Mason nominally embraced Pestalozzi's system, it is appropriate to determine the degree to which the method found real expression. To accomplish this, Mason's work will be considered in terms of the same three steps already used by Pestalozzi.

Number   The child was taught things before words. Objects were presented whole in order that the child could determine the number and kind of things being experienced. Mason maintained that "whole things are first observed and considered."[5]

[5] Lowell Mason and Theodore F. Seward. *The Pestalozzian Music Teacher*. New York: C. H. Ditson and Company, 1871, p. 8.

Children were first expected to enjoy a period of rote experience in order that a certain readiness or preparedness might be established for things yet to come. Through such exercise a *known* was established in much the same way that speech is known before reading begins.

However, in dealing with the *whole* in this most elementary stage, it seemed desirable that whatever elements could logically be pointed up *in passing* should receive attention during this initial stage. *The Song Garden Series* presented a very clear-cut picture of this aspect of the method. The series contained three books. Most of the songs incorporated into *Book I* were to be taught by rote.

The primary aim of that text was to initiate the pupil in "appropriate emotional and tasteful expression." The same reference indicated that this was the *natural* process of learning to sing, just as it was natural for children to speak before they read. Through this rote experience, mental exercise was involved even though basically recreational in nature. Through imitation the children were introduced to the problems of time and tune.

The child was first acquainted with the reality or object. This step preceded any knowledge of the name or sign of the thing being observed. If the lesson dealt with the elements of time, the child was introduced to the problem by hearing the differences in duration between one note value and another. This was done before any name, sign, or description was given. In other words, the whole was first presented for observation. That was the natural order of things.

Just as Pestalozzi insisted that arithmetic begin with counting objects rather than with abstract numerical concepts, so Mason called for the activity of music to begin with the cogent process of making music before abstract symbols were introduced. Once the *known* was established, then, and only then, was the child ready to proceed into the next concentric circle represented by the *unknown*.

Form   The second step, according to Pestalozzian principle, was to break the whole into its parts in order that the child might be led to a more precise understanding of the object. In the same way Mason moved to an analysis of the subject into its elements. After the *thing* had once been presented in its wholeness, the *Manual* called for the elements or parts of the object to be studied separately.

It is interesting to note that Mason's analysis represented a departure from the *Treatise* of Pfeiffer and Naegeli. According to that text, rhythm was studied completely before melody received any attention whatever; then melody was studied exclusively before dynamics could be investigated. But Mason preferred that all three topics be studied together, with one claiming no more attention in the process than the other.

Attention to *form* or minute *analysis* was diligently carried out. In melodies the scale was never taught as a whole, since Mason maintained that the *thing* was the individual note. In the scale the tones 1 and 2 were presented individually; next the two tones were combined into measures and sung in various combinations; then tone 3 was introduced, and tone 4, after which 1-2-3-4 were combined; then tones 5, 6, 7, and 8 were presented in the same manner.

Numbers were first assigned to the tones, the letter names being presented afterward. Intervals were then introduced, insofar as the tonic skips were concerned. Next the staff was presented in an interesting interpretation of the principle of simple to complex. The staff was taught one line at a time in the following manner:

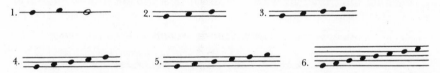

Still further evidence from *The Song Garden Series* supports the principle of *form*. With the presentation of *Book II*, a serious study of the parts became apparent through its minute treatment of the theoretical aspects of music in very exact and precise terms. *Book I*, representing the opposite extreme, presented much of the same material but in its wholeness. Pages 23 and 24 from *Book II* are reprinted below:

MELODIES

8. Melodies may now follow, and the pupils having become somewhat familiar with the first two tones of the scale, they may be named One and Two.

9. Commencement of the staff, the sign of pitch; a single degree or two degrees being presented, thus:

---

or pitch may be represented at first by figures, as the teacher may prefer. While the teacher now points to the line, the pupils should sing ONE; to the space above the line, and they sing TWO, with many repetitions, etc.

10. Notes in connection with a part of the staff; the former indicating the order of succession of tones, and the latter the pitch
of tones. Syllables,

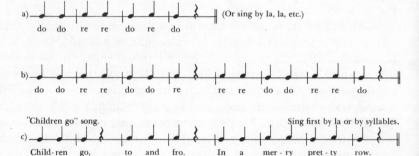

The teacher may take occasion to show that the space below
the line will answer just as well as the line itself to represent
the tone One, in which case the line will, of course, be taken
to represent Two.

11. The tone Three (reality) and a second line (sign) added.

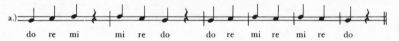

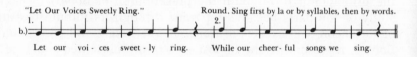

12. The tone Four (reality) and its sign.

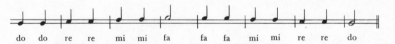

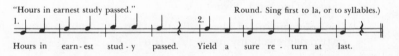

The pupils are now supposed to be practically acquainted with
the lower tetrachord (first four tones) of the scale. The other,
or upper tetrachord, being but a repetition of the same relation

of tones, at a higher pitch, may, if preferred, be given out at once, repeating the same syllables, Do, Re, Mi, Fa, but being careful to observe the proper pitch. The scale will then be complete with its eight tones; the syllables may afterward be changed so as to stand in the usual order, Do, Re, Mi, Fa, Sol, La, Si, Do.

13. The tone five (reality), and another line of the staff (sign) added.

"Better poor a whole life long."   Round. First to syllables

Bet - ter   poor a   whole life   long,   Than to   pro - fit   by what's wrong.

14. The tone six (reality), and the third space of the staff (sign) added.

"Men of Action."   First to syllables.

Men of   ac - tion, men of   might,   Haste ye   quick - ly   to   the   fight.

15. The tones seven and eight added to the scale. The scale completed, the fourth line added to the staff.

"Come Sweet Night."   Syllables first.

Come, sweet night, our   eye - lids   close,   O'er our   spir - its   shed re - pose;

That with morn - ing's   ear - ly   light,   We   may   wake both   calm and   bright.

16. Position of the scale as presented by the staff changed. One represented by the second space. Staff of five lines and four spaces completed. Line above.

do   re   mi   fa   sol   fa   mi   mi   fa   sol   la   si   do.

do   si   la   sol   fa   sol   la   la   sol   fa   mi   re   do.

17. One represented by the line below.

From Lowell Mason, *The Song Garden, Second Book* (New York: Mason Brothers, 1864), pp. 23–24.

Language   In the final step the parts were reassembled into a complete unity, with the child expressing verbally his understanding of the object or experience. The system might be defined as whole-part-whole. Mason supported this precept to the letter. He maintained that understanding could not take place until the object was first studied as a whole, then analyzed in its parts, and then reassembled once again.

It was the teacher's responsibility to lead the child on the road of discovery. However, what the individual took from an educational experience became completely a personal thing between the learner and the stimuli which the situation had provided. This discovering involved synthesizing single elements into a new and understandable order, a process which indicated reasoning.

Much attention in Mason's texts was placed upon a question-and-answer scheme. He might be accused of recalling the old catechistic approach but for the fact that he stressed the need for children to acquire knowledge by themselves rather than from the dictation of a teacher or through a laborious memoriter process. It seems clear that his question-and-answer technique was used to determine the level of understanding the pupil achieved through his own personal effort.

The Song Garden Series served as a particularly good example of this practice. The first two texts presented the elements of music, using techniques already described. *Book III* recapitulated the information in question form. The object of the third book was to place the *elements* or parts back into the *whole* from whence they were taken. Therefore, it may be assumed that the process of *putting back* was achieved by questioning an understanding of the whole. The answers given in the text were only approximations of those that Mason believed the individual would supply, provided he understood the material. A pupil's response was not to be the result of a mere repetition of what had been told him. On the contrary, the answers were to result from the child's own reasoning power and to reflect his real understanding of the subject.

Principle Versus Method

Pestalozzi regarded the work of Naegeli and Pfeiffer as a satisfactory representation of his principles in the field of music. However, he pointed out that the orderly systematization of elements described in that treatise would not lead to a complete realization of his educational aims. Method, then, although conceivably important, did not contain the sum and substance of the principles it intended to support.

Pestalozzi's aim, even in dealing with the intellect, was never merely to fill the student's mind with specific knowledge, but rather to set the mind in motion.

Pestalozzi saw the study of music as offering its greatest service to the moral rather than the intellectual development of man. It was not surprising, therefore, that he indicated his disapproval of the end value of the *Treatise* by Naegeli and Pfeiffer, which apparently dealt with methods directed more toward imparting a *specific skill* than contributing toward the all-round growth of the individual. Perhaps Mason could be accused of the same shortcoming. Mason's published materials indicated a very methodical and systematic arrangement of the elementary principles of music. All elements pertaining to musical proficiency were presented from the simplest to the most complex problems.

Mason, however, understood that a textbook could not teach. Its only function was confined, by the very nature of its composition, to define, describe, and provide symbols. He pointed out that the spirit of the text, or the reality, had to come from the teacher.

Mason acknowledged the fundamental position of philosophical and general psychological principles to education. While method had its place in dealing with the specific learning process, its position in the educational hierarchy was of secondary consequence.

Even if proficiency in reading a musical score was set as a goal, Mason never proposed that it was the *primary aim*. Like Pestalozzi he maintained that music should be included in the curriculum to assist in the development of the *whole man*. Further, he concurred with the Swiss educator that specific knowledge was of least importance. It was *through* knowledge that the individual was directed toward the *real* value of education, which was always represented as the moral aim. "Music's highest and best influence is its moral influence."[6]

Apparently Mason looked upon method as a means of projecting material which was to be used as an intellectual exercise, never losing sight of the supreme value—the moral element. Mason was too alert to the Pestalozzian spirit to have been vulnerable to the criticism Naegeli and Pfeiffer had received. Unquestionably method was subordinate to principle.

[6] Lowell Mason. *The Normal Singer*. New York: Mason Brothers, 1856, p. ii.

PART II

The Industrial Age

CHAPTER

4

An
Epoch
of
Utility

THE nineteenth century saw the United States shifting from an economy based on farming and commerce to one devoted to manufacturing and heavy industry. This change brought with it alterations in some traditional American values. Heretofore the acquisition of wealth had not been considered an end in itself as much as a means by which everyone might find a measure of security and happiness. Opportunities were available for all to live according to their effort and capacity in dignity and free from want. This had been the American dream, and to some degree it had been realized.

The advent of big business brought great poverty as well as great wealth. It became difficult for large masses of people who had moved to the towns and cities to acquire even the basic necessities of life. The small factory owner was replaced by corporations of tremendous size, which limited competition through monopoly or near-monopoly. Generally, leaders of the great corporations were men of little cultural background and enlightenment. Supported by the cult of rugged individualism, these men rose to undreamed-of heights of riches and power by the most ruthless means. The acquisition of wealth became the supreme goal, and the values of the Enlightenment and Christian humanitarianism stepped to a lesser position.

A Philosophy of Wealth

Andrew Carnegie, one of the most successful men of the period, published an article in 1889 entitled "Wealth," in which he endeavored to formulate a philosophy for the new industrial era. His thinking was based upon the doctrine of the divine right of property, a concept that had been supported by seventeenth-century Puritanism and also in the nineteenth century by American disciples of the Scottish common sense philosophy.

Wealth, according to Carnegie, came to those of superior energy and ability. Although a system of untrammeled free enterprise appeared at times unjust, it represented for Carnegie the most perfect system so far developed. It was for everyone to accommodate himself to the situation and permit business to be directed by the few whose strength and energy could guarantee its growth and success.

Nonetheless, Carnegie maintained, wealth brought with it certain responsibilities. A man of wealth was obligated to set an example of modest living, to see that those who worked for him were provided with a means of subsistence, and to consider the wealth he accrued as a personal trust to be used as he saw fit for the service and betterment of those less fortunate. The ultimate aim of the adventurous pursuit of riches was never wealth for itself but wealth that would improve society. This was Carnegie's ideal.

Poverty was to be looked upon as a blessing as well as a curse. Opportunity, according to Carnegie, was never more abundant. There was room for anyone with diligence to rise to whatever heights his ability would allow. Most of the great industrialists of the time had been poor and had achieved their success themselves. Carnegie's philosophy was distinctly individualistic. The poor man who could rise from poverty was to be respected, but the man who remained in poverty was to be shunned as one who had neither desire nor ability to rise to a position of worth.

Of course, Carnegie was protecting himself and his kind. However, his philosophy could not have caught on and prevailed for so long, if it had not fallen on fertile ground. His gospel of wealth became a working faith for millions of Americans. In spite of the depressions after 1873 and 1893 and the labor uprisings of 1877, 1886, and 1894, Carnegie's philosophy provided capitalism with a solid, theoretical foundation.

The worker became a cog in the wheel of industry according to his particular skill. As he succeeded, he was rewarded; as he failed, he was discarded and replaced by someone of greater ability. The entire philosophy indicated a continual testing procedure, with the fittest surviving. Although Carnegie's doctrine was never completely developed as a philosophy, it exerted a great influence upon the thinking of the day.

Expansion of Knowledge

The nineteenth century witnessed a remarkable expansion in organized knowledge. Specialized research uncovered more and more knowledge about smaller and smaller segments of subject matter. For example, early in the century natural history, as a branch of study, represented almost the entire field of organic life. Later in the century the study of natural history had been divided into such specialized subjects as botany, physiology, entomology, zoology, and a host of others. The available knowledge had so increased that no one person was capable of being a specialist in all these new fields; it was difficult to have a thorough mastery even of one of them.

Interest in science and the scientific method was sparked by the notable achievements of the German universities. But while the European occupied himself in research to learn more and more for the sake of knowledge and theory, American scientists were more apt to apply scientific information and methods toward utilitarian ends. Inspired by practical and profit motives to develop better transportation, invent more efficient machines, and improve the products of agriculture, the American scientist was pressed into such research as would solve purely functional problems.

According to the individualist-capitalist society, it appeared that knowledge must have a function to perform, must justify its existence through practicality rather than theory. Science provided a worthwhile office only as it could improve production and solve other difficulties allied to the world of business and industry. By the same measuring stick, education had worth only as it served the industrial economy, only as it prepared an individual to take his place in business or industry.

Changing Educational Ideals

Education could not help but be affected by the great force of the nation's powerful industrial corporations. Objectives of education had to be retranslated in terms of the needs of business and industry. The debate continued between advocates of the classical and the practical curriculums. With the triumph of business, the natural and social sciences assumed importance in the curriculum. As the century moved forward, not only was the college gradually forced to submit to new ideas but the public school as well.

Practical and vocational aims became primary. In this new civilization based upon capitalistic doctrine, the criterion was the practical use to which knowledge could be put. Those studies aimed chiefly at disciplining the mind were of little value to industry and business. Through the famous Morrill Act, the federal government rendered financial aid to colleges that provided instruction in agriculture and mechanical arts. Education of this kind was to supply industry with skilled workers, to provide more efficient methods of agriculture to the nation's farmers, and to support a growing movement to combine theory with practice. Educators desirous of furthering the cause of the public school continually underscored the value of a practical education not only for those who received it but for business and industry, which were the recipients of skilled and capable workers.

In order to understand the educational situation during the latter part of the nineteenth century, several important aspects must be discussed. For purposes of this study, three phases have been selected for consideration: philosophy, science, and psychology.

The Philosophy of Herbert Spencer

IN SEARCH OF DIRECTION

Education must have certain guiding principles, which can only be theoretically derived. The American industrial society that had developed a philosophy of wealth through Andrew Carnegie also set in motion considerable activity in the philosophy of education. As the century progressed, the industrial age demanded the knowledge that only the natural sciences had to give. The apparent utility of science directed many educators toward a new philosophy.

One of the first popularizers of science in American education was George Combe (1788–1858). Combe strenuously opposed an overemphasis on the classic languages and argued for a curriculum founded upon science. Between 1838 and 1840 Combe lectured in the United States in behalf of science and education. His arguments influenced many educators, among them Horace Mann. As a utilitarian and a moralist, Mann maintained that knowledge to have value, should be practical. As his report for 1839 indicated, he studied the knowledge that would prove of most worth to the fields of manufacture and commerce and incorporated them in his curriculum theory. Still another great popularizer of science in education was Thomas Huxley.

According to Frank Greaves, the most representative argument in behalf of the sciences, one that more or less coincided with Mann's, was that formulated by Herbert Spencer. Harvard's Charles Eliot also seemed to credit Spencer's thought with having had a distinct influence upon American education.

As an evolutionist Spencer emphasized the importance of material over spiritual values. While he was not opposed to spiritual values as such, he evaluated them according to strict scientific principles.

Spencer decried the emphasis placed upon classical studies and pointed up the value of those subjects that merited a place by virtue of their practical *content.* Much of his work regarding the aims of education and his method of determining the value of one study over another was new. However, he also pointed up the older educational principles of Pestalozzi in such a way as to establish those concepts firmly in the field of education for many years.

AIMS

Spencer considered education to be a preparation for life. He believed that the development of the whole man required an active consideration of three major capacities; the mental, physical, and moral. All three of these elements had to be considered in his philosophy. However, while Pestalozzi emphasized the moral aim above all others, Spencer stressed the mental or intellectual aim.

In his essay *Moral Education*, Spencer took a material rather than a spiritual view of his topic. The work was devoted to principles pertaining to the disciplining of children. He disagreed with Rousseau's proposition that all children were born good and endeavored to define the degree of perfection that might be expected of the young through proper training. Regarding the punishment of children, he endorsed the principle of penalty through natural consequences.

Spencer also treated the element of physical education as an entity unto itself and did not speculate, as Pestalozzi had done, as to possible values that certain other subject areas might contribute to the child's physical development. Spencer observed that excessive attention was often paid to the intellectual development of children at a time when their bodily growth should have been of primary concern. Therefore, he prescribed the establishment of a better balance between the two.

Spencer opposed the views popularized through Locke's philosophy in which physical development was seen as a hardening process that called for children to eat very plain food, to wash in cold water, to sleep in hard beds, and to dress in such a way as to become accustomed to cold. In place of this, Spencer provided in his essay on *Physical Education* scientific information regarding a child's proper diet and his need for suitable clothing. He further directed that play activities or sports were of greater benefit to the individual's physical development than formal exercises.

Spencer's doctrine seemed to answer the urgent requirement of an industrial age for a retranslation of educational objectives, for a criterion of knowledge not for its own sake but for its functional potentialities. Spencer's views on intellectual training seemed especially pertinent to the American educational needs of the times, coinciding as they did in considerable degree with the views of business and industry and of the general public as well.

According to Spencer the motivating influence behind the classical curriculum was that its traditional subjects had satisfied the general notion of what education ought to be. In other words, while a classical education was not necessarily geared to stir the child to action or to lead to any practical consequence, it conferred upon the individual the mark of distinction that society once held to be essential for anyone desirous of respect and position.

Convinced of the fallacy of such training in the light of an industrial world, Spencer presented a philosophy more in keeping with the educational needs of the time. Proceeding from the hypothesis that the real function of education was to prepare the child for life, he first set about to define and arrange those activities that constituted human life. In order of their importance, Spencer determined that education must prepare the individual for: (1) *direct self-preservation*; (2) *indirect self-preservation*; (3) *parenthood*; (4) *citizenship*; (5) *the refinements of life*.

Complete preparation in all the above divisions was the ideal. However, with achievement of the ideal doubtful, a *due proportion* in each area was held to be satisfactory. Exclusive attention to any one activity to the neglect of the others was looked upon as inappropriate. Nevertheless, some criterion had to be advanced so that an acceptable balance could be sensibly determined. Spencer directed that the average man had to avail himself first of training that would satisfy his basic needs—those things he held necessary to a complete life. Then he was expected to attend to other areas more remotely connected with his life and happiness. Further consideration of the five categories of activities that make up human life will tend to reinforce this hypothesis.

Direct Self-Preservation

Self-preservation was primarily an activity for which nature herself assumed responsibility insofar as it protected the body against organic damage. But there was a secondary kind of self-preservation that education had to instill—this was the prevention or treatment of disease. For that aspect of life, Spencer directed that education must provide a course in physiology.

Indirect Self-Preservation

Regarding the second activity of life, earning a living, Spencer argued that beyond the three R's there had been little, if any, training given that helped educate the individual in the methods of industry. Most men were employed directly in the preparation, production, and distribution of commodities. Therefore, education should provide individuals with the knowledge necessary to cope with the activities and responsibilities of such employment. In general, preparation would consist of methods directly compatible with those of industry, as well as a knowledge of the physical or chemical properties of things. In short, science became of first importance.

Parenthood

The third important division of human activities, according to Spencer, was the training and disciplining of children. When it came to rearing the young, classical studies offered no direct or practical service. Students, as future parents, should have instruction in the physical, moral, and intellectual principles of child care. Spencer maintained that children developed in mind and body according to certain natural laws and that unless parents were instructed in those laws through the study of psychology and physiology, their chances of succeeding in the responsibilities of parenthood would not be good.

Citizenship

Training in the proper function of a citizen was the fourth human activity that Spencer deemed essential in any good educational curriculum. History, the elected area for such training, was not to be a history of kings and battles. The practical emphasis in history was in the areas of descriptive and comparative sociology. Only through such study could the citizen learn to regulate his own social conduct. A dependence upon science was essential, for only through biology and psychology were reasonable and intelligent interpretations of social phenomena possible.

The Refinements of Life

The fifth activity pertained to those areas that made up the leisure part of life and that included the fine arts. Spencer maintained that the arts, because they contributed to human happiness, were a necessary part of education. Spencer maintained too that science underlay the fine arts just as it did the other four human activities. In all of the five areas of human activity defined by Spencer, science proved to be the underlying factor. That being the case, it would appear that education should be founded upon science.

The Meaning of Science

Spencer's contention that *science* was the sole foundation stone left cause for disagreement. There were those teachers who maintained that science could not be represented as a universal staple for child development. They argued that the processes were too involved for young children to grasp. Besides, all children were not naturally inclined toward the sciences, in fact teachers recognized that more children showed a greater bent toward other areas than toward science. Their position appears defensible only until Spencer's meaning of *science* is more clearly understood.

There was a tendency then, as perhaps there still is, to restrict the term *science* to apply to matter. This confined the word to mathematics and the natural sciences—areas of exactly predictable phenomena and natural laws. The term has often had a good many other connotations. The Greeks had several words to cover what we mean by *science*. The Romans, bequeathed us the extremely general term *scientia*, which translates literally as knowledge and which included at the least, all the many meanings ascribed to science by the Greeks. For this reason the definition of the word can, at best, be only vague.

Spencer not only accepted the broader connotation of *science*, but he extended the meaning to include an even wider reference. He assigned and described knowledge according to three different categories: knowledge of conventional value, knowledge of quasi-intrinsic value, and knowledge of intrinsic value.

Knowledge of conventional value represented information that was completely unscientific because it merely denoted an accumulation of facts which defied organization. It provided the individual with no instructive service in his quest for those principles that would guide his life's activities. Spencer pointed to the subject of history, for example. He held that names, dates, and battles typified conventional knowledge and that such information had no functional purpose or point when compared to the study of the phenomena of social progress.

Knowledge of quasi-intrinsic value was represented by bits of information derived from subjects of little utilitarian value that could find some application in areas that contributed toward complete living. An example of quasi-intrinsic knowledge was the information an individual learned about his own language through the study of Latin and Greek. This category still left things to be desired, according to Spencer.

From Spencer's definition of knowledge of intrinsic value, an understanding of what he means by *science* can be educed. All information having a direct bearing on an individual's preparation for complete living could be considered of scientific or intrinsic value if it satisfied two requirements: that the information contain an organized body of facts from which definite conclusions could be drawn, and that the knowledge be sufficiently structured as to make its acquisition a definite mental exercise. A subject area was evaluated from the standpoint of its practical content and its disciplinary value.

Spencer's emphasis on *science* dealt a blow to the classical studies. New subjects were defensible according to Spencer's standards if they satisfied the following essentials: they were practical, as determined by their contribution to Spencer's five activities of life; their knowledge represented an organizable body of facts; and the content could be properly judged as a worthy mental exercise. According to Spencer, the *arts* qualified as *sciences*.

The public clamored for the new scientific knowledge; this clamor had much to do with the development of the public school. The *elementary schools*—were so called because they were established to teach the *elements* of the scientific subjects.

Teaching became more of a science than an art. While the field of education belonged neither to the natural nor the social sciences, there was a tendency to stretch the meaning of science to cover a part of that field, which now made every endeavor to apply the scientific method.

It was pointed out earlier in the chapter that the success of the scientific method in German universities inspired much specialized research in the United States during this period. Because of the enormous increase in knowledge, the main trunk of science was divided into many associated branches. Where once a man could be a philosopher and include within that subject the study of psychology, as had been done throughout history, now psychology became a completely separate area in itself. In time scholars were even forced to specialize in but one of many fields of psychology.

Education was likewise affected by this application of the scientific method. Once it was possible for a professor to be responsible for teaching all phases of education. During the latter part of the nineteenth century, new knowledge so augmented the field that one university chair was insufficient to deal with all the required material. Like the field of science, education began to divide itself into many different branches of study, such as teaching methods, supervision, and educational psychology.

Between the years 1840 and 1860, a great deal of attention was given the general principles of teaching. At that time a number of books appeared offering many instructional practices which could be applied to almost any subject area. Of all such publications David P. Page's *Theory and Practice of Teaching* was one of the most successful examples of its kind. It was widely read for a period of about fifty years.

From 1860 on, more and more evidence testified to the fact that professional specialization was at hand. The publication of general principles gave way to the exposition of specific methods for individual subjects within the curriculum. The time had come when educational material had become so abundant, through scientific research, that no one book was capable of containing all phases of education. Books on educational psychology, school management, and methods of teaching were becoming more and more popular. The period could almost be referred to as an era of method.

Psychology

By the early nineteenth century several attempts had been made to construct a psychology more completely reconcilable with science. While the scientific movement held that *content* was of infinitely greater import than *form*, as the latter referred to the traditional disciplinary concept, the idea of mental discipline was very thoroughly rooted in educational thought. Moreover, in the middle decades of the nineteenth century, a widespread religious revivalism directed religionists back toward fundamentalism, making possible only a compromise position with science. Therefore, people were inclined to consider arguments in behalf of both faculty psychology and a more scientific psychology during this phase of educational history.

FACULTY PSYCHOLOGY

A renewed interest in faculty psychology became apparent from the middle to the end of the nineteenth century. One of its most well-known American adherents was Francis Wayland (1796–1865). Speaking before the American Institute of Instruction in 1854, Wayland maintained that faculties of the mind were both objective and subjective; that is, they brought to the individual not only a knowledge of the outer world but also an acquaintance with the energies of the world within him. Each group of those faculties were to be developed through training, exercise, and discipline; and by such means knowledge was acquired.

Related to this psychology was the doctrine of formal discipline. The mind was thought to consist of separate, independent, and naturally innate faculties, such as memory, judgment, and reason. These faculties were considered as potential powers of the mind, to be brought into being by practice and training. The exercise of one capacity was thought to transfer beneficially to another. Form was infinitely more important than content; as a result subjects that were by no means practical could be defended by the doctrine of faculty psychology. With such justification, traditionally prescribed studies held secure positions.

On the other hand, the adherents of the scientific movement advanced the idea that the *content* of the various studies was of greater moment than the *form*. However, after having argued effectively in behalf of content, most of the scientists turned around and defended the new subject areas on the grounds of mental discipline as well. Spencer himself provided an excellent case in point. While building his defense in behalf of science, he pointed out that acquisition of any kind of knowledge had value both as knowledge and as discipline. The result of one was to provide guidance for conduct, while the effect of the other was conducive to mental exercise. Both of those values should be considered when preparing the individual for a complete life.

The new thought threatened the once secure position held by the older subjects in the curriculum. Their traditional place in the scheme of things had rested primarily upon disciplinary grounds. The scientists seemed to indicate that a subject must justify its existence not only through its values as mental discipline but also by the usefulness of its content.

Supporting evidence for such thinking may be found through Spencer's justification of science over the study of foreign language. While learning a foreign language strengthened the memory, argued Spencer, it dealt with nonrational relations. On the other hand, science not only strengthened memory with its storehouse of accumulated facts but did so in a way far superior to the claims offered in behalf of a foreign language. Dealing as it did with rational relations, science exercised *understanding* as well as memory. Further, science cultivated judgment through the constant exercise of drawing conclusions from accumulated data and verifying them by observation and experimentation. While Spencer recognized science as the chief means of imparting content, he did not entirely dismiss the claims made for faculty psychology.

PSYCHOLOGY OF LEARNING

The scientific movement accepted the principle of formal discipline as part of its educational viewpoint. However, this was only a portion of the picture. In the way of developing the learning process, as it regarded the projection of knowledge and guidance through subject matter, Spencer re-emphasized Pestalozzi's psychological principles.

At first, it would appear contrary to all reasonable expectation that Spencer, a man of science, would be satisfied with a psychology that was developed only through empirical approximation. But Spencer was well aware of the shortcomings of existing psychological principles and went to some lengths to justify his position. He admitted that no genuine rational psychology was then in existence which could present a perfect scheme of things. Nevertheless, it was possible, with the aid of certain guiding principles, to establish workable premises that might eventually prepare the way for further scientific research. Spencer held that any criticism he made of Pestalozzi's principles was confined to *practice*, not to *theory*.

For purposes of clarity, the following discussion of Spencer's psychological principles will be divided into two parts: an exposition of the broad psychological view and a discussion of those principles most directly involved with the learning process.

Developmentalism

In general, the phase of Spencerian doctrine that dealt with the area of psychology emphasized developmental principles. According to this Spencer supported the proposition that the education of the individual was to coincide with the evolutionary development of man. This psychological position acknowledged three vital elements: (a) *the pattern of nature*; (b) *self-activity*; (c) *interest*.

The Pattern of Nature   In support of Pestalozzi, Spencer acknowledged that man develops according to the process dictated by nature. His faculties develop according to a certain sequence. As this growth occurs, the faculties require a very specific kind of knowledge in the same way that the body needs certain foods and senses a lack of one particular element or another. Educators must recognize this growth process and be ready with the proper knowledge at the appropriate time.

Spencer held that the child developed in a way corresponding to the way in which the human race itself had evolved. He emphasized, therefore, that all education should axiomatically proceed from the simple to the complex in the same way that man's knowledge grew through the centuries from simple beginnings to ever-increasing complexity.

Self-Activity Pestalozzi condemned the method of learning through memorization, suggesting that the child learned through interaction with external stimuli. Knowing and doing, he found, were bound closely together.

Spencer reflected this same attitude when he declared that *doing* was of far greater value than memorization. The child should learn through the activation of his senses. Observation was the keynote to learning, and only through the spontaneous activity of all his senses could the individual become acquainted with the visible and tangible properties of things. Rather than being told or required to memorize, children should be led to discover. Self-development was at all times encouraged as the natural way.

Interest   Of the new educational principles noted by Spencer, the element of interest was of particular importance. This was the prime stimulant for learning. All effort was to be directed toward making early education amusing and all education interesting. As a child indicated interest, he proved himself ready to digest the information presented. When he indicated disgust, the implication was that the work at hand was assigned either prematurely or in an indigestible form.

The Learning Process

Pestalozzi asserted that the individual was to develop according to the laws of nature. He further held that man must intercede with some intelligent control in order to assist nature with the learning process. Toward this end he proposed the *scientific* or *inductive* method.

Spencer accepted all this, and he recognized *observation* as the keystone. Both Pestalozzi and Spencer saw the education of the senses as basic to all learning—for by this means the individual received impressions from the outside world. The individual had first to acquire an accurate awareness of the visible and tangible properties of the thing to be learned, proceeding then from the simple to the complex and from the concrete to the abstract.

According to Pestalozzi, scientific knowledge was obtained through a process that involved three different stages: (a) number —how many and what kind of object, (b) form—their appearance or form, and (c) their names. Spencer indicated his support of this process when he stated that to learn according to the laws of nature, the individual derived his knowledge in three steps: (a) the truth of the number of objects, (b) the form or appearance of the thing to be learned, and (c) the relationship of one thing to another.

Number   As previously discussed, Pestalozzi's conception of number, form, and language could be restated as the method of *whole to part to whole*. Spencer's development of the elements of observation can be similarly condensed.

Observation, he maintained, was of prime consequence because without an accurate attendance to the object as a whole, the resulting conception would be erroneous. Education must first be content with a child's vague motion of a percept. The brain, like the rest of the organism, only reached its complete structure at maturity. Therefore, no child could be expected to deal with principles with the exactness of an adult. The instructor would have to be satisfied with a child's crude impressions at first. These first concepts could not be conveyed by abstract generalities but rather by concrete objects in their wholeness. Pestalozzi's principle of presenting *the thing before the sign* was undoubtedly inferred. As Spencer indicated, the particulars should precede the generalization.

Form   From a consideration of the object as a *whole*, the next step logically is analysis. According to Spencer, after the learner grasps a general notion, the instructor should make the concepts clearer by offering examples and practice. At this time, gross errors are corrected, and, gradually, understanding is refined and becomes more precise. It must be noted that Spencer's attitude toward *practice* did not suggest wearisome drill in nomenclature and definition. Rather he proposed that the child would learn by means of his own reasoning powers if elements of a subject were practiced or used in meaningful context. In this instance the object, particular, or thing, continued to be of prime consequence. By means of a further appeal to the senses, the object was more carefully scrutinized in order that the individual's perception of the particular could become more perfect.

Relationship   Pestalozzi referred to this step as *language* because it was at this point that the individual was to indicate his understanding by verbally defining the idea he had from observation and analysis. Principles or general formulas, Spencer emphasized, represented the unification of masses of single facts. Only after the individual has been thoroughly instructed in each particular, could he comprehend the complexity of an abstraction or a unification of many individual truths. This achievement occurred only when the child understood the relationship of one particular to another. Accordingly Spencer maintained that the *rule* was derived from *observation* and *practice*.

In support of this maxim, Spencer pointed out that the new method of teaching language placed grammar last. In this way the system was clearly set forth—first, a rudimentary or crude knowledge of the thing; second, an analysis or a more careful scrutiny of the parts; and third, an understanding and appreciation of the rules or principles of language.

It would simplify discussion to say that all music educators interpreted Spencer's learning process in exactly the same way. However, as education began to embrace the spirit and method of science, music educators, in company with those representing other subject areas, became more and more aware of the problems that cried for solution. As they formulated their hypotheses and tested them, their findings rarely met with unanimous acceptance. As one teaching method might gain the support of many adherents, it became equally possible for those same principles to attract a comparable number of opponents. The note versus rote method in the teaching of music reading makes a good case in point.

There were two important connotations to the meaning of rote singing: on the one hand, the activity referred distinctly to singing by imitation which offered no educational value beyond that of mimicry. Such an approach to music has always been signally deplored by music educators.

There is evidence available to indicate, however, that this type of work was frequently carried on in the name of music education during the nineteenth century. George F. Bristow, although he pointed out that by 1879 action was taken to improve the situation, represented the condition as follows:

> But when all the schools were furnished with pianos, good and solid instruction in music had to give way to rote singing. So it is easy to see the contempt musical instruction was held in by the authorities. Yes, rote singing was the prevailing epidemic at this time, in order to prepare for receptions which were held once a month.[1]

It may be understood, then, how the word *rote* fell into disrepute. Nevertheless, it seems unfair to judge all rote experiences by those carried on under such auspices. Earlier in the century under Lowell Mason rote singing was held in high favor among many music educators as a means toward the development of genuine musical training. As the century progressed, however, the acceptance of rote procedures was by no means universal with the result that some fiery debates ensued.

Benjamin Jepson and Hosea Holt may be considered two of the foremost opponents to the rote approach. The former made his point clearly when he said that, "The bane of all success in public school music is song singing, or to speak more properly, rote practice."[2]

Holt contended in articles and reports that rote instruction was entirely uneducational and placed music instruction upon a false basis. His words contained a similar ring to those of Jepson. To take an example, the following is offered:

> If the instruction in music in the public schools does not educate and develop power on the part of the children to make all music intelligible, then it is a failure.[3]

[1] George F. Bristow. "Music in the Public Schools of New York," Music Teachers National Association *Volume of Proceedings* (1885), pp. 30–31.

[2] B. Jepson. "The Science of Music Versus Rote Practice in Public Schools," Music Teachers National Association *Volume of Proceedings* (1887), p. 176.

[3] Hosea Holt. "Teaching and Teaching Reforms—Music in Public Schools," Music Teachers National Association *Volume of Proceedings* (1889), p. 113.

It is evident by this remark that his ideas centered upon a program based entirely upon music reading as a fundamental aim. In Holt's opinion, only after the child comprehended the printed page could he be expected to deal with music.

On the other hand, there were those music educators who supported rote singing as it connoted a specific method of teaching music reading founded upon educational principles that might very readily coincide with those of Spencer. According to O. B. Brown, the rote method appeared to be the only reasonable method which could be pursued naturally. After having visited a considerable number of schools where the note method was taught, decided misgivings of the results achieved were entertained by that instructor:

> I have visited schools of the youngest, in which most of the singing time seemed to be spent on various exercises, scalewise and in skips, and this goes on for a time with rarely a song to enliven or elevate. Sometimes, too, the discordant voices seemed to be almost in the majority. But how shall he learn? By hearing—by imitation—to use a much abused word, by rote.[4]

Of all those who supported the rote system, Luther Whiting Mason may be considered among the most active. Information is often found that connects this man as a distant relative of Lowell Mason. Sources of at least equal reliability disassociate the two great teachers from any family relationship. Supported by Christian Heinrich Hohman, the great German teacher as well as by James Currie of Scotland, Mason adopted a rote method which allied itself to the new language reading technics of the day. He argued that not necessarily words, but sentences, represented the unit of meaning.

> It is the idea as a whole, not the meaning of the separate words, which reaches his mind. So in music, fragments must not be presented to him at the beginning. It should be borne in mind that this musical sense is a matter of instinctive

---

[4] O. B. Brown. "Teaching and Teaching Reforms—Music in Public Schools," Music Teachers National Association *Volume of Proceedings* (1889), p. 108.

feeling with the child. It is in him by nature, and our object is to unfold it.[5]

With Mason, the musical phrase and period became the unit and received such stress as was heretofore common with note-for-note singing. He cannot be accused of teaching merely by imitation, as the following testimony indicates:

> In the first course, in connection with rote singing, the pupils have learned all the alphabet of music in a practical way. In this second book we keep up the practice of rote singing so far as learning the songs, but the pupils are expected to be greatly aided by their knowledge of notes, so as to learn the two-part songs by note after having heard them sung or played correctly once or twice. A plain chorale in two voices they are expected to sing at sight, so that the third time they will be able to apply the words.[6]

However, Luther Mason did not escape from criticism by Holt and his followers. About 1886 the Board of Supervisors of Boston apparently set out to expose the results of the rote system as it was taught by Luther Mason. To children who had studied under the method for eight years, they presented the following exercise and required them to sing it at sight.

According to the report, "The number of children who sang the piece at sight, and at least, passable well, varied from one-half to two-thirds of the whole."[7]

[5] Luther W. Mason. *The National Music Teacher*. Boston: Ginn Brothers, 1872, p. 12.

[6] Luther W. Mason *et al.* *The National Music Course, Book II.* Boston: Ginn Brothers, 1872, p. iv.

[7] Hosea E. Holt. "Better Teaching or a New Notation: Which?" National Education Association *Journal of Proceedings and Addresses* (1886), p. 5.

Holt seized upon this situation to emphasize the fallacy of following the rote-note procedure as well as to show the futility of expense Boston assumed when it invested $45,000 on pianos in order that the rote-note procedure could be accomplished.

With marked division among music educators over one problem or another, it will not be easy to draw them all under the canopy of a singular philosophy or psychology. However, in spite of the opposition that was evident between one theory and another, there is a surprising degree of unanimity that binds those forces of varying convictions securely together.

CHAPTER
5
Music
Education
in the
Age of Utility

FROM about 1850 scientific studies made important inroads into the general curriculum. If music education was to be accepted in the same way as the other new subjects, such as English, mathematics, and science, there was much to be done.

Specific instances show a movement in progress at this time to place greater emphasis upon content through the most scientifically designed methods available. Objections to Lowell Mason's system were expressed by Joseph and Horace Bird in a manual *To Teachers of Music* published about 1848. According to that publication it was necessary to present the elements of music in a more systematic way. This challenge helped to precipitate a change in the music directorship of Boston schools. Lowell Mason was relieved of his supervisory duties, although he continued as a teacher and was replaced by two of his former students.

The change in leadership did not completely solve what appeared to be the beginning of a re-evaluation of aims. Until 1857 music had been taught only in the grammar schools of Boston, though there had been some consideration given to extending that instruction into the primary grades. At that time the Boston school committee concluded that if music instruction was to attain the same degree of *proficiency* as other areas, it would have to begin in the elementary schools. The committee eventually recommended that in addition to the instruction already given, children in the primary grades would also be taught musical notation by the classroom teachers. The students were required, as was the case with their other subjects, to undergo proficiency examinations in order to receive credit. While the primary-grade teachers were allowed to use any music text they preferred, subject to approval by the school committee, it was hoped that some unity of method might result.

The new direction did not meet with any great immediate success although it did suggest that educators and parents were now ready to accept music into primary education. The only thing that retarded the successful extension of such training into this area of education was that no suitable texts or materials were available to stimulate activity in the right direction. That difficulty was overcome when Boston acquired the services of Luther Whiting Mason.

Even before going to Boston, he had earned a very fine reputation as a music educator. In 1853 the teaching of music in Louisville, Kentucky, was shared by two men, Mason and Fallin. A letter addressed to the former from members of the Boston Germania Band, then on tour, indicated their astonishment over the exceptional training given to children of school age in the rudiments of music.

The year 1857 found Luther Mason teaching in the public schools of Cincinnati. It was at that time he became acquainted with the music text of Hohmann, the great German teacher. Mason had the fifth edition of Hohmann's *Course of Instruction in Singing* translated, and it was published in 1860.

A perusal of that translated work will indicate how closely Mason followed the great German. With the youngest class of pupils, Hohmann expected the teacher to attend to the excitation of the musical sense. This unfolding of the child's "zeal and love for singing" became the aim for the first year. Instruction first emphasized imitation or singing entirely by ear. Rote work became a most important activity with the first classes.

However, the German found it possible to teach notation to children at a relatively early age. In keeping with his findings, the first year alone was devoted entirely to imitation, per se. The remainder of the course was given to instruction by *note*. As established in Hohmann's work, second year scholars

> . . . repeat the songs they have learned before; the younger ones listen, and thereby learn to distinguish between high and low, long and short, loud and soft tones, and thus acquire their first ideas of musical instruction. They are then led to *imitate* a sound that is sung to them, and in this way begin to sing by *ear*. At the same time, the note representing that sound is written on the board for the larger pupils. Both classes then sing together, the one by *note* and the other by *ear*, and the two are thus carried along evenly.[1]

Continuing with Hohmann's fifth edition, the staff, as a whole, is presented at once. In previous editions of the same work, one line at a time was studied, with the G line given in the first instance, the B line next, the D and F lines following one by one, and the E line introduced last. Hohmann emphasized the fact that this procedure was entirely practical to carry out, although experience indicated to him, at the time of the previous edition, that confusion sometimes arose when the incomplete staff was dealt with. Therefore, in all likelihood, the procedure appearing in the fifth edition seemed to him to prove somewhat better. The publication of that work by Mason was considered a great contribution to music education because it provided a suitable music text for the primary grades.

The city of Boston acquired the services of Luther Mason in 1864. With his appointment, a continuous music program was initiated to the extent that the primary, grammar, and high schools of Boston adopted a complete and unified system of music instruction. Mason taught the elementary classes, Sharland the grammar

[1] Christian H. Hohmann (trans.). *Practical Course of Instruction in Singing Prepared on School Principles*. Boston: Oliver Ditson and Company, 1856, p. 5.

schools, and Zerrahn the high schools. Mason instructed classes part of the time, and the regular classroom teacher continued with follow-up work between his visits.

In spite of criticism, there was still an overwhelming acknowledgment of his success as a teacher of music. His reputation spread abroad; he was known particularly in Germany, where Carl Reinecke acknowledged his contributions in the field of music education.

Music Education and the Spencerian Philosophy

AIMS

The influential philosopher Herbert Spencer was credited with stimulating a demand for scientific content and with the development of a scientific method. Scrutinizing music and the other arts, he demanded that they give precedence to those subjects having more direct bearing upon the responsibilities man was obliged to face in life. Nevertheless, he admitted that the fine arts should not be slighted. In fact Spencer recognized music as the most important of the fine arts in its service to human welfare. Beyond the mere pleasure it could induce, music had great benefits to offer mankind. Civilization tended more and more to develop the social elements of man's character by pointing up to him the satisfactions that derived from the happiness of others. This social development awakened the sympathetic side of man's nature and called for the development of a language of the emotions through which the individual could communicate his feelings to others. It was through music that this language, capable of projecting sympathetic intercourse, could be taught.

Spencer stipulated that if music was to become an effective element in the curriculum, it should be taught along scientific lines. Music, he argued, was an idealization of the language of the emotions and it succeeded or failed according to how well it conformed to the laws of the phenomena with which it dealt. While no musician could be great only by applying the rules correctly, he would be equally wanting if he relied on intuition alone. Genius, then, coupled with the science of *organized knowledge* represented the only plausible equation for success. Science, according to

Spencer, was necessary to the listener as well as to the musician. The truest and fullest appreciation of music, or any of the fine arts, was reached by acute perception of the theoretical content as well as the subjective aspects contained in a work of art. This faculty of perceiving was sharpened and educated through scientific instruction. Science, then, was a requisite to the knowledge and appreciation of music.

CONTENT

The degree to which music educators were influenced by Spencerian philosophy may be difficult to judge. Lowell Mason clearly acknowledged Pestalozzi as the source from which his aims and procedures had come. However, from the published texts in the field of music education during this Age of Utility, evidence of Spencerian influence is not immediately apparent. Luther Whiting Mason was profoundly influenced by Hohmann, a famous German teacher of music, whose methods were derived from Pestalozzi and Froebel. Hosea Holt and John W. Tufts, authors of the *Normal Music Course*, suggested Pestalozzian concepts when they referred to the moral, mental, and physical influence of music. But there were indications in the work of all three teachers of a new and more potent emphasis upon content.

According to Charles Eliot, acceptance of Spencerian doctrine was unconscious. The new industrial age precipitated a call for a more practical education based upon science. And, indeed, a strong new direction in education was evident; its goals—the pursuit of practical knowledge through scientifically devised methods. Changes in curriculum were to include a shift from classical to practical subjects, the introduction of electives instead of a prescribed course of study for all, and the beginnings of vocational training. These trends testified to a widespread acceptance of Spencer's views. Though Pestalozzi's philosophical foundations were laid aside, his principles of teaching received new emphasis through Spencer. This may explain why Luther Mason, Tufts, and Holt continued to mention and reflect certain Pestalozzian elements in their published works.

In line with the new thought, music educators offered new justification for the presence of their subject in the curriculum. Music was no longer in a category apart from other subjects but became integrated in the curriculum. Almost at once, instruction in sight-reading, or *prima vista* singing as it was sometimes called, began in the lowest grades. By emphasizing the study of the musical score, the child could be scientifically instructed in a well-defined subject area, and the class in music could be structured in a way comparable to other subjects.

The direction can be said to have been set through Spencer's philosophy. Music was now considered a *language*, and the methods used to impart that language were based upon the same systems as those employed in reading. Luther Mason's *National Music Course* presented a method of sight-singing based on a language-reading procedure popularized by Currie. The student derived meaning from the song as a whole rather than through the traditional note-by-note analysis. According to this method, a song should be presented in the beginning as a whole musical idea. Later attention could be directed toward its specific elements.

The aim of the *Normal Music Course* was to teach children to sing correctly by the note method in order to give them the knowledge that would enable them to sing any piece of music at sight. The authors of that series, while not in accord with the reading method that emphasized the rote-note method, directed attention away from the laborious system of learning the scale one note at a time. They claimed that the major scale rather than the individual note should become the unit in the study of pitch.

Other outstanding music educators of the period extending from the close of the Civil War to the turn of the century gave support to this goal. Frederic Ripley and Thomas Tapper, authors of the *Natural Music Course*, held that music was a language and that the responsibility of the music teacher was to impart to children the power to read that language. Sterrie Weaver, who devised a system for the development of individual sight-singing, was a firm believer in the teaching of notation.

In accord with Spencer, music educators referred to their subject as a *science*, representing an organized body of knowledge. Its subject matter was derived from the elements peculiar to its own construction. Music teachers considered a knowledge of the printed score as basic preparation for genuine appreciation.

Music, then, endeavored to justify its place in the curriculum on the basis of its practical content and intellectual discipline. As a science it conformed to Spencer's definition, *"a knowledge of the constitution of things."*

THE MARCH WIND

No. 19

Hear it   blow - ing   down the   street, whirl - ing   dust a - round one's feet.

Hear it   whis - tle,   hear it   roar;__   Do   not   let   it   in   the   door.

From Frederic H. Ripley and Thomas Tapper, *The Natural Course in Music,
The Music Primer* (New York: American Book Company, 1895), p. 39.

Music Education and the Scientific Spirit

The change in thought brought about by the Industrial Revolution created an emphasis upon the scientific method. Education was to be no exception to the craving for efficient systems.

Responding to this new spirit, music educators became increasingly aware of the many problems that called for solution within the confines of their particular subject area. It was the period of the invention of methods. Since it would be impossible to do justice to all the problems and methods in this work, four areas have been selected for discussion: (1) textbook revisions, (2) simplification of notation, (3) syllable names, (4) time and its unit of measure.

Textbook Revisions

Music books published in the last third of the nineteenth century projected very clear-cut procedures, and the authors insisted upon the presentation of their content in precisely the ways outlined. It is of particular interest to note the perpetual juggling of ideas that resulted from this marked attention to method.

Originally the *First Reader* of the *Normal Music Course* had a second part entitled *Child Life in Song*, which contained a considerable amount of rote work for the early grades. Later the authors felt that more exercises should replace the space formerly given to song in order to develop greater facility in music reading. For that reason the second edition gave itself more to wordless exercises. Rote singing, however, was not entirely abandoned, for a third section was added to the revised book, which contained *some* songs to be used for imitative experience. Later the publishers took the rote material and printed it in a separate book of the original series and entitled it *Child Life in Song*.

McLaughlin and Veazie found that eighth notes could be taught to children earlier than had been generally supposed. In their *Introductory Music Reader* they gave full treatment to that time problem.

The *National Music Course* by Luther Mason and others was originally based upon a rote-note method. On the other hand, the *Normal Music Course*, written by Tufts and Holt, indicated a more direct note-reading system. These two methods, the *National* published by Ginn and Company and the *Normal* published by Silver

Burdett and Company, had two active salesmen sponsors. The former series was the responsibility of E. W. Newton, who supported the rote-note method, and the latter series was represented by Robert Foresman, who, with equal zeal, advocated the note system. Incredibly, each man eventually converted the other, so that in the end both Foresman and Newton reversed their principles, with each adopting the views advocated by the other.

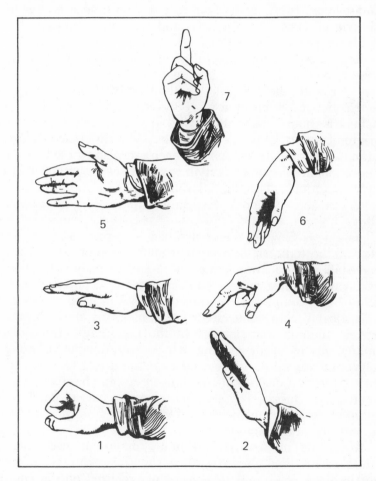

Hand signals from John W. Tufts and H. E. Holt, *Manual for the Use of Teachers: To Accompany the Readers and Charts of the Normal Music Course* (New York: D. Appleton and Co., 1884).

Simplification of Notation

There were several systems available, namely: the shaped-note method, Curwen's tonic *sol-fa*, the fixed *do*, and the movable *do*. Most of the tension and conflict resulted over the tonic *sol-fa* system of Curwen and the movable and fixed *do* methods.

The Curwen system   Briefly, the tonic *sol-fa* system needed no staff to indicate tones or time values. The syllables were written in abbreviated form, as d t l s f m r d. The time was represented by a series of cues involving lines and dots, which appeared before or after the pitch abbreviations.

Results of this tonic *sol-fa* system were successful enough in England to arouse interest among certain American music educators. True to the scientific method, two control groups were selected in a test sponsored in 1888 by a committee of the Music Teachers National Association. One group was instructed in Curwen's tonic *sol-fa*, while the other group was instructed in the staff notation. After twenty lessons had been received by the two classes, results indicated beyond question that the *sol-fa* method was completely victorious. Theodore Seward deplored the fact that the Music Teachers National Association had failed to publish its findings.

As far as Seward was concerned, acceptance in the United States of the tonic *sol-fa* system would not imply that the traditional staff notation was to be discarded. Although the abbreviations, as well as the symbols of lines and dots, were most ingenious, music of any complicated nature could not be transcribed readily or practicably into tonic *sol-fa*. His plea for the inception of Curwen's method was founded in the fact that it represented a simplification of music reading, which was thought to be capable of elevating students with less developed musical faculties to that elemental level a teacher might consider acceptable for the greater portion of his classes. Those students who wished to pursue music reading on a more advanced level would eventually be obliged to deal with the staff notation.

According to Seward and many others as well, Curwen's method in England proved sufficiently successful as to surpass even the most respectable achievements realized on the continent by any other system. Then why was it that the tonic *sol-fa* did not spread to any appreciable degree within the boundaries of the United States? One reason may be found in the fact that music from Germany, written in the accustomed staff notation, poured into America, while publishers in this country continued to print vocal music in staff notation. For any such system as Curwen proposed, music with the *sol-fa* indications would have had to be provided in order that the method could be used. Since the vocal music available in this country offered no such indications, there was little motivation for vocalists to desire a system they had no opportunity to put to use.

The Fixed Do vs. the Movable Do   While little if any argument in behalf of the fixed *do* is found in the writings of this period, the defense offered by those who preferred the movable *do* system makes it clear that the issue was debated. Coe Stewart, a very active music educator, favored the latter method which had already been used by Lowell Mason. He pointed out that the individual tone served no real or effective purpose unless it was situated among other tones in the expression of a musical thought. Therefore, the relative, rather than the absolute pitch, was the more important. In an effort to clarify his position he suggested that man was of little worth if he remained dissociated from society. It was only as the individual attached himself to all animate beings in his likeness that he became important.

Holt affirmed Stewart's stand. He argued that the individual should be guided toward acquiring musical ideas instead of merely the musical signs. All music was conceived on the principle that each sound was incomplete except in its *relation* to other sounds or pitches. Therefore, any agency that disallowed the conception of this relation acted to hinder the normal perception of sound. The fixed *do* did precisely this. For that reason it could not be used practically by the vocalist in reading music. Positive pitch, according to Holt, had no value in sight-reading. It would appear that of all the systems, the movable *do* method represented the most practical procedure. Music textbooks of the period testify to an acceptance of this concept.

According to Holt, syllables also had their limitations. They were useful insofar as they provided a focus of attention for younger children, who were stimulated to watch carefully the up and down movements of the noteheads. However, the sooner the child was released from the syllables and trained to focus complete attention upon the phrase or song as a whole, the sooner he would achieve the desired fluency with the printed score.

Syllable Names

Another argument was directed toward the pronunciation of the syllable names of the scale. The seventh note had been referred to as *si*. However, to use this term to designate both the next-to-the-last note of the ascending scale and the sharped fifth degree was confusing. It was therefore recommended that the seventh degree be called *ti*.

For some years *do* had replaced Guido d'Arezzo's *ut*. It was ventured by some to change the pronunciation of *do* to *doo* and *sol* to *sool*. In the opinion of some music educators, better intonation and tone resulted if the scale began with the *oo* sound. This suggestion was no sooner proposed when various interpretations appeared. One school of thought fully appreciated the importance of the *oo* sound but distinctly felt that it should not entirely replace the vowel *o*. As a result it was advocated that high and low *do* were to adopt the new sound of *oo*, but *sol* would retain the *o*, as had been the practice in the past. Others contended that high *do* alone would accept the designation of *doo*, while the first note of the scale, as well as the fifth note of the scale, would retain the *o*.

To be sure, such argument might be considered of little moment in the light of more profound discussion. However, the information is imparted as indicative of the mood of the period.

Time and Its Unit of Measure

A very popular system of teaching time problems had been through arithmetical explanation. To avoid involvement with fractions, which proved too abstract for young children, many teachers found that time could best be presented through imitation.

In 1829 M. Aime Paris invented time names as an addition or extension to the Galin-Paris-Chevé method. According to the Paris system the unit of time was one beat.

$\frac{2}{4}$ ♩ ♩   Tai Tai $\frac{3}{4}$ ♩ ♩ ♩   Tai Tai Tai

Between 1872 and 1875 Luther Mason devised a method in which the whole measure was considered as the unit. Time names were assigned each beat according to its metrical position in the measure.

$\frac{2}{4}$ ♩ ♩   Tä Tä $\frac{4}{4}$ ♩ ♩ ♩ ♩   Tä Tä Te Tĕ

The New Second Music Reader by Luther Whiting Mason

APPENDIX

Chapter I

SECTION I—*Double or Two-Part Measure*

First. The pupils are to be taught double time in the ordinary manner, with the names of the beats (Down and Up), accenting the down beat. *Second.* While beating time, the pupils, instead of saying *Down-beat*, are to say Tä (*a* as in fäther) and instead of saying *Up-beat*, they are to say Tā (*a* as in fāte).

Example 1

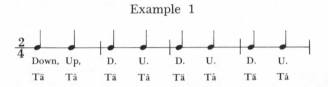

Where a sound lasts two beats, the vowel is changed *with* the Up-beat; as in

Example 2

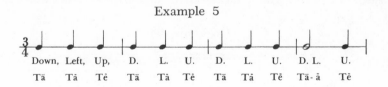

[Examples 3 and 4 not included]

SECTION II—*Triple or Three-Part Measure*

The beats in Triple Measure are Down, Left, and Up. The Down-beat is accented, and the Left- and Up-beats are unaccented. Some theorists say the Up-beat is slightly accented.

The Time-names are *Tä, Tā* and *Tē* (*e* as in mē.)

Example 5

[Examples 6 and 7 not included]

SECTION III—*Quadruple or Four-Part Measure*

The beats in quadruple time are Down, Left, Right, and Up. Accented upon the Down and Right beats. The Time-names are Tä, Tā, Tē, Tĕ (*e* as in mĕt).

Example 8

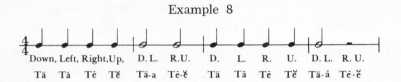

Down, Left, Right, Up,   D. L.   R. U.   D.   L.   R.   U.   D. L.   R. U.

Tä   Tä   Tĕ   Tĕ   Tä-a   Tĕ-ĕ   Tä   Tä   Tĕ   Tĕ   Tä-ä   Tĕ-ĕ

Chapter II
Two Sounds of Equal Length in Each Part of the Measure
SECTION I—Two-Part Time

When there are two sounds of equal length in each part of the measure, in two-part time, the Time-names are, Tä, fä, Tā, fā.

Example 19

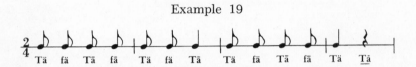

Tä   fä   Tā   fā   Tä   fä   Tā   Tä   fä   Tā   fā   Tä   Tä

SECTION III—Quadruple, or Four-Part Measure

Example 25

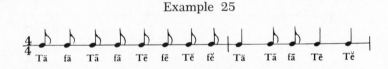

Tä   fä   Tā   fā   Tē   fē   Tĕ   fĕ   Tä   Tā   fā   Tē   Tĕ

Chapter III
SECTION I—Four Sounds of Equal Length
in Each Part of the Measure
Double Time

When there are four sounds of equal length in each part of the measure in Double Time, they are named, Tä, zä, fä, nä, Tā, zā, fā, nā.

Example 28

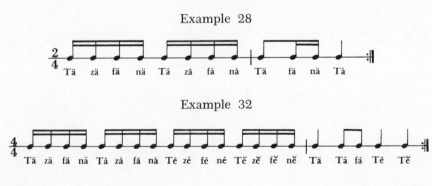

Tä   zä   fä   nä   Tä   zä   fä   nä   Tä   fä   nä   Tä

Example 32

Tä   zä   fä   nä   Tä   zä   fä   nä   Tē   zĕ   fē   nē   Tĕ   zĕ   fĕ   nĕ   Tä   Tä   fä   Tē   Tĕ

Chapter IV
SECTION I—*Triplets: Three Sounds of Equal Length
in Each Part of the Measure*
When there are three sounds of equal length in each part of a
measure, in Double Time, they are Tä, rä, lä, Tā, rā, lā.

Example 34

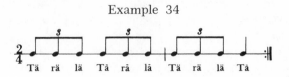

From Luther Whiting Mason, *The National Music Course, The New Second
Music Reader* (Boston: Ginn and Company, 1887), pp. 179–184.

There were those who preferred still other variations in those
systems, based upon the single beat as the unit of time. Note
values were grouped into rhythmic patterns and named.

Music Education and Psychology

In the field of music education, a need was recognized not
only for more effective music teaching but also for the creation of
some methods and procedures for the sake of establishing and
maintaining suitable standards. This was not to disparage the
specialized musical preparation of the instructors, many of whom
had studied with competent people and had arrived at an exceedingly high point of general performance ability. However, there
were no institutions to provide training for teachers who preferred
public school work. Most music teachers were obliged to manage
in the best way they could, whether or not their procedures proved
to be in keeping with the best educational practices.

Ralph Baldwin commented that with such diversity of method,
a corresponding unevenness in results was all too apparent. No
well-defined goal actually existed in music education, in direct
contrast to the carefully developed aims set forth for more traditional subjects. A child moving from one city to another would be
extremely fortunate if he found any continuity in his new music
situation. The condition revealed a need for immediate attention:
instruction in music had to be regularized to follow similar methods
and procedures used in the other studies in the curriculum.

In a paper entitled *Music Teaching from a Psychological Standpoint*, Hosea Holt directed attention to this deficiency. As a solution to the difficulty, he urged that music teachers should avail themselves of three years of regular normal school training. In this way they would learn principles of teaching applied to other subjects and would be able, in turn, to apply those ideas in the presentation of their own subject. A report by Silver, of Silver Burdett, corroborated the need for such training.

Since music educators began to recognize the need for a sound educational psychology, it would be appropriate to determine how faculty psychology, developmentalism, and the principles directly related to the specific learning process affected music education. It is also important to consider how those concepts were to be passed on to members of the music teaching profession.

AN ALIGNMENT OF PRINCIPLE WITH PRACTICE

In the preceding chapter, we saw that the adherents of the scientific movement were more concerned with content than form, but that they endeavored also to justify the new subject matter in terms of its value as mental discipline.

According to Spencer, each subject should offer a dual value in that it must not only prove itself to be practical but also to be a mental exercise for developing the faculties. He maintained that it was contrary to the economy of nature to present one group of subjects for the purpose of gaining information and still other subjects for the development of mental discipline. Therefore, subjects to be included in the curriculum must serve both purposes at the same time. As a result of the previous discussion, it was determined that two separate psychologies were considered. Faculty psychology was to apply in behalf of mental discipline. Developmental psychology, similar in principles to those of Pestalozzi, was to be employed in behalf of content.

Relationship of Faculty Psychology to Music Education

There is considerable evidence that faculty psychology had some influence on music education. Benjamin Jepson insisted that the study of music provided an unrivaled means of developing mental discipline. Tuft's *Handbook of Vocal Music* made the same point. According to Tufts and Holt, any teacher who followed the plan of their series would find that it provided a mental discipline equal in value to that achieved by other subjects.

Obviously music educators recognized the importance of faculty psychology. However, any subject seeking complete admittance into the curriculum must prove its worth as a practical subject as well.

As early as 1860, an article in *Dwight's Journal* defended music on the grounds that its value was not only of consequence as a *discipline* but equally as a *science*. Thomas Bicknell, in an article published in 1886, indicated that music education had ". . . its value as a means of intellectual culture and of mental discipline."[2]

Music, then, rendered a dual service according to Spencerian standards, providing training for the powers of the mind and developing the individual's musical potential.

A statement by Holt, "There is no teaching worthy of the name that is not scientific,"[3] shows him intent upon employing the most advanced psychological principles available at the time. Holt indicated a certain disposition toward Pestalozzi's psychological principles, as well as an accord with Spencerian thought. How music educators utilized these principles will now be considered.

Relationship of a Developmental Psychology to Music Education
In developing this portion of the psychology, the principles will be categorized in two distinct areas: first, the broad view will be considered, and, second, those concepts that deal most directly with specific classroom instruction.

Developmentalism Education was looked upon by developmentalists as based upon three essentials: (1) nature's method, (2) self-activity, and (3) interest.

Nature's Method According to Pestalozzi and Spencer, nature's method was of first importance. The latter philosopher proposed that the child developed in a way corresponding to the race itself even though a cultural epoch or evolutionary theory does not seem to be mentioned. Thus, the most natural way to educate children was derived from that hypothesis. Since knowledge had grown through the centuries from the simplest and most primitive begin-

[2] Thomas W. Bicknell. "Music in Public Education," Music Teachers National Association *Volume of Proceedings*, 1886, p. 178.
[3] Hosea E. Holt. "Conference on Public School Music and Popular Sight-Singing," Music Teachers National Association *Volume of Proceedings*, 1897, p. 103.

nings to more mature ideas and ideals, the child would progress from the simple things to the more complex.

Music educators were inclined to agree with Spencer that education should coincide with the child's growth process. As a result they evolved precise systems of instruction in accordance with their understandings of the pattern of nature. The sequence of material was so precisely ordered that supposedly a classroom teacher could instruct a music class with no difficulty.

Luther Mason held that music had an instinctive appeal for the child, which was given him by nature. It was the duty of the instructor to discover that gift. Each book of Mason's series imparted all material gradually, always moving from concepts in the simplest situations to those that became increasingly complex.

Musical notation and allied problems were broken down into the smallest elements and carefully reassembled step by step. According to the *Normal Music Course*, the *Cecilian Series of Study and Song*, as well as the *Common School Course*, a well-defined course of study was provided, with each exercise and song having a vital function. Holt and Tufts emphasized that the progressive order of the series had to be rigidly observed. McLaughlin and Veazie, authors of the *Introductory Music Reader*, maintained that every song and exercise had a very special purpose in their arrangement, which proceeded from the simple to the complex. For the teacher to depart from the given order would be to interfere with the natural way of presentation. The *Natural Music Course* similarly cautioned instructors to follow the systematic presentation of theoretic elements precisely as indicated in each text.

Music books were constructed according to the authors' understanding of a child's sequence of development. Texts began with the simplest rudiments and gradually led the child to more difficult problems. Any deviation from the proposed system was considered by the authors to be detrimental to the achievement of the prescribed ends because the growth process, as they understood it, would be disturbed. Education had to provide the proper knowledge at the appropriate time.

Self-Activity   The element of self-activity represented a refreshing change from the previous emphasis given in education to memorization. Much of the learning process was now left to the individual in order that he could crystallize his own understanding in a more personal and vital way.

Self-activity did not imply complete self-direction. The instructor provided the spirit and the motivation that set the learning process in motion, as well as the guiding influence that gave the activity proper direction.

Doing represented a vital element in the teaching procedures among music educators of this period. Tufts, for instance, stated that ". . . the classes should be kept constantly doing."[4] Evidencing their agreement, Frederic Ripley and Thomas Tapper wrote, "Everything in this system tends to cultivate the power to do."[5]

The interpretation of doing was not to be confined entirely to bodily motion or mere activation of the senses. Such a definition was too restrictive. Doing also connoted the sense or faculty of reasoning or thinking.

Luther Mason opposed songs that required bodily motion on the grounds that so much attention was given to the attendant physical activity that the music suffered in consequence. Nonetheless, his rote-note reading method was established in full recognition of the value of self-activity. The song became the unit of meaning. The act of doing, in the final analysis, was represented by the child observing the score, hearing it performed, and, through the instructor's guidance as well as the individual's own effort and process of discovery, learning to read. The learning was a personal process. Whatever the child's active mind could not draw from an experience, the teacher was at hand to provide.

Constant activity was advocated in the Normal Music Course. However, the authors advised against writing scales or intervals as mere mathematical exercises. Only after children were able, through practice, to sing their scales and intervals was any such exercise of worth. At that point the lesson became a practical ear-training activity because the work could be taken through dictation. Tufts and Holt further cautioned teachers against meaningless explanations of time values. They held that a knowledge and understanding of the relative length of sounds would be learned unconsciously through experience. The individual was thus led by the teacher to discover things for himself. Learning was his own responsibility through the exercise of his own reasoning power.

---

[4] John Tufts. The Normal Music Course A Handbook of Vocal Music. Boston: Silver Burdett and Company, 1896, p. 11.

[5] Frederic M. Ripley and Thomas Tapper. The Natural Music Course The Music Primer. New York: American Book Company, 1895, p. 3.

Interest   The developmentalists considered *interest* as the prime stimulant or motivation for learning. Since Pestalozzi, at least, this element had been an essential consideration in the educational process.

To educators of this period, *interest* had broad implications. It meant, for instance, that subject matter should be sufficiently appealing to the student to provide him with a continued interest in the material in adult life as well as childhood.

Music educators were very much aware of this vital ingredient in their teaching. So far as textbooks of this particular era can exhibit, every effort to motivate the child's love for music was made from the very outset of his instruction. Much attention was given to the collections of appropriate children's songs. In the beginning the rote experience awakened the child's interest, but it had other virtues as well. Besides the recreation and enjoyment it provided, some music educators maintained that rote singing gave the child a general familiarity with the language of music. The experience served as a foundation upon which to base more definite instruction in the science of music. In the same way songs were provided the more advanced classes, with similar attention given to the quality of the music and the appropriateness of the texts. Everything was done to encourage the free and sympathetic expression of the singers.

Rote singing was not the only means used to bring about a continued interest in music. There were teachers who maintained that interest could best be served if instruction dealt directly with the substance of the subject. For that reason the elements of time and tune represented the subject matter requiring attention. As a result, the music class spent its time learning to read the printed score.

Those music educators further maintained that music must always be taught through an appeal to the child's sense of hearing. They argued that if the study called for abstract theoretical problems to be solved on paper, music would be a dry and difficult pursuit. Instead, children learned to sing by singing. All theoretical principles were to be presented and practiced through performance. Teaching methods were made to conform to nature's laws as they were understood by those whose responsibility it was to develop courses of study. Knowledge was of interest if it was presented at a time when the growth pattern of the individual suggested his readiness to accept it.

The element of interest then was recognized by music educators, who satisfied its requirements on four counts: by rote singing, by presentation of the elements of music, by an appeal to the sense of hearing, and by founding methods upon natural laws.

The Learning Process   Spencer recognized with Pestalozzi that the laws of nature alone did not provide complete and sufficient control in educative matters. In order to assist the influence of nature, the scientific, or inductive, method was used to promote the learning process.

Observation, as representing the impact of impressions of the outer world upon the senses, came to be regarded as the source of all knowledge. Education, therefore, was based upon experiences of the outside world perceived by the mind.

Objects were first presented whole to the child. This permitted him to perceive the thing and derive some general notion of it. When the real thing could not be supplied, pictures or other acceptable representations were provided in order that the object could be observed.

Music teachers recognized the value of sense perception in their teaching. They appealed primarily, however, to the ear. As a matter of fact, some music educators considered that the sense of hearing could be developed faster than that of sight and for that reason was preferable. All difficulties in time and tune were made familiar to children through the ear.

Observation became basic to the learning process. While it was recognized and supported by music educators during this last third of the nineteenth century, the interpretation of the principle varied somewhat with the particular method of teaching music reading selected for use. The last chapter gave some indication of an intense debate between music educators as to whether the note or the rote system was the more effective method to pursue. Since both were in use, and there were texts in support of each, it will be necessary to consider how the principle of observation supported both points of view.

This particular aspect of the learning process included three steps which will now be discussed separately; they are: (1) number, (2) appearance or form, (3) relationship.

Number   It was considered that things must first be presented in their wholeness so that the child could draw a general impression of the number and kind of the object to be studied. The *thing* was introduced before the abstraction or the *sign*.

Those in support of the note method accepted this step as

basic. According to Tufts, "every new difficulty in tune or time should first be taught and named separately before the representation is given."[6] He further cautioned the teacher by saying that, "In the first stages, much time should be spent in training the voice and ear without any representation to the eye."[7] Additional support of this principle came from Ripley and Tapper when they wrote:

Care is taken to make the pupil familiar with musical effects before they are named; for instance, the words major and minor are admitted only when the effects which these words represent are perfectly familiar to the ear.[8]

It might be considered pertinent at this time to point out that those who preferred this note method, during the period under discussion, differed in their interpretation of this step from that established earlier in the century by Lowell Mason. According to Holt, Mason never understood completely the meaning of Pestalozzi's rule, "The thing before the sign." Mason maintained that the *thing* referred to a *single* sound. Consequently, each note of the scale was presented to the child as an individual object of thought. To learn the complete scale, therefore, became a relatively long and arduous task.

Contrary to that opinion, Holt contended that the *thing* referred to a *unit of thought*. With regard to music, this more correctly implied the whole scale. This idea gained importance. Ever since, the scale has generally been presented as a whole through scale songs rather than by the former method of note for note.

Holt and Tufts applied this same general concept to the teaching of time. Both men maintained that observance of the individual pulsations was not so essential. The more practical basis for emphasis was the regularly recurring accent. Instead of becoming involved with fractions by teaching one time value and then another, they presented time patterns which could represent a full beat. With the use of a swinging pendulum students were asked to think the accents of those patterns. Tufts said, "The Pendulum is infallible."[9]

Those music educators who preferred the rote method were

[6] Tufts. *Handbook of Vocal Music.* pp. 10–11.
[7] Tufts, p. 19.
[8] Ripley and Tapper. *The Music Primer.* p. 3.
[9] Tufts. *Handbook of Vocal Music.* p. 25.

also in complete support of presenting objects or things to children in their wholeness first. However, they went a step beyond Holt's concept of a *unit of thought*. Luther Mason argued that music was a language and should follow the language-reading technics of that day. Sentences, then, represented the unit of meaning rather than the individual word. Things would have to be dealt with in their completeness because it was the idea as a whole that was of consequence. Mason contended that through rote singing the pupils would initially become introduced to the *thing*, or, in other words, the entire alphabet of music. His method of dealing with time problems also shows that he preferred to consider larger wholes than did either Tufts or Holt. Rather than taking the whole beat as a unit, he devised a system which emphasized the rhythmic structure of the whole measure.

Appearance or Form   This step suggested an analysis of the thing. Once the object or particular as a whole had been presented, the next step required the teacher to help the child refine what had initially represented a rude concept of the object. The process called for analysis or a careful scrutiny of the parts of the thing observed.

Those who preferred the note method of teaching had already presented the scale in its wholeness. Now the individual tones were to be used in every possible relation to each other.

From the *First Reader* of *The Normal Music Course*, twenty-four exercises were devoted to the drill of the first two notes of the scale as for example, 1,2,1,1,2,2,1. As the exercises progressed, other notes of the scale were added until the whole scale appeared ascending and descending. Thus, after the scale had been taught as a whole, the individual tones were scrutinized more carefully in relation to the others. Later, intervals were introduced through many exercises and some songs. *The Natural Music Course* proceeded in a similar way to impart elements of the whole to the child. The little studies were composed in a way that closely resembled those used in *The Normal Music Course*, dealing first in short, stepwise exercises and gradually adding more and more notes of the scale. Songs only appeared after a considerable number of exercises had been presented.

Those who had a preference for the rote-note method also used this step in the process for analysis where explanation and comparisons could be made. According to *Book II* of *The National Music Course*, a considerable emphasis is placed upon music reading. However, it appears that the analysis is not dealt with in a fashion quite so extreme as that used by those who favored the note method. Rote singing continues to be carried on, and while a knowledge of notes becomes important the responsibility for analysis is left primarily to the individual child. Mason seemed to recognize that, while the parts had to be studied in relation to the whole, no universal method could be invoked as a suitable means to acquaint every individual with the same analysis. Since every individual is different, so will his analysis differ from all others. An interesting reference to Mason's method was written by J. Baxter Upham, a member of the Boston School Committee in 1871. He said:

> "In the lowest class in the grammar school the pupil is rapidly led over the whole ground taken in his primary course. . . . The child is now expected to begin to read the notation of simple musical phrases at sight.[10]

Relationship At this point in the educational process the individual was led, through a unification of all the elements, not only to an understanding but also to an appreciation of the complexity of the abstraction. In keeping with the scientific method the music educators used this step to culminate the teaching process. All particulars had been presented to the child in their wholeness and the concepts had been further refined by a study of the parts. It now remained to draw the particulars together into a new and meaningful whole.

The music educator could determine how well the individual had achieved an appreciation and understanding of the musical elements by the degree of sight-reading skill a student displayed. Prima vista singing was indeed a primary aim. Tufts clearly spelled out this objective when he said:

> To teach a proper use of the voice, and to give the pupils a command of their musical powers until they acquire the ability to sing any composition at sight, should be the aim and object of all instruction in music.[11]

---

[10] J. Baxter Upham. "Music in our Public Schools," *Dwight's Journal of Music*, XXXI (May 20, 1871), pp. 26–27.
[11] Tufts. *A Handbook of Vocal Music*, p. 14.

Holt, one of the strongest exponents of the note-reading method did not, however, maintain that syllables be used excessively, particularly during this last step of the learning process. While he believed that syllable names could be attached to musical sounds,

> . . . to practice singing with them as such until the singer finds it difficult to think or give the sound unless he also thinks and sings the syllables is narrowing in its effects and prevents that freedom in thinking which every singer should possess. The syllables are very useful in elementary teaching if properly used. . . . If they are properly used little children will outgrow them as naturally as they outgrow their garments.[12]

While it cannot be denied that reading was a very important goal to be realized at that time, there is sufficient evidence to indicate that music reading was not representative of the entire sum and substance of music education. Holt stated that "Sight reading alone is not the object of the Normal Music Course,"[13] it rather opened the door to a knowledge of music.

Those who preferred the rote method still emphasized music reading as a primary objective. However, beyond a comprehension of the relationships between the elements of music, there was a more subjective goal . . . growth in musical understanding.

Beginnings of Teacher Training

Music educators became more and more aware of the need for placing music instruction upon a sound educational basis. Necessity required the establishment of institutions where proper training could be provided for those selecting music education as a profession.

Before music departments were organized in normal schools and colleges, leading music publishers rendered an invaluable service to the profession by providing summer training schools. Each of these institutions naturally devoted itself to the particular

[12] Hosea E. Holt. "Music in Public Schools," Music Teachers National Association *Volume of Proceedings* (1883), pp. 43–46.

[13] Hosea E. Holt. *The Normal Music Course, Introductory Third Reader*. New York: Silver Burdett and Company, 1887, p. v.

method the sponsoring publisher favored. However, as Edward B. Birge indicated, the general tone of those institutions was far from commercial and they maintained a high educational level. The first of those music schools was directed by Hosea Holt in Lexington, Mass., in 1884, followed in 1886 by the National Summer School of Music in Boston. At Lake Geneva, Wisconsin, Silver Burdett and Company launched the American Institute of Normal Methods, with Holt again in charge. The American Institute, incorporated in Boston in 1892, represented a continuation of Holt's Lexington school but with a different name. This institution had an impressive staff which included H. E. Holt, Samuel Cole, Leonard Marshall, and John W. Tufts. In the latter part of the 1890s, The American Book Company sponsored in Chicago the New School of Methods under the directorship of Thomas Tapper, with such men as Aiken and Dann assisting.

A few year-round schools also developed in those early days. Under the auspices of Ginn and Company, the Emma A. Thomas School of Detroit was started in 1892 as an organization maintained for summer courses only. Eventually it offered year-round training, a service which the Crosby Adams School of Chicago also advanced at that time.

PART

III

Seeds
of
Progressivism

CHAPTER
6
Child-
Centered
Education

A GREAT DEAL OF EDUCATIONAL ACTIVITY became apparent toward the end of the nineteenth century, inspiring a sense of urgency in this country to create an educational system that would meet the exigencies of a maturing America. While Pestalozzianism had done much to break down traditional educational procedures, there was no reason to believe that any great reformation in American education had taken place.

The industrial age also brought certain changes in educational thought through Spencer's influence. However, what seemed at first to be a logical aim of supplying industrial demand with skilled labor eventually proved otherwise. Opponents pointed out shortcomings that had far-reaching implications. The real question seemed to be, should children be exploited in industry's behalf with no thought to individual development or to the demands of society?

Through a re-evaluation of educational aims, new and challenging ideas came to the fore. Acknowledgment must be given to the educational thought that came to this country from Europe. Froebel's writings were very favorably received, far beyond the measure generally associated with the success of the kindergarten movement. The philosophy of Herbart, brought to this country by Charles De Garmo and advanced by Charles and Frank McMurry, had an influence that cannot be dismissed.

The new principles were endorsed by those educators who recognized that in education a balance had to be established between the demands of society and the needs of the individual. They began to challenge the content-centered education that was supported by industry and by much public opinion as well. In place of vocational emphasis, these educators called for a child-centered education, which they considered more in keeping with the ideals of democracy. Two very important movements got under way in support of that view; the New Education and the New Psychology.

I

The New Education

The New Education may be traced directly through Rousseau, Pestalozzi, and Froebel, and also to the Oswego system as evolved by Sheldon. However, more than anyone, the man most responsible for the New Education was Francis Wayland Parker.

The "New Education," or the "Quincy Methods," or the "New Departure," began its development in 1875, when Parker was invited to undertake the supervision of the schools of Quincy, Massachusetts. The position was particularly well suited to his progressive thought because of the unusual attitude of the members on the board of education. They sensed that the existing system left a great deal to be desired and sought an educational philosophy which Parker was destined to develop. So successful were his five years at Quincy that in 1880 he accepted an invitation of a similar position at Boston, where he remained until 1882. Parker was then called to Illinois, where he assumed the principalship of the Cook County Normal School. To this institution he was to contribute a great deal. Upon retirement he was succeeded by John Dewey.

Parker was an evolutionist. Before examining his educational thinking, it is necessary to review his philosophical position.

Foundations of a New Philosophy

IDEALISM VERSUS NATURALISM

A widespread view, held in prescientific days and acknowledged by some in more recent times, maintained that the child was a miniature adult born with independent knowledge. He became able to use this innate gift as soon as he reached the estate of accountability, that is, when he was able to manage his mother tongue with some degree of fluency. At this age—about six—he attended school to be trained and drilled. Failure to learn indicated stubbornness and disobedience. Under that philosophy, and certainly in accordance with Christian theology, the child was born essentially evil. It was the function of education to discipline the individual in this life in order that he might eventually achieve goodness for the world to come.

The more secular belief, which was likewise in accord with this philosophy, held that the child was to be made over in order to fit into a prevailing culture or political and industrial system. This view presupposed a body of absolute knowledge, value, and truth—the world of the idea, which transcended nature.

Those who held this view fostered a reaction at the turn of the century that protested the emphasis being placed upon naturalistic philosophies. Many educators reasserted a dualistic humanism, which rested more upon the traditional philosophy of idealism. William T. Harris, superintendent of schools in St. Louis and later U.S. Commissioner of Education, was particularly active in exerting his influence in this movement. Statements of Nicholas Murray Butler in *The Meaning of Education*, 1902, seemed to serve as testimony that he, too, pointed toward that type of humanism.

IDEALISM AND NATURALISM

After the Civil War there developed a philosophy of idealism that incorporated the theory of evolution. Its foundations rested upon the hypothesis, popularized by Darwin, that the world was a natural product of natural forces and that it had taken eons to develop. The process of growth would progress only so long as the product and the forces continued in endless interaction. Parker, with others, believed that man was a part of this same process. Man's bodily structure and his mental makeup were all products of an interactive experience derived from an environment of both physical and social forces. Man, therefore, was a reflection of the natural world.

These same men, while alive to the ramifications of evolution, also saw man as a spiritual being. This traditional philosophy of idealism was represented by many forms; at its heart was the affirmation that the physical world took its being from the creative and guiding power of God. Similarly man himself was somehow an expression of this same spiritual force.

The concept of evolution was woven into this philosophy by some. Other idealists held that the world was in a continual process of change, rather than being the result of purely natural forces, these changes represented progress toward perfection through the guidance of an unseen Absolute. The same process was thought to govern man's spiritual life.

Educators accepting such a view never lost sight of purely naturalistic tendencies which most traditional idealists refused to heed. Those who recognized nature's contribution to education proceeded from the hypothesis that the endowments of the child—his physical, intellectual, and emotional capacities—precisely determined the limits of his development. Therefore, any educational philosophy must consider individuality to be of special consequence. Education must help each human organism to reach only that fulfillment of which its endowment would permit. No body of knowledge could be selected as holding the key to an individual's perfection. It was through the child's own capacity and activity, aided by the teacher's guidance, that the individual's potential could unfold and develop.

Even though it was contended that God created the child in His own image, which should have made each human being perfect, the physical and mental imperfections that were frequently evident led many to believe that nature intervened in the child's development. Such thought, precipitated by Darwin's theory of evolution, had an impact upon idealism. For some, philosophy could no longer be considered complete unless Darwinism was included.

Parker's work, finding particular application in the primary school, presented a restatement of an epistemology that took into consideration the values of the naturalists. It also did much to lead American education away from the kind of traditional idealism that emphasized imitation and memorization. In his writings he acknowledged the works of Pestalozzi, Froebel, and Herbart as sources that distinctly inspired his thinking.

Philosophy of the New Education

The central point of Parker's philosophy was that education should serve the harmonious development of the whole being. The human being was born good and was placed upon this earth to exercise the highest moral power. Despite tendencies toward evil, the individual was the creation of God. Therefore, education had to present conditions that best drew out the inherently good qualities and developed the moral character of those to be educated. This was the aim of the philosophy.

A broad curriculum, comprehending all possible educative experiences, was made available for the many-sided development of the child—its body, mind, and soul. Skill and knowledge became merely the *means* rather than the *end*, and no real distinction was made between education for intellectual and moral ends.

Such thought was quite discernibly inspired by Pestalozzi. The Swiss educator urged simultaneous moral and intellectual education. However, he implied that each represented a separate entity, with the heart maintaining the highest place in the general scheme. To awaken the moral sense, he appealed to the hearts of children through his example rather than through forcing upon them verbal precepts.

Froebel, too, had emphasized moral training but in a more clearly defined way. Morality was actually the fulcrum of Froebel's entire educational philosophy. Unlike Pestalozzi he did not consider that the child learned entirely from the example of others. A moral life could only be attained through practicing morality, taking its inspiration from the life of Jesus and from the fatherhood of God. Without this relationship to God the Creator, man's work would have no meaning other than to provide him with the necessities of life—food, clothing, and shelter. Froebel reasoned, that since God created man in his own image, man should reflect his Maker, in his own creativity.

Education began by stimulating the individual into action through external stimuli. It was expected that the values the child derived through this directed activity would become impressed upon his inner spiritual being. Once the individual became conscious of his innermost nature, he would be motivated to manifest his true essence in outward creation.

The function of the educational process was to establish unity between the inner and outer man. The inner essence of the individual could be recognized through outward signs: man's achievements were the result of the deep reflections of his innermost soul.

Returning to Parker, it may be said that his aims were greatly influenced by the educational thought of both Pestalozzi and Froebel. However, he interpreted his aims in a more temporal manner. While he contended that the individual was Divine, his philosophy aimed toward a social or democratic end rather than to something individualistic or religious. Industrialism had taught Americans to respect the "self-made" man. In nineteenth-century America the *individual* was the primary concern rather than the welfare of *society*.

Among the first to anticipate the need for sociological considerations in education, Parker took a broader view of morality and character building as it affected society at large. It became important in the New Education to be concerned primarily with *motive*, that condition which could stimulate action. According to Parker, even the most primitive motive—self-preservation—was worthy of attention. Gradually the child might exhibit through his training still higher motives, ranging from an interest in the preservation of family to that of community, or, and best, that highest human action represented by the desire for dedicating personal life for the betterment of mankind. Coinciding in some degree with Froebelian thought, Parker recognized that the inner man had first to be reached because it was the inmost recesses of the self where motive could be sparked. Once the individual became conscious of this inner self, he would find a guiding influence that could direct him toward worthy achievement to the full measure of his capacity.

Psychology of the New Education

In order to effect the many-sided development of the individual, Parker ventured close to another German philosopher-psychologist. This was Herbart, whose principle of apperception commanded considerable attention in the United States toward the end of the nineteenth century.

HERBART AND THE PRINCIPLE OF APPERCEPTION

Those who followed Pestalozzi supposed that reason was a high form of sense perception. Toward the end of the nineteenth century, a reaction against this concept began to emerge. Leibnitz, in his *New Essays on the Human Understanding*, launched the principle called *apperception*.

According to Leibnitz *perception* belonged to empirical psychology, that science of the mind which dealt with cognition, feeling, and other anthropological and ethnological characteristics. The mental act he called *apperception* was assigned to rational psychology which was concerned with fundamental distinctions of inner man such as the soul, its personality and immortal destiny. Leibnitz maintained that objects and events could be *perceived*. However, the nature of the mind was *apperceived*.

Herbart took this new doctrine of apperception and broadened its sphere to include all recognition, interpretation, and explanation. He agreed with Pestalozzi in accepting *observation* as basic to the learning process. However, Herbart reasoned that from the impact of the external world upon the individual, certain ideas were produced. These concepts had a life of their own and fought their way toward the highest point of man's consciousness. Along the way they aided similar thoughts to reach the same destination. Conversely, they endeavored to discard antagonistic concepts. This process involved like ideas to fuse together into a substantive unity.

The principle of apperception did not necessarily distinguish between vastly different concepts. Between black and white, or right and wrong, for example, there were intermediary grays which were likewise accepted or rejected by this apperceptive mass according to the value of their contribution to the clarification of what was being apperceived. It was conceivable that an overabundance of gray could change the initial tone of the given color that represented one of the given poles. Such procedure permitted total acceptance or rejection of some ideas while allowing others to be transmuted or modified into a form appropriate for unification with the existing apperceptive mass.

Herbart maintained that information had to be so offered as

to allow the connection of ideas to take place within the mind. Without this all the material from the many areas represented in the curriculum would total nothing but one large, chaotic mass of information. Therefore, special arrangements were made in order that each subject be related carefully to the next. One study center was established through history or literature, and all other courses allied themselves in support of the chosen center. Such a system, thought Herbart, would so present subject matter as to allow the child's mind to grasp and assimilate material into an understandable whole.

PARKER AND THE PRINCIPLE OF UNITY

Parker assumed that as in God and in all His creations there was unity, a system of education had to conform to the same postulate. Accordingly he urged the correlation and unification of subject areas which had originally been evolved and developed by Herbart.

As an example, a child's learning to plant a flower represented in itself, only a small and special skill. But participating in such an experience was bound to make the child somewhat aware of the soil best adapted to the condition, the effects of water and sunlight, and nature's cycle of birth, growth, disintegration, and death.

Such thought moved Parker to suspect that geography could never be taught without also teaching geology and minerology, since all three areas existed in the closest relation. As he progressed, he recognized that such unity remained incomplete without further adding meteorology, botany, paleontology, zoology, anthropology, ethnology, and history, as well as concepts of form and number. These formed the *central subjects* of the curriculum. No one area was presented as a skill but rather as a contributive element toward the all-round development of the individual. Should one of the subjects be omitted, the others would be affected and perhaps could not exist. Each study was viewed as completely dependent upon its interrelation to all other subject areas.

Through experience the child learned, during the preschool years, a multiplicity of things through their connection one to another. As suggested previously by the planting of a flower, it was the normal, natural way, that directed the learning process throughout the individual's early school years. Parker, therefore, worked toward free and spontaneous activity. The child then learned in the way nature intended he should. Lessons dealt with meaningful units as well as with the position of particular wholes in their relation to other wholes. The child made discoveries through his own insight rather than through a laborious memorization of meaningless and unrelated facts.

The teacher could do no more than aid the child by setting up proper physical and mental conditions so that understanding could occur unconsciously and automatically. To clarify further, three important elements have been selected for consideration, namely: (1) observation, (2) self-activity, and (3) motive.

Observation

According to Parker's psychology of learning, the physical organism had the capacity to receive and retain ideas created by the attributes of external objects. The concepts derived through observation, if they were to be accurate, represented the same number of elementary ideas as those attributes contained in the object observed. Further, the ideas had to be related, arranged, and be as vivid as the objects themselves. Upon the adequacy of these concepts depended the individual's knowledge of the external world. While Parker asserted that the brain did not have the physical basis for perfect adequacy in the observation of an object, it had to be trained in the power to receive elementary ideas as accurately as possible.

From a casual reception of the object's attributes through the senses, only an inadequate concept resulted. However, the continuous impression of that same object upon the consciousness led to a more distinct approximation of what had been observed. The educative value of such observation rested in the fact that more and more adequate concepts resulted. In turn, this permitted the individual a more complete basis for analysis, comparison, classification, and generalization.

Conscious activities, Parker held, were made up of units of elementary ideas as well as the inferences derived from them by the ego. While these states of consciousness were experienced by every human being, there were comparatively few people who really became educated. It was not enough, therefore, to receive through the senses external energies. Observation was only the beginning.

Self-Activity

Parker considered the central law of education to be self-generated effort. Only those experiences that evoked an interaction between outside stimuli and the organism he conceded to be educative. Observation was only part of the picture. A learning situation was satisfactory only when the organism responded to given stimuli with activity and effort. Education depended upon how effectively the educand made use of the conditions surrounding him. Individual development was the result of self-activity.

Self-activity did not mean complete self-direction to Parker. It became the responsibility of the teacher to stimulate within the individual the effort to grasp each elementary idea and seek further ideas that would lead to total understanding. The New Education stood for continual self-generated effort and activity.

Motive

Motive, according to Parker, was the power that stimulated all activity. The driving force behind all human action, it was fundamental to all acts of learning.

With children, immediate pleasure was considered the prime motivating factor. However, motivation could also be based on anticipated interest, or that pleasure that would result upon completion of an act.

Lessons were selected on the basis of the interest they aroused. Once the motive had been sparked by appropriate external objects, attention could be sustained. The thoughts derived from the initial activity stimulated emotion. The resulting need or desire for an expression of those ideas prompted the organism to become a willful medium for the required action. This unit of action between inner and outer man represented the "central educative moment." Since motive seemed to be the most basic force in the act of learning, there was nothing else but motive to be developed. From there, all else followed. Just how this element could be directly achieved must now be given some attention.

MODES OF EXPRESSION

Introduction

Parker's aim was to devise an educational system which would provide for full individual development. Through the central subjects, skill and knowledge became means to moral power. *Man*

Thinking was the primary concern. The child was offered experiences consisting of realities brought to him by objects and conditions from the outside world. The educative act was consummated through the child's own self-activity and effort.

However, self-effort and action could only be sparked by motive. Without motive there could be no thought and consequently no execution. Since this element stimulated the being into action, it not only had to be activated and sustained but also trained to be as noble as the limitations of the child would allow. It becomes evident that *Inner Man* was also of considerable importance.

Beyond the central subjects discussed earlier in this investigation, another group of studies, qualifying under the term of *modes of expression*, were used to intensify educative activities. Included under this heading were music, painting, drawing, modeling, making, gesture, writing, and speech. Parker maintained that each of these subject areas had a unique function to contribute in the development of those motives which he considered to be the highest and noblest.

The Function of Music in the New Education

Music was assigned the cultivation of the emotions. It was accepted as the means by which joy, grief, pleasure, and ecstasy could best be expressed. From its earliest beginnings it had been considered capable of calling forth the deepest religious emotions as well as those of truest patriotism.

According to Parker, man was nothing without emotion, as his whole being depended upon the nature of his inner being. Music had always been successfully used to arouse in the individual the most profound feelings of reverence. Its history reflected the history of the development of man's emotions. Rightly, then, the service it could best render was the cultivation of inner man.

This assignment was unique, since the area of the emotions had not been stressed before to such a degree. Heretofore, the intellectual dimension had been of greater import. In the eighteenth century Rousseau asserted that emotion played an important role in the make-up of the individual. However, the realm of feelings was destined to remain virtually unexplored for many years.

Not until Darwin's *Expressions of the Emotions in Man and Animals* in 1872 did scholars begin to note from his observations and experiments the importance of emotions. The work furnished a good deal of information that subsequently drew greater attention to the subject. Justification of this statement may be found in the James-Lange theory of the emotions brought forth independently by the two men almost simultaneously—James' theory in 1884 and that of Lange, the Danish physiologist, in 1885. Hall, Titchener, and Dewey are examples of men who later dealt even more thoroughly with the subject.

The position of music in the New Education became precisely defined. Its place was one of decided import, since the satisfactory culmination of its service would help set the learning process into action. Emotion inspired motive which, in turn, set the mind and body into activity and effort. The proper interaction between self and external conditions resulted in the development of moral power within the individual.

By inflating the contribution of any study beyond proper proportion the entire plan of the New Education would be destroyed. Music was not to have an intellectual service any more than geography was to aid in training the emotions. Man Thinking and Man

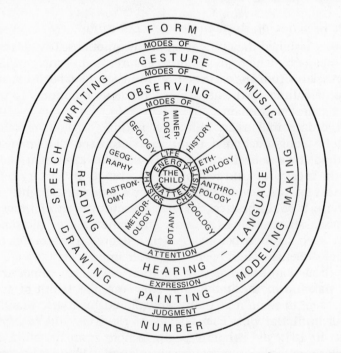

From Francis W. Parker, *Talks on Pedagogics: An Outline of the Theory of Concentration* (New York and Chicago: E. L. Kellogg and Co., 1894), p. ii.

Feeling were each to command attention through the unique service of specific subjects.

CRITICISM OF A PREMATURE SOLUTION

The New Education suggested that music could serve man best by developing the emotions. Responding to this trend, some music educators discarded all the theoretical substance that had once occupied a prominent position in any acceptable music course. Singing became the only means of achieving the aim prescribed by the new philosophy. As a result the study of music degenerated into a recreational activity, providing little else but rote experience. While this subject had held a place in the curriculum for only a few years, this practice had already proved to be undesirable.

At the opposite extreme were those strenuously opposing the new direction, maintaining that music was to be based on purely disciplinary grounds. Through reading, the child's faculties could be developed to their fullest extent. At some future time the individual would finally gain a sufficient knowledge of the fundamentals of music to permit an understanding of the esthetic dimension. Skill had to emerge before appreciation was possible. Their argument had very little tangible evidence to support it.

After over half a century of music education, there were few concrete successes. According to Pommer, when sight-reading became the sole motive for music education, the pupil was apt to leave the subject as soon as he left school. From an account by Miller, children were more apt to dislike than to like music when reading became the end rather than the means. In some instances educators became so displeased with the way in which the study was carried on that some cities removed music entirely from the curriculum until such time as a more satisfactory approach could be adopted. In very singular instances, where particularly strong teachers held forth, results were good. However, such cases were so rare that music generally came to suffer disfavor when it should have become one of the most enjoyable courses in the curriculum.

It would appear that many differences of opinion arose in regard to the teaching of music. There were those who taught music from a purely esthetic approach. The very substance of the subject was removed with the result that no reality existed. Music left itself exposed to criticism and mockery from both student and educator. Any subject worthy of a place in education must offer a breadth and depth, resting on something firm and specific. On the opposite side there were teachers who almost exclusively emphasized the technical aspects, completely neglecting artistic expression. Music became a wearisome grind that did more to destroy than engender a love for art. Extremes in either direction then proved unsatisfactory.

Parker's interpretation of the function of music did much to reaffirm the fact that the subject had another aspect beyond that of sight-singing. However, his thought directed music toward another objectionable extreme, namely, a purely esthetic approach. Not until the advent of new principles of psychology could an appropriate balance between the two approaches to music be proposed.

II

The New Psychology

The New Psychology, unlike the New Education—an exclusively American development—took its name from an international movement. Although experimental psychology was recognized earlier, it is generally conceded that the laboratory of Wilhelm Wundt in Leipzig, which he established in 1879, marked the real beginnings of those techniques generally associated with the movement. (Granted, the controlled studies pertaining to *sensation* by William James at Harvard had begun five years before, but James' laboratory never seemed to compete with Wundt's.) Consequently the University at Leipzig became the mecca for those students interested in the new direction. Psychology now divorced itself from speculative philosophy and restricted its work to the study of mental processes by the experimental methods already universally recognized in other scientific fields.

Americans were no less interested in this new study than Europeans. Therefore, it was not surprising to find among the first students at Leipzig, a number of American scholars. G. S. Hall, James R. Angell, and J. McKeen Cattell were among the first to attend. Upon returning to this country, they set up their own laboratories and continued their studies in psychology. Their explorations often carried them some distance from the well-defined areas set by Wundt. In any event much of the new psychological thought developed in the United States at the end of the nineteenth century could be traced to the Leipzig laboratory. Child Study was one of the movements that may be thus classified.

The Genesis of Child Study

Sparked by Darwin, an interest developed in child study along biological lines to determine more accurately the nature of the child. Harris believed that child psychology had a definite service to perform for education. Russell insisted that some attention should be given to external observation even though introspection was still relevant and useful. Parker saw the advantage of the new psychology almost at once. Educational periodicals supported the call for a scientific psychology, particularly during the decades of the eighties and nineties.

The history of the child study movement is generally considered to have begun in the United States in 1879. This was the year G. Stanley Hall supervised Mrs. Quincy Shaw and four kindergarten teachers in their endeavor to probe the contents of children's minds. The results of that study were published in the *Princeton Review* in 1880. Another early prelude of the new psychological movement was Jacobi's *Physiological Notes on Primary Education and the Study of Language*.

G. Stanley Hall was the undisputed leader of the new movement. Through investigation and study with his disciples, he endeavored to present the field of education with certain reliable psychological principles. Although many of his methods must now be considered crude, and the validity of some investigations seriously questioned, there can be no doubt that his findings contributed much to educational progress.

Principles of Child Study

Child Study presented some notable principles, which had a considerable impact upon education. Those that are of particular importance to the field of music instruction will now be considered.

RECOGNITION OF CHILDHOOD

Hall pointed out that children could not be considered little adults whose faculties and attributes were the same as those of their seniors, though on a reduced scale. Instead they were an entirely different species whose concept of truth, instincts, and attitudes could hardly be said to coincide with those of mature persons.

Each species—the child and the adult—had its own special set of reactions and adaptations to an environment. Individuals represented a wide range of differences with one another, not only in age but in physical and mental growth sequences. From such findings Hall made every effort to point up materials and methods suited to children. Teachers were no longer to present mature concepts in a fashion which they might conceive, *a priori*, could be absorbed by infant minds.

THE RECAPITULATION THEORY

According to Hall, an evolutionist like Parker, the soul developed in a very similar way to that of the body. Rather than separate mind and body, the two were treated together. Therefore, as man continued in his process of development, both were considered entities in the process of becoming. This hypothesis led Hall toward the evolutionary principle of recapitulation, maintaining that man repeated generally the outline of his evolutionary development. As he progressed, certain very distinct phases or stages were passed through, stages revealing the historical periods of man's development.

The Early Years

In forming his educational views, Hall found himself in fair agreement with Rousseau, who prescribed that during the prepubescent years (between eight and twelve) the child should be allowed to follow his recapitulatory tendencies of savagery through play. Realizing that this solution was hopelessly idealistic Hall tempered the plan with something more practical. He advised that through stories of heroism, the child's need for reviving ancestral experiences could be satisfied. He further directed that, because of the child's need for the skills civilization demanded of him, this period had to begin at approximately age three and end at the age of eight.

The Period of Drill

Hall considered age eight as the beginning of a new stage in individual development. In terms of the recapitulation theory, the child was well beyond the simian period but still before the historic period.

For the next four years reading, writing, arithmetic, instrumental technique, and other skills were deemed appropriate areas of attention. It was a time for the disciplines of drill, habituation, and mechanism, with only a limited appeal given to understanding. According to Hall, the child at eight had hardly reached the age of reason. Therefore, this period was to be devoted to laying a foundation for thought and morals.

The Adolescent Period

Education had to recognize that the individual now required greater freedom if he were to succeed in this phase of his training. Hall pointed out that the adolescent's power to appreciate was far more advanced than his power to express. While reasoning developed quickly at this age, the individual's ability to verbalize had not reached a comparable level of accomplishment.

The period of adolescence demanded educational techniques quite different from those for the earlier age group. Drill methods were to be relaxed and an appeal made to the student through interest. There was no restriction placed on what should be taught. The curriculum could contain all worthwhile knowledge. Subject matter was to be presented to the individual in comprehensible wholes, so as to capitalize upon the child's natural receptivity. While drill might be required at times, the methodical method of spoon-feeding morsels of information could not continue. Even though the individual lacked the power to express himself clearly in a testing situation, the instructor would have to progress with the presentation of new material. The whole process would break down under reverse conditions, with the result that progress would be impeded instead of promoted.

In a general way a modest outline of Hall's psychology of learning has been provided. The early years, from age three to eight, suggested a revival of prehumanistic experiences; the period to include the ages of eight through twelve emphasized drill and habituation; and in the adolescent years drill was relaxed, and an appeal was made to interest and freedom.

Applications of Hall's Psychology to Music Education

Because singing was a means by which man could express his innermost feelings, Hall rated it as the most universal of languages.

To study this mode of expression was to awaken the soul to a love of nature and to all sentiments both racial and domestic. Affections could be trained. The vehicle best adapted to the development of the highest moral qualities was music. The most practical basis for this instruction was through the voice.

The Early Years

Rhythm was considered the most basic of all primitive music. It represented the very earliest of primeval origins. For this reason Hall maintained that the individual in the early stages of schooling would naturally respond to music that was strongly rhythmic in character.

Little children would begin their musical development more readily with experiences representing primitive types of music. Rhythm was the natural point from which to start since it appealed to the motor senses. Step by step they would eventually pass through the various stages of civilization and arrive at that level where they would achieve a real appreciation of the present culture.

The child would respond deeply and early to Nature's sounds, for it was the first music master of the race. Such melodism had its effect on the soul throughout the immemorial past. Unless the child experienced such sounds which had previously controlled his moods and elicited imagery, further music training would have no effect because there would be nothing within his soul to which he might respond.

The child's singing experiences might start at age two or three with short little melodies learned by rote. After several years of such training a repertory of songs would be built through which not only piety, patriotism, and other sentiments could be recognized, but from which a reading readiness could be established.

Important as it might have been to prepare to cope with the printed score, Hall asserted that music reading was of little consequence compared to the education of the feelings. The prime function of the music teacher was to direct a "gymnastics of the emotions."[1] It was through the theory of recapitulation that this would be accomplished. Through music, children could revive many of those historical experiences of the soul. ". . . [Music] is

[1] G. Stanley Hall. *Adolescence, Volume II.* New York: D. Appleton and Company, 1915, p. 31.

the art of arts because it is most prehumanistic and also most prophetic of the superman that is to be."[2]

The Period of Drill

Between the ages of eight and twelve, music maintained an important place in the child's education. Although this was the time when the character of training was primarily devoted to development of skills, Hall admitted that the music class should also continue with rote singing.

The function of music in education was to deal with the cultivation of the emotions. Even during those years when disciplines of habituation and drill were emphasized, nothing was to precede or disturb that aim. Music education was not admitted into the public school, according to Hall, in order to make musicians. Its chief objective was to build character.

He admitted, however, to the desirability of learning to read the musical score. In those instances where this specific pursuit was recommended, he cautioned that such training should be made subordinate to the established direction.

Hall acknowledged the improvements being effected in language-reading methods and translated them into the music situation. First, a readiness period had to be established. Through much rote singing children would become familiar with the language of music before being subjected to any abstraction of the printed page. It would be as absurd, he said, to begin immediately with the study of the musical score as it would be to teach language reading before the child acquired the power of speech.

The child would not only derive an emotional benefit through rote singing, but would also become familiar with the language of music itself. By a process of imitation, the individual would be taught the song by phrases or meaningful wholes, a method that took account of the unity of the child's mind.

According to Hall the music teacher should realize, along with the language-reading instructor, that the technical aspects of both subjects could best be taught from the song or from the words with which the child was thoroughly familiar. Only after the unit

[2] Hall. "The Psychology of Music and the Light It Throws Upon Musical Education, National Education Association *Journal of Proceedings and Addresses* (1908), pp. 848–854.

of thought was established in its wholeness could a closer inspection of the parts be initiated.

Music reading was acknowledged as an important skill but it was to have a secondary place in the scheme of things. So long as reading was a *means* of bringing music to the training of the emotions to the child, it was acceptable. Under no circumstance was it to represent itself as the *end*.

The Adolescent Period

The technical aspects of music continued to be considered of minor consequence even in the education of the adolescent. As a matter of fact, this was the period when drill methods were relaxed and a greater freedom given to the individual. Subject matter had to be made more appealing if interest was to be sustained and information had to be offered in meaningful wholes as opposed to the tedious methods of spoon-feeding minute facts in succession.

Hall argued that at this point in the development of the individual it was natural that the voice would be raw and awkward for a time. Any attempts to direct the child toward the production of a pure and correct tone not only limited the services which the subject was capable of providing but also induced throat strain and certain discomfort. No matter how good or well intended, all technic was bad if it prevented the individual from the experience of expressing those feelings which were both normal and worthy.

In education the substance of music dealt with the language of the emotions. All experiences that awakened the soul to sympathy and social solidarity held the center of attention. Rules pertaining to structure, voice production, and reading remained in the background. It was the moral aim that continued to be supreme throughout the educational process.

III

A Summary of Principles

The latter part of the nineteenth century saw the United States busily engaged in constructing an educational system that could be reconciled to a new and rapidly developing civilization. While still in a relatively adolescent period of its growth, it was natural that this country still looked to its mother continent for guidance. It was not surprising, therefore, to find an immigration to the United States of many European ideas which were favorably received. Of particular note were those of Froebel, which exceeded those pertinent to the Kindergarten movement, and also those of Herbart. Pestalozzian principles as well as Spencerian thought were still not without their effect.

Interestingly enough, however, it would appear that none of those foreign philosophies were accepted at that time in their entirety by the country at large. Rather, those innumerable principles proved to be merely the seedlings of what eventually became truly American educational principles.

Aims and objectives were evolved in this country even though many of the new and challenging ideas could be traced to European sources. As a result, it seems fair to state that a debt of gratitude is due Francis W. Parker and G. Stanley Hall. A work of this kind cannot possibly give a complete review of each and every element. However, it is hoped that the following will offer a summation of principles which may fairly represent the work of those two men, insofar as they affected the field of music education.

Philosophy

Parker was not a traditional idealist. Strongly influenced by Darwin's theory of evolution and inspired by Pestalozzi, Froebel and Herbart he saw man not only as a spiritual being but also observed that through the individual differences and imperfections apparent in the divine being, nature intervened, having an effect upon the child's development. Since the human being was divine, his reason for existence was to exercise the highest moral power. Education, therefore, had to provide the right conditions for the development of morality. The process became that of uniting inner and outer man, or *Man Thinking* and *Man Feeling*. No separation was made between intellectual and moral training; motive became the primary concern. External experiences awakened motive which in turn stimulated outward action. Once the individual became conscious of this inner self, he would recognize an influence that could direct him toward worthy achievement.

Hall's philosophical concepts were similar to those of Parker. He, too, was an evolutionist and believed that the soul developed in much the same way as the body. As man proceeded through his process of development his soul followed a similar process of becoming. Intellectual and moral training were considered together.

The preceding pages of this chapter seemed to disclose that both Parker and Hall recognized music as that subject best qualified to cultivate the emotions. According to Parker it became the means of expressing joy, grief, pleasure, and ecstasy. From the earliest beginnings it was the agency through which the deepest religious emotions as well as the truest feelings of patriotism were expressed. Hall asserted that music was the language of feeling and that the teacher was to use it to open the child's soul to social solidarity and sympathy. Music's fundamental purpose was to be found in the finer development of the emotions, the feeling, and the sentiments. *Man Feeling* was to occupy a position beside that of *Man Thinking*.

Psychology

These same men, however, did not meet in unanimity with regard to *how* the objective could be achieved. Parker regarded music, painting, drawing, modeling, and such, as modes of expression. It was the goal of these areas to intensify educational activity by developing motive—that element which could stimulate self-effort and action. Since Parker accepted music as the best means of expressing man's deepest feelings, he designated music as that subject best qualified to cultivate the emotions. This interpretation of the role of music in education did much to call attention to values beyond notation and technique. Those who responded to this assignment, in the field of music education, discarded all theoretical substance. The study degenerated into an activity that provided little else but rote experience and found itself exposed to mockery from all sides.

According to Hall music was the language of feeling and had as its chief aim that of refining the emotions. He expected that such training would have a direct and positive effect upon the will and character of the child. However, he suggested that such growth was not necessarily achieved through the mere singing of songs. Since no real separation between moral and intellectual power could be made, the skills and knowledge of music must also be recognized as worthy educational substance. These, however, would be only acknowledged as a *means* toward which the proper objective could be directed.

The early years, insofar as music was concerned, were to be devoted to a revival of the historical experiences of the child's soul. He would be given a rich experience of melody and rhythm upon which further musical training could be based. The intermediate years, ages eight through twelve, emphasized drill, habituation, and mechanization. From this, music education took its cue and stressed the skill and knowledge of the art as a *means* toward the fulfillment of music's objective, namely, the training of the emotions.

During the period of adolescence, technique was subordinated in favor of interest. A relaxation of drill methods at that time was considered necessary as well as desirable. Rather than focus on the mechanics of technique, an appeal to the child had to be gained by presenting larger wholes. Hall contended these could be understood by this age group, even if at that time their power to express might be rather limited.

Modern Technique of Reading

By now improved methods in language reading were not by any means new in the field of education. The alphabet system had long been questioned, and had been superseded in places by the word method. Even the plan that conceived the sentence as the basic unit was conceded to have certain possibilities. Parker emphasized these techniques in his *Talks on Pedagogics*. Hall not only recognized the new methods of teaching reading but indicated those possibilities for use in music instruction.

The child learned to read in a spontaneous way in the same fashion as he had learned oral language. Reading did not concentrate at once upon the form of the word but rather upon the meaning it conveyed. The need for analysis was recognized, but this much was primarily up to the individual during his act of learning. While the child could be quite unconscious of any analysis, he could find points of identity in numbers of new words that had already occurred in a previously acquired vocabulary. To observe, and through his interest in what he observed, self-activity and effort would be thrust into motion, thus leading to the desired educative act.

Insofar as music education was concerned, the song approach was considered most desirable because it paralleled the new reading technics. By this means the child would experience tone and rhythm in meaningful situations. Upon his ensuing response, the way would be prepared for a later emphasis upon the abstractions of reading according to the most acceptable language-reading principles.

Recognition of Childhood

While not an entirely new concept, when the work of Rousseau, Pestalozzi, and Froebel are considered, Parker and Hall must be credited with contributing further support to the recognition of childhood in education. Parker challenged the content-centered curriculum that had been strongly supported by industry as well as by a great deal of public opinion. In its place he recommended a child-centered education more in keeping with the democratic ideal. His work found a particular place in the primary school. It also did much to direct American education away from that kind of traditional idealism which stressed imitation and memorization. However, through the psychological contributions of Hall, a more thorough understanding of the new direction was realized.

According to him, the child could not be considered a miniature adult whose faculties were almost identical to those of his seniors. Rather, the child was a product of nature. He gradually matured as a result of a continual interaction with his environment in a process similar to the evolutionary development of the human race itself.

The child could not be expected to think, feel, and understand in the same way as an adult. He could develop and mature only to the degree permitted by his natural endowments. Education could best lead the child toward personal fulfillment by appealing to his natural capacity with those experiences relevant to his particular stage of growth. The successful accomplishment of this depended entirely on how well the learning activities were selected and presented.

Educators were called upon to retrace their steps to the world of childhood. In that way they tried to find the key to those principles, methods, and materials that would prove adaptable to children's needs. Education began to realize that it must give back to childhood that which was childlike.

The Child-Study movement spread like wildfire. It became a major topic with parents' groups, woman's clubs, organizations of Sunday school teachers, and summer schools. A noticeable lessening of such spirit was apparent toward the closing years of the century. However, there is too much evidence to support the argument that child study had not spent its force at this early date. It may be said more aptly that, although child study suffered criticism and withdrew from box office popularity, those truly engaged in the work offered more pertinent and profound results every year. Dewey seemed to sum up the situation when he said:

The feature of child study against which criticisms have been justly directed are the results partly of the exaggerations incident to all large movements in their inception, partly of the misdirected gyrations of those camp-followers who, hanging about education as about all other progressive forces, attempt to use child study for their own advertising and aggrandizement, and partly of the unwise zeal of those who, lacking in stability, are blown about by every new wind of doctrine and lose the just perspective.[3]

[3] John Dewey. "Criticism Wise and Otherwise on Modern Child Study," National Education Association *Journal of Proceedings and Addresses*, 1897, pp. 867–868

CHAPTER
7

Patterns
of
Music Education
in a *New* Era

A<small>RT</small> had barely made a beginning in the United States during
the colonial and early years of nationhood, but what had been
done was the work of men who *felt* and *thought* in their own terms.
This was culture in its truest sense, no matter how primitive it
may have been in comparison with older civilizations. Before the
middle of the nineteenth century, a few Americans had become
famous and influential in the world of arts and letters. Despite
these isolated successes it would be impossible to say that there
existed at that time a mature American culture. There were forces
that did much to retard its progress.

The new rich, who rose to positions of wealth and power
during the nineteenth century, were self-made men whose interest
in art was primarily acquisitive. It was quite common for these
titans to contribute great sums of money for the development of
large music and art projects, more for praise and to flaunt their

success than from any real appreciation for art. These bequests may have had a more negative than positive effect upon culture in the United States. For many, art became a status symbol, a dead relic of the past to be respected for its cost and rarity rather than to be enjoyed for its living value. This, with other factors, caused enthusiasm for a characteristically American culture to wane and to be replaced with ever-increasing worship of European art.

In mid-century Ralph Waldo Emerson and Walt Whitman emerged to awaken America to its own cultural possibilities. They condemned those who conformed to standards of European origin and pointed out that art was dynamic rather than static. Both men did much to convince the people of this country that a class of native artists could arise and provide a creative spirit that was truly American. This new art, emancipated from European traditions, would explore and celebrate the experience of the free man in a free society. Rather than being something to be admired for its scarcity and cost, art was to have a vital function: to substantiate man's inner life, which was the source of his outer existence. This concept was to find application in the American schools.

As industry developed in America, child labor became an increasing problem. Educators awakened to the ramifications of the exploitation of children in behalf of industry, with no provision for their social or self-development. Child labor might impose a ceiling upon the child before he realized his own selfhood. The school could provide him with useful skills for service in industry; however, these skills would be of little consequence if still greater natural endowments went undetected and certain social values remained undisciplined. Surely, *Man Feeling* was of equal social importance to *Man Thinking*.

In the area of music, it became apparent that an overzealous pursuit of sight-reading skills did more to prevent than to assist the child to achieve the ultimate goal—his affective and moral development. Courses of study were minutely planned in order to pass the tests upon which all school work was evaluated; and so long as the student could perform a sight-reading exercise fluently and accurately, he fulfilled the important requirements. Unfortunately, his interest in pursuing the subject after he left school did not receive the attention it deserved. Apparently music educators were more concerned with *preparation* rather than with *fulfillment*.

It would be unfair to single out music as the only area that failed to stimulate in the individual a continuing interest. This criticism, while specifically pointing up discrepancies in the teaching of music, also levels a general indictment at the other subjects as well. However, a change of direction was soon to become evident.

I

The Liberal View

Changes in educational direction seldom occur in such a clearly defined way as to make distinct chronological treatment feasible. It is rare indeed that the end of one sequence of events can be precisely partitioned from those that herald the advance of another. Music education proves in no way to be an exception to this condition.

While principles of the New Education were discernible during the last quarter of the nineteenth century, they were by no means representative of the sum and substance of all educational thought. Nevertheless, as older systems and philosophies persisted in many quarters, a music teacher here and another there indicated that the elements of a child-centered education were gradually making progress.

A significant keynote of the new direction may well have been struck at a meeting of the Music Teachers National Association, when Millicent McKenzie said: "Gentlemen, I want fewer methods and more music."[1] This suggested that too much attention may have been paid to system and that the presentation of the subject with its proper aim and focus was in danger of being lost.

Marie Ruef Hofer pointed up the general difficulty very well in an article written toward the end of the century. She complained that so much elaboration had been given the technical side of music that its emotive aspects were nearly forgotten. In her view the artistic presentation of music was more important than theoretical abstractions.

Samuel W. Cole, too, testified against the proposition that reading was the total sum and substance of music education in the

[1] John Towers. "Teaching and Teaching Reforms—Music in Public Schools," Music Teachers National Association *Volume of Proceedings* (1889), p. 129.

public schools. He insisted that the sight-singing tests given to school children before the public did not represent the capabilities of the average class or the musical ability of the average scholar. Cole contended that to serve its purpose successfully, all children must derive benefit from music. The public school, therefore, should not have tried to assume the responsibilities of a conservatory of music, but should endeavor instead to create a musical atmosphere in America.

No longer was music to be represented entirely as a skill. Now it was to become the medium through which the child's esthetic nature could be developed and a foundation upon which his character could be formed through proper emotive experiences. In essence this was child-centered education. The development of *Man Thinking*, or outer man, was not to represent the all-embracing goal; this new American civilization called for more attention to the development of *Man Feeling*, or of inner man. The degree to which music educators were to accept the principles set forth by the New Education, and that phase of the New Psychology known as Child Study, will now be examined.

Music Education and a New Philosophy

Music education was fortunate to have in its ranks men and women who not only accepted the new philosophy but understood its ramifications and implications. Some of the most notable of these leaders were David M. Kelsey, C. H. Congdon, W. L. Tomlins, Alys E. Bentley, and Eleanor Smith.

Kelsey projected the spirit of the new philosophy when he said that music in the New Education was devoted to the expression of feeling in the most esthetic forms. Similarly Congdon offered his concept of music in the curriculum when he indicated that music's moral influence was more lasting than the word or precept. Its effectiveness, he warned, was not realized through constant drill and practice in solfeggio.

In the introduction to *The Laurel Music-Reader*, Tomlins said that he had endeavored to ". . . bring to the student the riches of an uplifting sentiment or ennobling thought." This same spirit can be found in the work of Alys Bentley, author of *The Song Series*, as well as in Eleanor Smith's *Modern Music Series*.

While music educators provided abundant support for the direction indicated by both Parker and Hall, it will be remembered that there was some conflict in the way the objective would be achieved. It was pointed out in the previous chapter that the logical solution, with regard to Parker's premise, was through the exercise of pure rote singing. On the other hand, Hall did not entirely dismiss knowledge and skill as means by which the primary aim of music could be realized. Further study reveals that music educators preferred this latter view.

Kelsey argued for concrete skills, namely, sight-singing, theory, and harmony, suggesting that for music to cultivate the emotions, it was necessary to inject substance into the course, if only as a *means* by which the moral aim would be achieved.

Supporting Kelsey's view, Congdon said that while educators looked more toward the moral influence of music, the reading aspects of the study should not be dropped. A careful study of *The Laurel Music-Reader*, *The Modern Music Series*, and *The Song Series* provides further supporting evidence. Therefore, while affective development remained the primary aim, music educators generally agreed with Hall that a body of knowledge represented a means rather than an end and that intellectual and moral faculties should not be treated as separate entities. The specific aims of the music educators may be summed up as follows: (1) the cultivation of the musical sense, and (2) the development of an understanding of the elements of music.

Music Education and the New Psychology

Hall argued that if there was no real separation drawn between moral and intellectual powers, each subject must use its own special content to realize basic objectives. His recapitulation theory seemed to support this premise.

THE EARLY YEARS

According to the psychological principles set forth by Hall, the early years of childhood had to be devoted to the development of appropriate musical experiences, upon which further training and appreciation could be based. He pointed out that up until age eight, children, like aboriginal savages, would respond more readily to primitive types of music. Step by step they would achieve a greater understanding of music in the present cultural context just as civilization slowly developed its refinements from primordial beginnings. Throughout man's development music has had its effect upon the soul. Until the most primitive experiences with sound and rhythm were enkindled within the child, through which the moods and imagery of his genetic past could be recalled, there would be no foundation upon which to build a genuine esthetic appreciation.

Music educators recognized that rhythm as well as tone could not be grasped by the intellect alone, but must be experienced through listening and singing. An appeal to the senses became the first step. In bygone days the mother's lullaby and the recitation of nursery rhymes seemed to establish this foundation in the very earliest days of childhood. Since these activities seemed to be carried on less and less in the home, the feeling for rhythm and tone within the child became the responsibility now of the teachers.

Increased importance was placed on singing in the school. According to Congdon and others, it was the general opinion that musically the first three years of school life, to include the kindergarten, should be given over to the singing of rote songs, to instill in the child an interest and a love for music. As a further value the song would be established as a comprehensive unit through which the child would receive impressions that could gradually be associated with the musical scene.

The emphasis upon rhythmic experiences seemed quite new, at least in the way they were presented. C. A. Fullerton believed that rhythm could best be developed by carefully pointing it up as it occurred in real musical situations, without isolating specific problems for drill. His assumptions were supported and carried further by Marie Burt Parr, who maintained that through singing the child would awaken to the pulse of the rhythm in such a way that even his muscles would respond to it. She suggested also that as songs were sung children might march, drum, and even illustrate the songs with pictures.

Frequently nature study, along with other subject areas, was mentioned in connection with music. This not only suggested correlation, as developed by Herbart and pointed up by Parker, but also a technique that would underscore Hall's principle of recapitulation. Casterton spoke of using songs relating to the harvest, to autumn coloring, to the preparation for winter, and so on. Hofer pointed out that such experiences would stimulate in the child thoughts and feelings of the world about him and awaken in him certain feelings and emotions that would call up the age-old relationship between man and nature.

The Modern Music Series was patterned along the lines of Hall's psychology. The series proposed that knowledge was achieved through experience and that the quality of the child's experience determined the quality of his enlightenment. It was not sufficient that children could read music with great facility. Success was determined according to how the learning process stood the true test of art education.

It was of paramount importance that the individual be given a rich musical basis for his training. Music offering immediate appeal should be used to awaken within the child the true spirit of song. This direction was apparent in both *A Primer of Vocal Music* and *A Second Book of Vocal Music* from the same series. Similar testimony can be found in *The Song Series* by Bentley, in *The Laurel Music-Reader* edited by W. L. Tomlins, as well as in *The Congdon Music Readers*.

The Period of Drill

From the ages of eight through twelve, the child was to be subjected to the disciplines of drill and habituation. Hall thought that this was the time to present note reading. However, he warned that at all times technique was to be subordinated to those activities that trained the child's sentiments, feelings, and emotions.

According to the second book of *The Modern Music Series,* considerable attention to technical work was evidenced. Each song and exercise appeared according to its position in a graduated sequence of theoretical problems. The book contained a carefully planned method of sight-reading to coincide with the child's mental capacity. Emphasis was placed upon reading the printed score, as Hall had indicated was appropriate at this stage of development.

In further testimony Book Two of *The Song Series* stressed music reading and gave copious directions as to just how such ability was to be developed. *The Congdon Music Readers*, as well as *The Laurel Music-Reader*, appears to have embodied the same spirit.

The Adolescent Period

Educational approaches necessarily had to be altered considerably for the child as he reached adolescence. For that age, a relaxation of drill methods was thought to be necessary and desirable. The educator was charged with a greater concern for the child's interest. Rather than stressing the mechanics of technique, an appeal was made to the child's interest through the presentation of larger wholes. Complex as those concepts might have been, Hall contended that adolescents could well understand them, even if their power to express them might be rather limited.

The Modern Music Series acknowledged this principle in the third book. By the time the child reached grades seven and eight, it was presumed that he had mastered the elementary principles necessary for reading and understanding songs written by the great composers. The basic purpose of this last book was to make clearer the principles already presented and to lead the student to greater enjoyment through more advanced and challenging musical experiences. With these goals in mind, the author hoped to continue the fundamental principles upon which the entire series rested, namely, to enhance the musical sense and create an understanding of the elements of music. *The Song Series*, as well as *The Congdon Music Readers*, gave further support to this view.

The Song Method

In the field of music education, those sensitive to the newer concepts recognized with Hall that reading must be taught, but only as it served the spirit of song. Congdon warned against antiquated drill methods in the fostering of reading ability. All drill should be taken from good musical literature. He said that unmusical exercises, composed only for the purpose of clarifying problems, defeat the intended objective. They are uninspired tunes and dull the child's musical sensibilities.

The indications were that music reading was moving away from the old note-for-note reading method to one that emphasized larger thought units. Hall and Parker acknowledged the improved methods of language reading. A very adequate exposition of the system can be found in Parker's work in terms of his own psychological principles.

According to the leader of the New Education, the word-method, although not considered perfect, should be emphasized because the word represented a whole. The child was not directed to analyze the word into its parts; any attempt at analysis at this stage was considered unnecessary and unnatural and diminished the action or appropriate activity the word suggested.

A child was introduced to the problem of learning to read

after approximately six years of life. By that time he had become accustomed to learning oral language spontaneously. The reading method had to conform to his most natural disposition toward learning—putting names to those objects that interested him. Association was considered a fundamental power of the mind, continually recognizing and classifying, by analogy, new and unfamiliar things.

While the child might be unconscious of any analysis, many new words contained points of identity, which he would recognize from previously acquired reading experience. In this way, he naturally would enlarge his reading vocabulary. Although analysis was acknowledged as necessary, it was acceptable only when the situation prompted it; the appropriate timing and degree of analysis depended primarily on the needs of the individual.

Parker hypothesized that through observation the child's interest would be aroused which, in turn, would spark self-activity and effort, the culminating force in the achievement of the educative act. Thus, through these elements—observation, interest, and self-activity—the child's reading power could be developed.

OBSERVATION

Parker maintained that observation represented "the continuous action of an object upon consciousness for the purpose of developing and intensifying its corresponding individual concept."[2] While this principle alone was not completely sufficient for the clarification of concepts, it was accepted as basic to the educational process.

Music educators contended that observation was one of the foundations upon which music reading could be developed. Alys Bentley seemed particularly in accord with this concept as it applied to the development of music reading. She maintained that sight-reading must be developed through observation, that the concepts derived through the continuous action of the object upon the consciousness could be as vivid and real as the object itself.

From Book Two of *The Song Series*, Bentley contended that sight-reading was not dependent upon one organ or faculty. At one moment the sense of sight, and at another the sense of hearing, might contribute most to sight-reading; at other times sight-reading

---

[2] Francis W. Parker. *Talks on Pedagogics*. New York: E. L. Kellogg and Company, 1894, p. 122.

might depend most upon memory, imagination, or the sense of rhythm. Concepts arrived at in this way would be made more adequate and perfect through the variety of experiences and contexts in which they were used.

All experiences were so presented as to clarify concepts derived through observation. The continuous action of the object upon the consciousness meant to Bentley an appeal to the powers of observation through all the senses and by a variety of means.

The primer of *The Modern Music Series* proposed that knowledge was primarily the result of experience and that the adequacy of ideas was measured by the accuracy of observation. Written for the kindergarten through second grade, the primer began with rote singing. However, rote singing did not suggest pure imitation. Children were urged to observe the rhythm by indicating some recognition of the pulses. They were also asked to note tonal characteristics through the comparison of phrases with the scale itself. After gaining a general familiarity with the elements of time and tune in this way, additional song material was provided to lead the child to increased awareness of intervals and rhythmic contrasts. Through pleasant singing experiences the child's musical vocabulary was enlarged.

In an effort to make the child's observations more acute, the primer proposed six modes of procedure, as follows: (1) rote singing; (2) song-inspired interval drill, with the child learning to sing intervals and scale fragments; (3) sight-singing, with help from the teacher when necessary; (4) singing by note and by ear in combination, a technique in which the child imitated the teacher in singing familiar tunes with syllables rather than words; (5) studying songs by note and by rote, which permitted the child to read and sing more difficult songs, with the teacher assisting him on the more involved phrases; and (6) writing melodies from memory, which helped the child to become familiar with the staff notation. According to the primer, all technique was to be gained from observing and studying music itself. Understanding was best derived from actual singing experience.

The other books of the series followed in similar patterns. The child was expected to read the score with increasing independence. At no time was song-singing de-emphasized.

Observation became an important feature in the teaching of sight-reading. The rote-note process made the child more attentive to the printed score. The teacher was at hand to analyze when the situation prompted it, but only as the specific instance required it.

However, as Parker pointed out, observation was only the beginning. Something had to succeed it if the educative process was to be carried on: this next step was represented by the act of *doing*.

SELF-ACTIVITY

According to Parker, a learning situation could be satisfactory only to the degree that a child actively responded to the given stimuli. Music educators became equally concerned with this second principle as it affected the rote-note reading process.

Properly carried out, the system called upon the child's own activity to direct him toward greater and greater understanding of the printed score. The child observed the score, heard it performed, and through his own mental activity acquired the power to read. The learning was a personal process, with the teacher acting only as a guide.

According to Bentley, "Sight-reading requires musical power. Musical power develops through its *use* in sight-reading. . . ."[3] From Eleanor Smith came further testimony of the importance of self-activity when she said that the only real training the individual received was that acquired through his own personal effort. Congdon recognized the same principle, stating that a child learned to read by reading. Too much teaching tended to retard rather than accelerate the process.

Through self-activity the child learned in the way he wanted to learn—this was most natural. The child's discoveries were not the result of a series of facts instilled in him through memory, but came rather through the child's own insight. It was further asserted that the child would learn by himself only if he was *interested* in what he observed. Therefore, the element of interest rose to a position of particular consequence.

INTEREST

Many music educators were of the opinion that rich musical experiences through song contributed a great deal toward establishing and perpetuating among pupils a continuing interest in and a love for good music. Once children were properly introduced to the

[3] Alys E. Bentley. *The Song Series, Book Two.* New York: A. S. Barnes and Company, 1907, p. 163.

subject through singing, the theoretical aspects of music could be taught more satisfactorily.

Bentley maintained that from beginning to end the basis of instruction was the song. Through songs an interest in music was first secured; technical problems could be considered later, although interest had to be kept continually alive. Without a love for music, the development of sight-reading skill was considered impossible.

In *The Modern Music Series* Eleanor Smith stated that a rich musical experience was the first essential and that only when the element of interest supported experience, could knowledge of music and its elements be developed successfully.

Interest as a basic force in music education found strong support in Hall's New Psychology. Hall's recognition of the principle will now be considered.

Music Materials Reflect a Recognition of Childhood

The Child-Study movement pointed out that the materials used in the education of children had to be childlike. The educational substance was to suit the interests and capacities of the individual child, no matter what his stage of development. Verses had to conform to children's interests. The vocabulary itself needed careful scrutiny. The words had often proved either too difficult to pronounce or entirely beyond the comprehension of the child. Melodies had to be selected primarily for their beauty rather than as unmusical backgrounds for abstract technicalities. Casterton indicated that a recognition of the child's interests was just becoming a consideration.

The Modern Music Series presented many lovely songs in support of the Child-Study movement. According to Gehrkens boards of education were invariably impressed by this new series. Their judgment was based almost entirely upon the beautiful songs that were included within the pages of the texts.

The Congdon Music Readers must be counted as one of the important series of the time. The author endorsed the principle that only through good song material could a true understanding of notation and a real appreciation of music be developed. Tomlins supported the thesis in *The Laurel Music-Reader*, stating that complete musical self-expression could best be taught through a number of beautiful songs.

Whether children were able to read music or not, the general spirit of the period gave song-singing the first importance; all other values were reduced to secondary positions.

MORNING SONG

John Karl   Eunice Goodspeed

Wake, song - birds, - 'tis sun - rise, come sing a roun - de -
lay.   'Tis morn - ing, 'tis morn - ing, and night has flown a -
way, come out, come out, and greet the day.

Suggested Lesson in Song, Observation, Testing the Ability Of The Eye.

With the books in the hands of the children, the teacher sings the song while the children follow.

The keyboard work may be applied here. The class telling in what key the song is written, on what pitch it begins and ends, etc.

The teacher sings with "la," different intervals or phrases. The children find each interval or phrase as it is sung. The following suggestions are given for the analysis of this song.

The teacher sings the following phrases. The class find phrases like them.

The teacher sings the following phrases. The class find and sing each in turn and compare them.

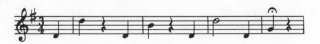

In like manner, sing and compare these phrases.

SKIPPING DANCE

STEP—Simple Child Skip.

MOVEMENTS—
1. Forward.
2. High skip, straight ahead.
3. Side skip.
4. Round skip.
    Children in groups of three.
    Right hands joined overhead.
    Skip around in a circle.
    Turn at measure six and skip in opposite direction.

SPANISH DANCE

Rocking movement, forward on strong beat. Alternately strike an imaginary tambourine on raised knee, and shake it overhead.

From Alys E. Bentley, *The Song Series, Book Two* (New York: A. S. Barnes & Co., 1910), pp. 3, 35, 36, 151, 154, 155.

II

A More Conservative View

Another group of music educators refused to break entirely with the more traditional concepts established when Spencer's philosophy prevailed. These men stood for the supremacy of content both as a means to develop mental discipline and as a foundation and preparation for the genuine esthetic experience that could eventually be realized. This reluctance to recognize the new educational direction did not suggest that they were entirely insensitive to the spirit of the times.

At the end of the nineteenth century, there were educators who reasserted a dualistic humanism, which supported a content-centered curriculum and the development of mental discipline. This suggested the traditional philosophy of idealism. Hegel was the philosopher who most nearly represented this school of thought. He maintained that morality was the chief aim in education, although his means of fostering it differed from those of Pestalozzi, Froebel, Spencer, and others. According to Hegel the child commenced life as an organism of nature, being good in only a negative way. The potential of the individual was to be drawn out by education. Through the disciplines imposed by the school, the individual would be led away from the material, which was unreal, to the spiritual, which was real.

The school years represented a period of preparation. Subject areas served their purpose best when they proved distasteful. In that way they satisfied the disciplinary development of the mind by turning the child away from his natural inclinations to those that would direct him to spiritual things. Education had the duty of presenting the individual with a predetermined package of knowledge, which would be the key to the kingdom of the spirit. Hegel's influence was only a contributory factor in American educational philosophy, but it served to re-emphasize a subject-centered curriculum.

This study has discovered nothing that would indicate that those music educators who supported content and mental discipline were traditional idealists. In fact, there is more evidence to the contrary.

While upholding the more conservative position, these men did not shut out any new thought that might serve their field of endeavor; instead they recognized much of the contemporary thought that affected their work. It will be noted, as this discussion continues, that principles of both Hall and Parker were contained in the work of those who continued to support the more established point of view. This indicates that they did not resist principles established through the philosophy of naturalism.

Music Education and a Subject-Centered Philosophy

In 1905 Frank Rix argued that because language study required the child to learn to read so that he could eventually become acquainted with the greatest literature and highest thoughts, the same demands should also be made in music. Sight-singing was not only an excellent exercise for the development of character and mental discipline, but it was the only way an individual could read and understand the world's great music.

Baldwin reflected a similar attitude when he said that a knowledge of the mechanics of music was the only real preparation for an appreciation of the esthetic side of the subject. Its language had to be taught first. A call for a return to fundamentals was urged by William T. Harris, who argued that schools existed for the purpose of imparting definite knowledge. The music educator should teach facts, which would eventually build within the child the knowledge necessary for an ultimate appreciation of music.

Further evidence may be found from the results of a group that reported to the Music Teachers National Association in 1907. Under the chairmanship of R. L. Baldwin, the committee consisted of such distinguished people as E. B. Birge, Julia E. Crane, E. G. Hood, and H. E. Owen. Their report stated that the aim in music education was achieved only when the child could manage all principles of time and tune, had gained some knowledge of the great composers, and had an acquaintance with their representative works. Specific knowledge became the means to man's complete fulfillment.

Many music textbooks of the period reflected a more traditional philosophy as indicated by the principles contained in The New Educational Music Course by McLaughlin and Gilchrist; The Melodic Music Readers by Ripley and Tapper; and The New Normal Music Course by Tufts and Holt.

A review of one specific series may be pertinent as final testimony that a form of conservatism continued to maintain a place

FIRST MUSIC READER

Part I
Rhythmic Type, One Sound to the Beat, in Various Keys and Kinds of Measure

Two-quarter measure. *Phrase* Mark. *Tie*

Clear the school-bell calls to-day. "Come, O come!" it seems to say.

Intervals
5 - 3
1 - 3
7 - 5
5 - 8

THE VILLAGE GREEN

Jane Taylor   German Folk Tune

Allegretto

Breath mark

1. On the cheer-ful vil-lage green, Skirt-ed round with hous-es small.
2. See them frol-ic hand in hand, Mak-ing now a mer-ry chain;

All the boys and girls are seen, Play-ing there with hoop and ball.
Now they form a war-like band, March-ing o'er the grass-y plain.

LEAVES AT PLAY

Frank Dempster Sherman   M. White

Allegro

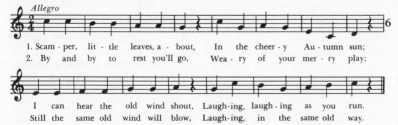

1. Scam-per, lit-tle leaves, a-bout, In the cheer-y Au-tumn sun;
2. By and by to rest you'll go, Wea-ry of your mer-ry play;

I can hear the old wind shout, Laugh-ing, laugh-ing as you run.
Still the same old wind will blow, Laugh-ing, in the same old way.

From James M. McLaughlin, George A. Veazie, and W. W. Gilchrist, *The New Educational Music Course* (Boston: Ginn and Company, 1903, 1906), p. 1.

145

of importance in spite of the inroads made by the New Education and the New Psychology. Without being bound to previously conceived principles, as were the revisions specified above, it seems fair to assume that *The Hollis Dann Music Course* was free to embrace whatever philosophy it chose. A product of the old singing school, Dann was sensitive to that type of training founded upon more traditional thought. Therefore, it is not surprising to note that he approved of the methods contained in *The Normal Music Course* of Tufts and Holt. *The Natural Music Course* by Ripley and Tapper appeared in 1895. The authors had endeavored to simplify and improve the Tufts-Holt Series, which had by then enjoyed ten years of success. Dann found the new books sufficiently satisfying to use in his classes for several years. More important, the series became the source from which he derived important principles that were later incorporated into *The Hollis Dann Music Course.*

He was convinced that a mastery of the language of music was essential to the achievement of any real and lasting appreciation. Dann argued that since an instrumentalist must read in order to participate, those following a choral track must also read. He insisted that the old-fashioned singing school had proved capable of developing the skill of music reading among its constituents.

NAMES	SEQUENTIAL EXERCISES SERIES A,B,C,D,E AND G	WRITING BOOK	REMARKS
John Bright	A, B, D, AND G	90	
Robert Burns	Cannot Sing	0	Evidently has adenoids Needs medical attention
Mary Smith	All o.k.	95	Enjoys playing teacher
John Stout	Series A only	50	From another town Never had music before Improving rapidly.

Example of January Report (Third Year): Musical Dictation, Study of Tone and Rhythm. Hollis Dann, *Manual for Teachers, Book One* (New York: American Book Company, 1912), p. 113.

Therefore, it seemed that at least the same level of achievement could be attained under the improved conditions of American education at the turn of the century.

In 1912 the American Book Company released the first volume of *The Hollis Dann Music Course*. Each book was so organized that the teacher did well to use the material as it appeared according to its chronological dependence. Both exercises and songs followed in much the same arrangement as in the previous music books of the Tufts-Holt and the Ripley-Tapper vintages.

Recognizing with the more progressive teachers that music education must not emphasize intellectual development to the complete neglect of the esthetic, Dann endeavored to maintain a balance between the mechanical and artistic sides of the subject. However, in order to attain this goal, he worked on the premise that music appreciation must be achieved through participation. To Dann sight-singing was a necessary tool through which the student could derive true appreciation. As a matter of fact, one criticism leveled at him was that he expected esthetic and spiritual qualities to follow naturally from the capacity to deal with the printed score. There is too much testimony to Dann's teaching excellence and to the success of his textbooks to take this criticism seriously. It might be more to the point to accept as possible the premise that some teachers who used his materials might have been so diligent in their projection of the subject matter that they lost sight of the spirit of the course. According to Dann, "True success lies in developing both sides of the subject."[4]

Dann was an expert in the development of the child-voice by virtue of his own experience and the influence of William Tomlins. His work emphasized beautiful singing. Heretofore those interested in music reading were often too ready to sacrifice everything else for the success of sight-singing. On the other hand, those who looked to music as the primary means for unfolding the individual's affective nature sometimes lost sight of thoroughly good voice training.

Dann was among the first to advocate that the compass of songs for the classroom be limited to the notes of the treble clef.

[4] Hollis E. Dann. "An Anomalous Situation, With Suggestions for Improvement," National Education Association *Journal of Proceedings and Addresses* (1902), pp. 618–621.

This would permit a flutelike head tone rather than the coarse chest quality resulting from songs with a very low range. The popularity Dann's books enjoyed would indicate that his series contained a quality and spirit that rendered them useful and inspiring.

The Herbartian Influence on Music Pedagogy

By 1890 some Herbartian ideas had made inroads in American education. It has already been noted in Chapter 6 that the principle of apperception supported Parker's theory regarding the unification of subject areas. At the close of the nineteenth century, Herbart markedly affected much of the day-to-day teaching techniques used in classroom instruction.

THE FORMAL STEPS

To render his psychology more effective in an educational situation, Herbart evolved his so-called *formal steps*. Before describing the processes involved, a distinction between *absorption* and *reflection* must be made. Absorption refers to the acquisition or contemplation of facts or ideas; reflection relates to the mental assimilation of facts acquired through absorption.

The first step was called *clearness*. Facts and ideas were presented to the pupil, who was expected to acquire and contemplate the material as the process of absorption demanded. The second step was *association*. It was expected that the newly acquired ideas would unite with the mass of facts already assimilated in the mind. This procedure again called for the principle of absorption, but with the addition of some reflection. *System*, the third step, called for the logical arrangement of those facts and ideas that were associated and unified as a result of step two. The process of reflection became uppermost at this point. Lastly *method* was established, calling for the practical application of what the child had learned through his apperceptive experience. According to Herbart this involved an active reflection.

These four steps seemed to suffice for Herbart. However, some of his disciples felt that the procedure was not altogether comprehensible to those who were not completely acquainted with Herbartian principles. Ziller and Rein, both devoted disciples of the famed German educator, augmented the steps to five in number. The steps were defined as follows: (1) aim and preparation, (2) presentation, (3) comparison and abstraction, (4) generalization, (5) application.

THE FORMAL STEPS AND MUSIC METHODOLOGY

According to Butts the last two decades of the nineteenth century saw Herbart's ideas influencing education as much as Pestalozzi's principles had earlier in the century. The formal steps found a definite place in the presentation of subject matter. There is reason to speculate that these steps might also have affected lesson development in music education at the same time.

In his *History of Public School Music*, Birge supported this premise when he said that a great interest in Herbartian pedagogy was apparent in the 1890s. Music methods and lesson plans were based on those principles. Further evidence for this contention may be deduced from the *Summaries of the Course in Methods*. This publication was prepared by the Alumni Association of the Institute of Musical Pedagogy. Founded by Sterrie Weaver in 1900, the Institute was carried on after his death by such men as Ralph L. Baldwin, Will Earhart, and Thaddeus P. Giddings. Every lesson plan included in the *Summary* was constructed according to the following plan: (1) aim, (2) preparation, (3) teaching, (4) application. It would seem unlikely that these headings, so comparable to those of Herbart, could have been conceived by mere coincidence.

The methods of Percy Graham, a pupil of Hollis Dann, reflect similar thinking. Developed in about 1910, Graham's *Vocal Music in the Elementary Schools* serves to suggest that he was also influenced by Herbart. Each lesson proceeded according to the familiar plan: (1) aim, (2) preparation, (3) teaching, (4) application.

The Traditional Philosophy and Child Study

There was one aspect of the Child-Study movement that those music educators who held to more traditional methods and principles absorbed to considerable degree. This was the concept that childhood needed to be recognized. In support of that phase of child study, they revised their melodies and words to reflect the interests of childhood.

MUSIC TEXTBOOK REVISIONS

A great number of music textbooks for public school use were rewritten in order to comply with the new view. *The New Educational Music Course* by McLaughlin and Gilchrist was published in 1904. Holding to the principles of *The Educational Music Course* of 1898, the revised work indicated a great effort in behalf of really good song material.

The Natural Music Course by Tapper and Ripley went through a similar revision in 1903. According to the authors the general plan of the first editions was carried over into the revised versions. However, the song material was greatly enriched to include well-known songs from America's best folk music. In 1906 *The Melodic Readers* by Ripley and Tapper was published. As in the case of *The Natural Music Course*, upon which this new series was founded, music reading was the foundation of the course. Nevertheless, a great deal of enrichment was evident in the new texts.

Meanwhile Tufts and Holt revised *The Normal Music Course*. As with the series mentioned above, *The New Normal Music Course* held completely to the features of the original texts. However, childhood interests were given consideration. There was a noticeable effort to improve both melody and words. Hollis Dann and his contributors—namely, Laura Bryant, Arthur E. Johnstone, and H. Worthington Loomis—succeeded in offering a collection of truly beautiful song material in their books.

The Child-Study movement had not been without effect. While in some areas it was accepted with reservations, in other instances its impact proved so great as to become the seed from which the next era was to grow.

PART
IV
A Period of Protest and Reaction

CHAPTER

8

Progressivism

The Genesis of Progressivism

Political and Economic Factors

THE term *progressivism* has often been considered the exclusive property of education. Actually the Progressive movement originated as a result of political and industrial factors.

Abuse of power turned public opinion against the giants of industry and their political allies. As the muckrakers succeeded in indicting the leaders of industry on charges of ruthless business practices and of buying their way to ever greater power from government representatives, the public demanded that the situation be remedied. Corrective measures by the old order had been nothing more than ineffective patch-up jobs. Thoroughly impatient with conservative reform, the new progressives vigorously challenged the status quo.

There were conflicting views in the progressive camp, which were evident in the presidential campaign of 1912. Those who followed Theodore Roosevelt committed themselves to a severe reorganization of the American political and economic system. On the other hand, the Wilsonian platform of progressivism was relatively more conservative. No matter which of the two candidates the voters supported, it was clear that the American nation had awakened to the need for a re-examination of principles which deeply affected its life.

Progressivism, then, was a mass movement representing and uniting the expressions of many political trends and social attitudes. It is difficult to define the philosophy of this movement, which was, as Ralph H. Gabriel described it, ". . . a potpourri of social theories and beliefs."[1]

EDUCATION AND THE PROGRESSIVE MOVEMENT

Neither political progressivism nor its educational counterpart was a completely systematic philosophy. As older and more conservative ideas were protested and challenged, progressivism emerged, its character and aims shaped by the reaction against conservatism.

Progressivism and the Philosophy of Pragmatism

It is important to distinguish progressivism from the pragmatist philosophy of John Dewey. The upheaval that gave birth to progressive ideas took place before Dewey achieved educational leadership. Whereas pragmatism is correctly identified as a philosophy, progressivism was first a *practice*, from which a philosophy eventually evolved. Although an affinity may have existed between them, they were two quite separate movements.

While there were experimental schools founded upon the philosophy of pragmatism, as early as 1918, their aims and values were not generally accepted. Only later was pragmatism to influence education widely. According to Sidney Hook the acceptance of the principles of progressivism did not by any means suggest acceptance of the tenets of pragmatism.

---

[1] Ralph Henry Gabriel. *The Course of American Democratic Thought*. New York: The Ronald Press Company, 1940, p. 332.

The Individual and Society

Soon after the Civil War many educators recognized that education was not entirely satisfactory. Children were found to be well trained in the memorization of many facts and definitions and highly developed in certain skills. However, after these students left school, they carried with them little or no intellectual curiosity, which might lead to continued growth and the further acquisition of knowledge. No apparent taste for art seemed to result from the traditional school; and all the information that had been poured into the students' minds appeared to have no moral effect upon them at all. Further, even though they were well-versed in the facts of history and government, they lacked a sense of citizenship.

It was probably this last problem that caused the greatest concern. Many leaders began to fear that social cohesion was imperiled. Any new means for the conservation of society would have to be supplemented by education. The conservatives favored a course that emphasized morality imparted through strict disciplinary means. But progressives, differed in their major plans as to how a new social cohesion could be accomplished. They insisted that repressive measures were not appropriate for schools in a

Winslow Homer, *The Country School* (1871). Oil on canvas, 21⅜″ x 38⅜″. City Art Museum of Saint Louis, Missouri.

democratic society, where expansion of the mind and spirit should be fostered instead. Such thinking led to a serious questioning of the traditional curriculum and a renewed interest in a liberal education.

It is too early to draw a valid definition of the progressive philosophy. Only as it developed, did its philosophy emerge. Because the movement embraced many schools of thought, a consideration of its practices must provide the initial focus.

Some Progressive Principles of Psychology

Until almost the turn of the new century, philosophy included both a theory of knowledge and psychology. Gradually the material of both became so vast that a division of the subject was inevitable. Men of one temperament naturally found the rationalistic method of philosophy more appealing, while others preferred the experimental methods of science. Psychology as a separate field began to stand on its own feet as the offspring of philosophy.

The nineteenth century was marked by a series of impressive scientific discoveries. Americans could not help but become extremely conscious of the importance of science and the scientific method. They became suspicious of any system that was incompatible with experimental science. People credited psychology rather than philosophy with the capacity to provide solutions to problems. There was a widening gap between the two disciplines, even though they were related in principle. Education reflected a kind of impatience with metaphysics. By the turn of the century, the emphasis was on practice rather than theory.

The confusion that existed in the United States during the 1890s in the realm of educational psychology is difficult to imagine. In most colleges and teacher-training institutions, the old faculty psychology continued to dominate. About the time that Hall started the Child-Study movement, Frank M. and Charles A. McMurry, with Charles DeGarmo, introduced the Herbartian pedagogy.

William James launched an all-out attack on faculty psychology in 1890 with his *Principles of Psychology*, following it in 1891 with *Talks on Psychology of Interest to Teachers*. The Child-Study movement did not prove entirely effective in establishing a science of education. As to the Herbartian movement John Dewey in 1896 attacked its doctrine of interest in a paper entitled "Interest in Its Relation to Will" before the National Herbart Society. This was done with such success that "Herbart" was dropped soon afterward from the name of that well-established organization. However, it must be conceded that Herbart's principles still contributed considerably in the area of method and classroom procedures.

With the advent of the twentieth century, the older psychologies that stressed introspection and mind-body dualism were replaced. The last of these to go was Structuralism, which, under the leadership of Edward B. Titchener, continued on into the present century. While structuralism, combined with a study of images, thoughts and feelings, withstood the test of purely scientific precision, it was not destined to fit the popular American notion of what psychology should offer.

Americans preferred a science that could direct and improve the business of everyday living. They were not interested in the real complexities of the mind. Psychology in this country had to be practical and to focus its attention upon the mind in use. Darwin's theory of evolution directed its course. Man, as a child of nature, had to develop by adjusting and adapting to his environment.

According to Edward H. Reisner the arrival time of experimental psychology could be pinpointed at some time between the publication of O'Shea's *Education as Adjustment* in 1903 and Bagley's *The Educative Process* in 1905. Of the various psychologies that developed during this period, those most pertinent to this discussion are Functionalism, Behaviorism, and, if not in the strictest sense a *school* of psychology, the movement of Tests and Measurements.

FUNCTIONALISM

Evolution maintained that man was a part of nature. His intellectual and moral achievements were developed in the natural processes of biological adaptation and adjustment to his environment. To the psychologist things looked very different when *functions* of a whole organism were considered. Animals and plants had survived the evolutionary struggle as complete living things rather than as cells, organs, or tissues. If individual differences had accounted for survival, enabling some living things to adapt to changing environmental conditions, then individual differences were clearly of the greatest importance. Those psychologists who stressed adaptation and adjustment became known as Functionalists. Their field of study was accepted as practical, a condition that suited American temperament.

Educational procedures were bound to be influenced by the changed conception of the nature and functions of mind. The school began to realize its place as the initiator of activities appropriate to the child's interests and capacities.

Adaptation and Adjustment

Dewey's article entitled "The Reflex Arc Concept in Psychology," published in 1896, marked the beginning of the functional school. He theorized that psychological activity could not be analyzed into parts but had to be considered as one complete whole. Dewey did not believe in treating physical and mental experiences as entirely separate phenomena: any act included both the physical and the psychical. The older conception of the dualism of mind and body was discarded. By considering only total coordination, every act was studied in its totality. There was no clear-cut division between stimulus and response. Functionalism studied mental activity from a biological point of view. The genetic approach was emphasized not only as it applied to psychological but to educational problems as well.

George E. Partridge, in his *Genetic Philosophy of Education*, stated that philosophy had to play a secondary role, permitting genetic psychology to provide educational progressivism with its basic concepts. Of all the new thoughts evolved, the dominant principle seemed to be that of *development*, which emphasized, according to Charles Judd, ". . . a progressive fitting of a species more and more fully to its environment."[2] From this general idea stemmed certain pedagogical ideals.

Most important was the principle found in the recognition of individual differences. Different standards of judgment were adopted for each level of development. Perfection was considered a relative term. Progressivism promoted the ideal that the school should recognize individuality, not as one entity among like entities but as a mark of differentiation. Pupils had to do things in their own way. As long as the child indicated in his work an appropriate method, that method was permitted; but when the method was seen to be faulty, it was corrected.

[2] Charles Hubbard Judd. *Genetic Psychology for Teachers.* New York: D. Appleton and Company, 1907, p. 106.

There had been a great deal of discussion concerning the question of whether a child was by nature good or bad. The progressive position emphasized that the child was neither good nor bad. The doctrine of development maintained that at birth the child was not adapted to his environment. It was to be expected that he would perform acts that were not always in accord with conditions as they really were. However, by the very fact that he had the power to vary and adjust his actions, he eventually could and would adapt.

A Theory of Knowledge

Progressives were opposed to the older premise that education should aim at a refinement of functions. Instead they pursued the broader ideal of adaptation. At that time there was much pressure upon the school to offer vocational courses. While the progressives supported this movement, they did not agree that a refinement of function in those areas represented the educational end-all. Instead they fostered vocational training only as it contributed to the immediate environment. Specific knowledge had its place. However, no educational system could be considered worthy if the training it supported only resulted in the development of memory. With the mastery of only the formal content of a subject, which tended to confine its meaning to something fixed, learning was considered incomplete.

Progressives asserted that the child would not continue through life in the environment represented by the present. Therefore, concrete facts had to be fitted into a system of meanings and understandings in order that the individual could adapt to the new and ever-changing situations he would meet in the future.

Learning to Do by Doing

From child study, biology, and sociology, a very important tenet was emphasized. It was no longer believed that rigid order in the classroom was necessary to concentration. More importance was placed upon what the child expressed as a result of his impression than upon the quantity of facts that could be poured into his mind to be memorized.

Judd asserted that an impression had to modify the active life of the individual. It was the motor consequences that gave it meaning. After an impression had been received, an activity of some kind followed. As action became associated with the impression, the idea or experience became more significant. The functional school dismissed the older concept of the dualism of mind and body. It maintained that an act must include both the physical and the psychological.

General Learning

Some psychologists held that there were generalizing effects possible in learning. They contended that the child learned more than just the specific subject matter upon which attention was immediately focused, that transfer of learning took place where similarities of relationships existed. These generalists maintained that experiences must be related in such a way ". . . that what is gained at one point will redound to the advantage of the individual in many spheres of thought and action."[3]

Associated knowledge   W. H. Kilpatrick's association with the project method has identified him with this wider, generalist procedure. He maintained that the child did not learn one thing at a time but a number of things associated with the principal object of the child's attention. Not only was it possible for one activity to reveal to the child associated knowledge, but also ideas and attitudes that would lead on to more activities when the lesson itself had been completed.

Concepts were of no consequence unless they could be learned in connection with real and living challenges. As they became tools for living, they could, as meaningful entities, transfer to many applications. The history teacher became more concerned with the child's development in character and citizenship than with his retention of every detail of the Civil War. In the same way the arithmetic teacher directed the child's attention to the values of the study in actual life situations rather than toward a refinement of arithmetical acumen. Meaning and understanding took precedence over mere fact.

Reading   The foremost educators indicated a strong dissatisfaction with the way in which reading was taught. They held that only by strength of tradition did the subject maintain such an important place in the lowest grades. Supported by science, child-

[3] Lawence E. Cole and William F. Bruce. *Educational Psychology.* New York: World Book Co., 1950, p. 514.

hood was considered a time for other subjects. The reading process could not be undertaken successfully until the pupil's nervous system and sense organs became stronger and more fully developed.

Dewey pointed out that the child should be about eight years old before anything other than incidental attention to the subject of reading was offered. He agreed with physiologists that such confining work was inadvisable with little children whose sense organs and nervous systems were yet not sufficiently developed.

According to others such training was not to be undertaken seriously until the child reached the age of ten. The finer movements of eyes and fingers adapted themselves to such techniques only after they had become developed. The nervous and muscular systems in the child's early years were just not ready for such specific work. The recapitulation theory indicated that reading came late to the race; therefore, other matters should mark the child's primary education.

The child was obliged to linger in the oral stage during his first years of schooling. When, according to Edmund B. Huey the reading activity was introduced, the pupil would progress as he saw and heard new words in contexts that would suggest their meanings. A reading vocabulary could be developed more easily by allowing the child to accomplish it in the same way as he had achieved his spoken vocabulary, by learning new words through content and through using them to his own purpose. Phonics was dangerous before the age of eight or nine.

By studying the causes of learning plateaus Judd and others supported the theory that learning had to begin with larger wholes. After an exposition of such units, a period of analysis would follow. Then a concluding time allotment was given to the reconsideration of the whole. Learning followed a pattern of whole-part-whole, or synthesis-analysis-synthesis.

Judd pointed out that modern reading techniques were structured to develop economical ways of deriving meanings. The active side of reading, particularly the articulation of the eye movements, was to be established before meaning could be drawn from the printed page. The first important fusion in the reading process took place when the child connected a written word with the spoken language by the process of synthesis. However, instead of looking to the next seemingly natural step of moving from word to sentence, Judd warned that a period of analysis must come next. The child had to be taught how to break up the written word into its elements. This prepared the child for a more complex synthesis of words into phrases and then into sentences. Only when this process of synthesis to analysis to synthesis was achieved could eventual meaning be derived from the printed page.

Creative Thinking   Learning could not be considered complete with the mastery of only the formal content of a subject. To repeat a given fact confined meaning to something fixed and unchangeable.

In protest to the older concepts of repression, progressives tended toward a development of initiative and expression. Creative experience became the means, by allowing flexibility within a learning situation, so that each child could derive from his experience not only lessons pertinent to his everyday life but also an interest in further pursuits suggested by the original activity. The creative experience was considered a valuable element in the development of the child's educational growth.

BEHAVIORISM AND CONNECTIONISM

Behaviorism was officially inaugurated in 1913 by John B. Watson. In company with his followers, he challenged traditional psychology on the grounds that it depended entirely upon introspection. According to the behaviorists such a method fell short of scientific demonstration. They argued that by observing behavior, the success or failure of certain learning situations could be accurately measured. According to the new thought all learning could be reduced to conditioned reflex.

This school became concerned with the study of the child's outward behavior. Learning was viewed as a process where connections between stimuli and responses were established. Connectionism found its way into educational doctrine, especially through the efforts of Edward Lee Thorndike. It must be said, however, that in spite of an undoubted alliance between Thorndike and Watson, Thorndike never attached himself to Watson's school. Nevertheless, his thinking, in regard to habit and attitude formation, indicated an unmistakable inclination toward behaviorism.

Specific Learning

Thorndike objectively dismissed assumptions regarding faculty psychology and mental discipline. What a man was and what he accomplished were the results of his original nature—the constitution and disposition with which he was born—and the environment that acted upon him before and after birth. Ideas were established when connections were formed between a situation and a response. Any skill a man attained represented an appropriate reaction to a certain situation. Learning was no longer looked upon as a training of certain inborn faculties. Instead it became a process of building connections or bonds between stimuli and responses. Several important results, which had a profound bearing upon education, can be attributed to Thorndike.

According to Thorndike's concept of transfer of training, no carryover could take place unless there were common elements in the subject areas involved in the transfer. From the study of Latin, it was possible for some transfer to take place to the study of English, because certain words in English were derived from Latin. If good citizenship included, among other things, a knowledge of the best hygienic practices, the formation of good hygiene habits could result in a transfer to better citizenship. It appeared, then, that certain subject areas could be considered the source from which common knowledge was derived. Attention had to be given to specific accomplishment in these areas.

As a result Thorndike and his followers proceeded to develop economical methods of teaching each specific subject within the curriculum. Every area called for its own special methodology; it was the duty of the psychologist to determine the most effective techniques to be utilized in each instance. While this method could be considered narrow, Kilpatrick acknowledged that it had merit in the development of specific skills.

The Expanding Curriculum

An attack had been made upon the theory of mental discipline in American education. It had been presumed that the classics were of utmost importance; they disciplined the mind, though their *practical* contribution to the student's life was questionable.

Thorndike pointed out that no one study could be favored over another for the general improvement of the mind. Therefore, students who wished to pursue a certain goal would not attain it through study of the classics but rather through those subjects that bore directly on the end in view. This concept, coupled with a host of pressures from outside educational circles, opened the doors to a vastly expanded curriculum.

The prevailing attitude in the field of education made change a distinctly difficult problem. For centuries education had been considered the means of developing the individual for the professions or for the "good life" enjoyed by the leisure class. Any attempt to prepare an individual for productive work had been thought unworthy of an educational institution.

This attitude did not go unchallenged; there were too many forces at work. Industrialism was rapidly making itself felt among the entire population. Scientific management, with its "efficiency engineers," had proved its worth to both factory and laborer. Industrial occupations were considered less degrading, and with coincident changes in the social situation, the public demanded that youth be given the opportunity of preparing for practical employment. The conviction deepened that the chief function of the school was, by specific instruction, to aid the industrial population in acquiring the means of earning its living.

As a result of such pressures, and substantiated by psychology, classical education was no longer to be the dominating influence in the high school. The curriculum was to be greatly enlarged.

Tests and Measurements

Another of Thorndike's contributions to education was in the new field of tests and measurements. Darwin's conclusion that all living things showed slight variations had paved the way for the study of individual differences. Francis Galton and Karl Pearson may be credited with initiating the idea of educational testing; but it was the publication in 1890 of James McKeen Cattell's *Mental Tests and Measurements* that led to the Measurement Movement, which would make testing a common feature of the American school. Refining and systematizing the work already done, Thorndike, a student of Cattell, adapted quantitative tests and measurements to the field of education.

Thorndike's publication of the *Hand-Writing Scale* in 1910 marked the beginning of a long series of tests used in the evaluation of the work of children. Other early efforts, which are worthy of note, were *The Steon Arithmetic Test, the Hillegas Composition Scale*, and *The Trabue Language Scale*.

The testing of so-called general intelligence is credited to Alfred Binet and Theodore Simon. In 1905 these two Frenchmen offered tests to determine which children would and which would not benefit from regular schoolwork. Almost at once American educators became interested in using these tests. Certain changes were made by William Stern in 1910 and by Terman and Childs in 1912; and in 1916 the Stanford revision appeared. The testing movement grew by leaps and bounds with the appearance of a long list of tests that enabled teachers to measure the results of their instruction.

In Search of a Philosophy

Education could not confine itself to a pattern based solely upon science and psychology. Educators had to be guided by explicit aims; and these aims must be grounded in a theory of knowledge. There were many schools of philosophy from which to choose.

HUMANISM

There were those who redirected attention to humanism, fostering a reaction against the emphasis being placed upon naturalistic philosophies. This group reasserted a dualistic humanism, which rested upon the traditional philosophy of idealism. In general, they advocated a liberal education, but they harked back in their arguments to mental discipline and to the development of individual faculties, which would make possible the transfer of learning to other subjects.

Sufficient testimony has been offered to support the contention that progressives represented a group of thinkers who were respectful of all scientific findings. Their interest in the new and improved procedures provided a momentum that generated the spirit of the movement. It was highly improbable that they could have been guided by any philosophy that would have reacted against the very principles that served as a foundation for their thinking.

REALISM

The philosophy of realism, at the time of the progressive movement, maintained that the dualism of inner consciousness and outer world incorrectly assumed consciousness to have reality. It held that consciousness was a nonentity, was actually a *function* of experience. While there were conflicting theories within the school of realism, it was unified on the proposition that knowing was a process that effected a reconciliation between an organism and an object. Through science civilization had accumulated a fund of knowledge, which had become basic to its existence; it was the responsibility of the learner to master that inheritance and build upon it.

Since realism dealt with the world of the here and now and was extremely sensitive to the findings of science, the realists quite naturally went along with a stimulus-response type of learning that led toward scientific tests and measurements. The position of the realists, even including Breed's *Education and the New Realism* of 1919, never exerted a direct influence upon educational philosophy, but had its effect upon education through the work of the determinists.

IDEALISM

Idealism had a tremendous impact upon instruction during the nineteenth century. This philosophy could be expressed in several forms, of which two most directly affected education.

There were the traditional idealists who opposed naturalism and believed that the purpose of teaching was to discipline the child in such a way as to prepare him for the world to come.

Opposed to this school were the idealists who recognized the ramifications of Darwinism. Although man was still seen as a spiritual being, there was too much evidence to support the premise that nature had much to do with his development. This evolutionary idealism, which represented a compromise between idealism and naturalism, seems to have had a particularly potent effect upon American education.

Looking back to Pestalozzi, it was impossible to associate his thought with a specific philosophy beyond that of Rousseau's naturalism. While Pestalozzi's principles identified him in some ways with sense realism, his emphasis upon the moral aim would have better suited an idealist than a realist. Though he had not tried to erase the distinction between heart and mind, Pestalozzi had urged that moral and intellectual education proceed together, with the *heart* maintaining a place of the highest importance.

Froebel, though clearly an idealist, was not wholly allied with traditional idealism. He had received his impulse to teach not only from the writings of Pestalozzi but also from firsthand experience with the Swiss educator at Yverdon. While Froebel attempted to inspire his charges with the life of Jesus and with the image of God's fatherhood, still he asserted that a child's education had to conform to nature.

Herbart, fired by what he had learned at Burgdorf from Pestalozzi, set himself to render those ideas more scientific. Herbart's principles came to this country at a time when the desire to emulate industrial efficiency in the public school was at a peak. Because his psychology appeared so sympathetic toward scientific principles, it was hastily endorsed. His philosophy, on the other hand, did not enjoy the same recognition. Character development, or the establishment of a good moral life, provided the basis of his educational philosophy. Virtue was achieved when a child's acts were in genuine accord with a good understanding of right and wrong. The aim of education was to inculcate within the pupil those ideas that would contribute to his comprehension of the accepted moral order and would help him carry it out.

Parker, influenced by both Froebel and Herbart, was fundamentally an idealist. He contended that the physical world could not be, or continue to be, without the creative and guiding power of an Absolute Mind, or God. Similarly man himself must somehow represent an expression of that same spiritual force. However, Parker never lost sight of the views inherent in naturalism. He proceeded from the hypothesis that the child determined the limits of his own development; therefore, any educational philosophy had to consider individuality of special consequence. No body of knowledge could be pointed to as the key to an individual's perfection. It was the child's own capacity and activity, aided by the teacher's guidance, that eventually would unfold to realize the individual's potential. The natural way was the only way the organism could readily develop.

Idealism—subscribed to in whole or in part by every major contributor to the development of child training, including Pestalozzi, Froebel, Herbart, and Parker—had become a foundation stone of American educational philosophy. This same philosophy of idealism continued into the twentieth century. According to Horne there was an outward world order as well as an inner world of experience, and both were in need of attention. Man's continual quest was for self-realization. From the outer world he would construct an inner world, which approximated external reality. Man was born with certain potential; and learning clarified what at the beginning was inchoate. Learning was an unfolding of what was within the individual from birth.

In some of its aspects idealism leaned toward essentialism. As matter was apprehended through the senses, ideas were apprehended by the mind. Ideas were considered eternal. They became the essentials of the child's education.

Partridge said, in his *Genetic Philosophy of Education*, that educational principles had to be in agreement with the external realities of life and also prove harmonious to the inner values as represented by ideals and imagination. Where educational effort was directed toward the child's mind, attention had to be focused upon nature's way. This principle suggested naturalism. Such attention to the dualism of inner consciousness and the outer world re-emphasized what had by then become a more or less traditional American educational philosophy.

The abundance of philosophical activity makes it impossible to say that speculative thought was laid aside in the formation of educational aims during the period of progressivism. However, it would be impossible to select any one particular philosophy until principles and practices are more carefully scrutinized in real educational situations. The next chapter will explore the particular philosophy that guided education in the progressive era.

A Conflict of Views

The fact that music education hitched its wagon to the progressive star by no means signified that it did so without real cause. Music educators recognized that many problems still called for solution but the new principles and methods held forth a great deal of promise. In spite of the growth that music education had enjoyed during the nineteenth century, a serious conflict of views between two opposing schools of thought still remained unresolved.

Perhaps the basic argument can be represented best by Frank McMurry's work in the New York City School Inquiry which estimated the quality of teaching, the courses of study, and other important points in the elementary schools of that city. Among his findings he indicated that the subject of music, with other studies, placed emphasis on technical efficiency. The course was considered badly abstract with little appeal to the children.

Although there were those in the field of music education who were careful to avoid this emphasis upon technical efficiency, they were not allowed to enjoy complacency either. Some agreed with Osbourne McConathy when he said that the reaction to an emphasis upon sight-reading led to a type of instruction in which hearty and spontaneous singing became the focus of attention with the aim that music be studied for joy and inspiration. Such work, according to McConathy, represented the pendulum swinging much too far in the opposite direction. Therefore, the music educators looked for new aims and methods which might provide a necessary balance between both schools of thought.

Summary of the Principles of Progressivism

A number of ideas have been pointed up in this chapter in an effort to characterize the progressive movement. For convenience, some of the more important elements are reviewed below.

I. A Period of Protest
    A. Progressivism was a movement of protest and reaction against traditional beliefs that had no scientific basis.
    B. It cannot be assumed that educational progressivism and the philosophy of pragmatism were identified together as one and the same thing. Progressivism as a movement could not be assigned any one accurate definition since it represented a collection of many theories and beliefs.
    C. Progressivism dedicated itself to the development of the individual, without failing to realize that society as a whole must be improved.

II. Some Progressive Principles of Psychology
    A. Functionalism
        1. The most dominant principle was that of development that emphasized a progressive adaptation and adjustment of the individual to his environment. Perfection was considered a relative term, with different standards of judgment adopted for each level of development. Individual differences were recognized.
        2. Progressives reacted against the older premise that

education should aim at a refinement of functions. A broader ideal in a theory of knowledge was pursued.

3. The progressives maintained that bodily activity was as necessary as mental activity in the learning process. An effective educational situation had to provide a total experience, with as much attention accorded to the expressive interpretation as to the impression received.

4. Generalists held that the child learned a number of things associated with the specific object of his attention, so that a number of things were learned at one time. The project method gained particular favor. There was a tendency also toward the development of initiative and expression, with creative experience the means.

B. Behaviorism and Connectionism

1. The spirit of connectionism found its way into educational doctrine through Watson and Thorndike. Attention was directed to the scientific development of economical methods for the teaching of each specific subject.

2. From Thorndike's ideas on the transfer of training, the doors to a great curriculum expansion were opened.

3. Tests and measurements provided instruments by which the child's potential and progress could be scientifically evaluated.

III. Philosophy

A. Philosophy was still needed to provide aims and direction. Three schools of speculative thought were particularly active; namely, humanism, realism, and idealism.

9

Music Education
and the
Progressive
View

A Period of Protest and Reform

FROM THE TIME OF THE FRANCO-PRUSSIAN WAR, the Germans used the term *Kultur* to refer to the whole socio-politico-scientific activity that was growing up among them. The word *culture* was often used to encompass the entire range of man's activities, connoting civilization rather than the narrower meaning, esthetic development.

Around the period of the Civil War, science guided the intellectual progress of the American people and emphasized that same meaning of culture. Recognizing life as a biological function, scientists emphasized the absolute necessity of the individual's adaptation to his environment. Immediate interests were satisfied by supplying the demand for creature comforts, labor- and time-saving machines and devices.

171

Educators were also becoming more aware that adaptation necessitated the recognition of immediate interest. However, while they agreed that vocational courses had valid services to render, they resisted any pressure to make such studies the educational end-all. Education should not only help the child adapt to the present but also to the future. The only way in which such broad ends could be accomplished was to permit a practical education to form the foundation upon which a truly liberal education could be constructed. Education was to serve remote as well as immediate ends.

Educators in the art fields wished to re-emphasize the esthetic aspects of culture referred to by the Germans as *Bildung*. Although they acknowledged that science had a rich contribution to make, they pointed out that it had not enhanced virtue, improved taste, or enriched man's inner life.[1]

A PHILOSOPHY OF ESTHETICS

Until World War I esthetics remained in the grip of traditional idealism, which insisted upon art for art's sake. But a new point of view was steadily gaining acceptance.

An earlier chapter noted that Emerson and Whitman had been influenced by Darwin. They maintained that no part of life could be separated from the whole. Further, with the new divisions of society, the culture that had ornamented the lives of the upper classes was of little consequence unless it could render a functional service to all.

For fifty years these thoughts had lain almost neglected until they were picked up by the American architect Louis Sullivan. He believed that an original American architecture could only result from the integrated personalities of real Americans and that the ideas and techniques must come from *both* science and art. Sullivan maintained that the power in culture had to come "from the vast human plenum we have called the multitudes."[2] What he partially realized, Frank Lloyd Wright carried much further. Wright's conviction that architecture should prove functional to the needs of a changing culture reflected the evolutionary outlook.

[1] Charles Gray Shaw. *Trends of Civilization and Culture.* New York: American Book Co., 1932, p. 76.

[2] Harold Rugg. *Culture and Education in America.* New York: Harcourt Brace and Company, 1931, p. 177.

Music also seemed to adopt this viewpoint. Basing his approach upon that of Herbert Spencer, who applied Darwin's theories to science, psychology, and ethics, C. Hubert Parry considered the art of music from a similar standpoint in his *Evolution of the Art of Music*. The American composer Edward MacDowell expressed similar thoughts in *Critical and Historical Essays*.

Through a change in esthetic principles, the musician began to consider *Man Thinking* and *Man Doing*. It was the whole man toward which attention now became directed—his mental and physical growth as well as his spiritual and emotional development. The whole man meant inner man and outer man, man as an individual as well as man as part of society. Esthetics began to point away from the refinements that had made it the property of the dilettante to the practical, or functional, which made it the property of the many. Art was to be for all, not for the few.

Music Education as a Social Force

Progressives supported the principle of individual development. Recognizing, however, that in the past so much attention had been given to individualism that social cohesion had suffered, it became evident that education must become an instrument for the preservation of society. Educators began to recognize the service that music was capable of rendering in this regard.

Karl Gehrkens emphasized this point in his *Introduction to School Music Teaching*. Group singing, he said, fostered group feeling. Because music was a language of the emotions, it was capable of inspiring a deep sense of patriotism and a susceptibility to other necessary social values. *The Universal School Music Series* endeavored in its texts to encourage this aspect of music.

Peter Dykema was very active in promoting group singing, even beyond the confines of the classroom. In 1913 the Music Supervisors' National Conference published a pamphlet of "18 Songs for Community Sings." This marked the first real attempt by music educators to suggest to the adult community what it should sing. The pamphlet appeared just prior to the community Christmas celebrations. These songs, along with the carols children were taught at school, formed a very important part of holiday festivities.

The success of the pamphlet was so overwhelming that early in 1917 the "18 Songs" was expanded into "55 Community Songs."

This was later revised into the famous "Twice 55 Community Songs," which probably inspired a score of similar songbooks that appeared soon afterward. This interest in community music, supported so avidly by Dykema, actually grew more quickly than any other movement music educators had ever sponsored. Dykema credited this to the mood of the war years, when expressions of national feeling and unity were strong.

Music Education and Progressive Principles of Psychology

FUNCTIONALISM

Adaptation and Adjustment

One of the most outstanding characteristics of the progressives was their insistence upon a developmental approach. Perfection was considered a relative term, with different standards of judgment adopted for each step of the way.

Progressive music educators recognized that content and materials had to be adaptable to the stage of growth and development of the children they taught. Intellectual growth was gradual; and only as the elemenary capacities of the child's mind were enlarged by experiences that complimented those faculties could the educator lead him to greater musical attainment.

The work was planned from a psychological concept rather than from inferences arrived at through armchair speculation. Courses of study were developed from the standpoint of the child's mind and experience. There were considered to be three well-defined stages of growth: the sensory period, the associative period, and the adolescent period.

In the sensory stage, which included the first three grades, a collection of rich musical experiences was presented as a basis for the child's further musical education. By a variety of means, the child was gradually introduced to music reading.

The earliest attempts to sing provided him with a background of musical ideas from which further knowledge could be developed. His voice went up and down in pitch, and he articulated short tones and long tones. Although no precise knowledge resulted from such primitive beginnings, these experiences carried him through the

PICTURING

To help first-grade children to listen intently to the music they sing and hear, have them compare the auditory impressions which they are now for the first time trying to analyze, with certain types of visual perception already familiar. . . .

"Swanee River"

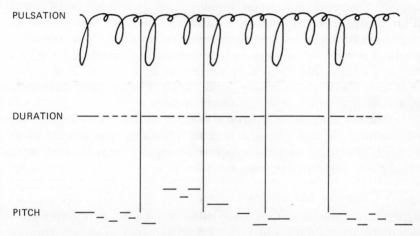

PULSATION

DURATION

PITCH

A fuller discussion of this whole matter will be found in the valuable book entitled "Education Through Music," by C. H. Farnsworth to which the editors are indebted for the original idea.

From Walter Damrosch, George H. Gartlan, Karl W. Gehrkens, *The Universal School Music Series, Book One* (New York: Hinds, Hayden and Eldredge, Inc., 1923), pp. 173–174. Courtesy Barnes & Noble, Inc.

same kind of process he had encountered in speech, that is, from mere babbling to the articulation of definite words. The teaching of music started in the same way as language techniques, from rote or imitation. This was accepted as the natural way of learning.

The associative period, grades four through six, emphasized the cultivation of specific skills. This was the time to train the finer muscular and mental coordinations. Reading and its allied activities were pursued because drill and discipline were more easily accepted at this stage than at any other period of development.

Gehrkens warned of the danger of dwelling too much upon such activities: while a departure into a disciplinary realm was psychologically admissible, the music teacher should never lose sight of the primary aim, that of fostering in the children a love and appreciation of the subject.

During the adolescent period, grades seven and eight, the work was planned from a more adult point of view. This last period found the child dominated by his emotions more strongly than before. Concentration upon molding the character, encouraging high ideals, and cultivating a taste for the finer art forms was urged. Training was more general than specific. New phases of musical development were introduced, with singing activities taking less of the time than they previously had. It was at this point that the study of composers and music history was introduced, along with a study of instrumental works.

Music educators endeavored to cater to the child's natural way of learning. It was thought that by following the procedure described, the right musical experiences might be presented to the child at the appropriate time.

A Theory of Knowledge

Progressives declared that knowledge could not be represented by the mere accumulation of facts. Education had to satisfy two conditions. One immediate aim was the mastery of specific subject matter areas such as the three R's. A more pressing responsibility demanded that schoolwork was to prepare the child for life; meaning and understanding were of prime consequence.

Charles H. Farnsworth maintained that music material had to be so presented as to relate to preceding experience. In this way the elements incorporated within the whole became integrated into meanings instead of remaining separate and unrelated parts. Ideas were developed so as to form a foundation for further ideas, and the child was led to newer and richer experiences. The same thinking was reflected by Gehrkens, who offered every possible activity in order to achieve a development of meaning and understanding.

The Music Education Series emphasized that only songs and not exercises were to be used. Previously, according to the authors, as soon as a child learned a fact in one situation, the underlying precept was presumed learned. Progressive thinking reasoned that no such thing could be taken for granted, that only when the individual had experienced the precept in many contexts could it be considered understood. Therefore, a wide range of experience appeared essential to the progressives if proper meanings were to be derived. A similar expression of that principle was clearly offered in *The Progressive Music Series*.

Learning to Do by Doing

The old conception of the dualism of mind and body was discarded in favor of the proposition that any act must include both mental and physical activity. Learning became entirely related to doing. This tenet was given genuine support by those music educators generally accepted as spokesmen of the period.

In a general discussion of his principles, Farnsworth pointed to the necessity of providing a combination of bodily and mental activity in the work. He so arranged his material as to make ultimate use of the principle of self-activity. As an example the child stepped in response to rhythm and clapped to indicate duration.

Gehrkens lent support to the general precept when he said that rote singing and bodily response to rhythm by marching, clapping, and swaying should receive great emphasis. In this way the child could derive the proper meaning and values. Further testimony for this concept was provided in *The Universal School Music Series*, to which Gehrkens was a contributor.

The Progressive Music Series underscored the need not only for singing but also for rhythmic experiences. Rhythmic activities were developed through bodily action to include singing games, folk dances, marching, and dramatization.

While most music educators agreed with this tenet in principle, they were at variance as to the best means of implementing it. Satis Coleman and Will Earhart may serve to emphasize this point.

According to Coleman rhythm was the foundation of music, but the feeling for this element first found expression in the body. Physical movement displayed a sensitivity to the different pulses of music, and the dance was a natural preparation for the understanding of form. Next in sequence came singing. When children proved ready for reading, the skill was undertaken.

Earhart, on the other hand, insisted that tone was the most natural element. By beginning with tone, the groundwork could be laid for higher esthetic response. Rhythm became the second important factor, but it should not be detached from music if it were to be associated with beauty. However, since rhythm was more physiological than aural and could best be created through bodily movement, Earhart recommended its presentation through eurythmics.

THIRD GRADE—SYLLABUS

  I. ROTE SONGS. (Books in the hands of the children)
      1. Development of artistic singing; use of the voice
      2. Enlargement of the musical vocabulary
 II. RHYTHMIC DEVELOPMENT
      1. Growth of the rhythmic sense
          (a) Through rote songs
          (b) Through singing games
          (c) Through folk dances
      2. Study of rhythmic notation
          (a) Through scanning the poem
          (b) Through comparison and association of the phrases of new songs with those of familiar songs
          (c) Through study of comparative note values
III. SPECIFIC WORK IN EAR TRAINING
      1. Organization and development of the figure vocabulary acquired in the previous grade
          (a) Tonic-chord figures
          (b) Diatonic figures
          (c) Interval figures
          (d) Additional chord figures
      2. Further enlargement of the vocabulary
      3. Development of the ability to sing any tone of the scale by relating it with the tonic
      4. Creative work
 IV. SPECIFIC WORK IN EYE TRAINING
      1. Visualization drills for figures made familiar through ear training
      2. Finding staff position of tonic chord from the key signature
      3. Written work
  V. DEVELOPMENT OF THE SYNTHETIC PROCESS
      1. Reversing former analytical process
      2. Re-reading familiar songs
      3. Reading new songs classified with regard to figure content
      4. Reading unclassified songs

From Horatio Parker, Osbourne McConathy, Edward Bailey Birge, W. Otto Miessner, *The Progressive Music Series, Teacher's Manual, Volume I, for First, Second, and Third Grades.* Copyright, 1915, 1916 by Silver Burdett and Company, p. 74. Used by permission.

According to the Teacher's Book of *The Music Education Series*, of which Earhart was an author, the study of music was based on tone. Bodily action, used to develop a sense of rhythm, was to be employed with care. Action songs could do much to destroy tone; therefore, such activities were to be all but excluded from the formal music period. In spite of this attitude, bodily activity was recognized as helpful and was used to a degree.

General Learning

Because progressive education embraced many ideas, conflicts were not unusual. As a result of the disagreements that arose over the principle of individual differences, two sets of solutions were proposed. Thorndike, Watson, and others supported the *specific method*, which provided for certain definite techniques of learning for each subject area. In opposition, Dewey, in the company of such men as McMurry and Kilpatrick, favored the *general method*.

Actually the acceptance of both of these two proposals could contribute toward good teaching. As Kilpatrick acknowledged, the narrow or specific method was particularly useful in helping the child achieve a specific skill. However, he pointed out that there were other values that had to be dealt with by more general methods.

Earhart accused science of overemphasizing man's physical or outer being and of promoting only material ends. Specific knowledge might develop efficiency, rational power, speed in learning, and other allied values; but moral qualities, creative thinking, imagination, direction of taste, and ennoblement of feeling would be lost. Education had been symbolized as a ladder, but this linear symbol was insufficient; education had to have depth, breadth, and richness, as well.

According to *The Universal School Music Series*, facts of music theory could only be of value as they led toward general musical intelligence. Although music theory was important, the time allotted to it must not interfere with the broader aim of music, namely, the development of a genuine love for the art. Gehrkens wrote in *An Introduction to School Music Teaching* that sight-singing had been overemphasized, that it was not really the skill that was the objective but rather the development within each child of a distinct love for music.

Associative Knowledge   The general method held that the child did not learn one thing at a time but rather a number of things associated with the immediate object of his attention. Earhart indicated his endorsement of the principle of the project method in three specific ways. The first involved the music auditorium. Here instrumental and vocal programs, planned and executed by the children to include solo and small ensemble performances, could be presented as a project. Second, the improvisation of melodies might serve a similar end. Such an activity directed that children work together to write a song. Third, a project dealing with a toy orchestra could also serve the ends of a general method, with pupils developing their own score together.

Correlation was by no means new. It had originally been conceived by Herbart. The principle of apperception, which was of importance in his educational thinking, naturally recommended a unification of similar elements from several subject areas.

According to Elizabeth Casterton music would correlate well with nature study, geography, history, and literature. For example, when music was used in association with nature study, songs could be planned to coincide with the seasons. In the case of geography, music could offer folksongs of the lands studied. Her enthusiasm was echoed by W. A. Putt, who emphasized that instead of pressing for more time to be devoted to the area of music education, the energies of music educators would be better spent in giving more attention to correlation of music with the rest of the curriculum.

Satis Coleman referred to correlation in regard to the construction of primitive instruments such as pipes and drums in the music class. She contended that such an activity carried the child beyond the mere practice of instrument-making and led him into the physics of sound as well as the manual arts. It further directed the children toward the history of many different peoples, their methods of making musical instruments, and also toward world geography and a knowledge of natural resources. Such training contributed toward a broader education.

The Music Education Series offered testimony in support of this principle. It specifically called for correlation with the other arts, most particularly recommending the use of poems and pictures to re-create the mood expressed in the music.

Music Reading Techniques   New techniques in the field of language reading were quickly absorbed into the area of music education by progressives. Hardly a text failed to indicate a recognition of the latest procedures.

Earhart declared, as did most of his contemporaries, that instruction in music reading had to be offered. Tonal meaning, symbolized by the staff, was to be derived from notes through repeated use rather than by memory drill. Songs were to be sung by syllable in imitation of the teacher. In that way the tone syllables would be encountered in many different contexts, and the ability to read could be developed.

Rhythm was to be taught in the same way. The symbols acquired meaning first through imitation and then as they were used in a piece of music. The class responded first collectively and then individually. As the reading process continued through the grades, dependence upon imitation decreased until it almost completely disappeared.

The concept of word reading was adopted by Earhart. He pointed out that motives or phrases represented musical thoughts rather than the single note. Therefore, it was essential to emphasize a connected series of notes. According to Judd and his followers, this technique called for a period of reading readiness in the early school years. Earhart subscribed to that same thinking.

This view was held by many important music educators of the time. Experiences based primarily upon observation and imitation commanded major attention during the sensory period. Learning in larger wholes was not confined only to tonal patterns but took in rhythmic patterns as well.

As in the case of language reading, it was noted in the last chapter that educators could not agree completely as to exactly when reading *per se* should begin. This held true in the field of music.

Thaddeus Giddings, in his *Grade School Teaching*, held that while reading readiness was essential, readying experiences should be completed by the end of the first grade. Sight-singing should begin in the second grade. Farnsworth, on the other hand, asserted that the child's first three years of schooling should be spent learning songs as complete wholes through imitation. Later the child would be led to recognize parts as they occurred in relation to the whole. The intermediate years would be the time for more careful analysis and attention to the elements of reading. Gehrkens, taking a more general view, said that reading might start in the first, second, or third grade.

The associative period was the time when the reading specialists called for analysis in word reading, that phase of work requiring the child to break down the whole word into its elements. This technique was carried on by music educators, although some emphasized it more than others. According to Giddings this analysis began in second grade.

The Music Education Series reflected Earhart's thinking as well as Giddings'. A review of that series indicates that their procedure took the motive as a unit. By emphasizing the measure or even the phrase instead of the single note, it was maintained that children could grasp more properly the whole melodic idea. This was consistently carried out through the rote and note experiences. However, as need for analysis was indicated, it was presumably treated more diligently in the early grades than by some other texts. Gehrkens reflected this same procedure of whole to part, stressing analysis continually in his reading program.

The Progressive Music Series supported Judd's theory more specifically. During the sensory period, in the elementary grades, a vocabulary of ideas and experiences was offered. During the associative period, in the intermediate grades, more care was given to fluent sight-reading. Here the analysis of the motive and rhythmic figures could be accomplished for a more complete understanding of the whole. The Eleanor Smith Music Course followed a similar procedure, whereas The Universal School Music Series directed attention to phrase and figures, with analysis where necessary.

In all cases the newer language techniques were indeed accepted in kind. Nowhere was Judd's ideal of synthesis-analysis-synthesis specifically mentioned, but it was clear that the first two parts of the process at least were followed. Apparently further singing experiences in the junior and senior high schools were relied upon for the completion of the last synthesis.

Creative Thinking   According to Earhart, if a broad view in education was preferred, attention had to be directed toward developing the child's creative power. Since two children might derive very different effects from the same experience it was unwise for the teacher to restrict meaning to something fixed and unyielding. Creativity required a flexibility for each child so that he might call his imagination into play. Improvisation of melodies was one exercise Earhart offered. He suggested that there were many other types of creative activity that would promote the child's musical growth.

Coleman's emphasis upon both thought and action fostered a great deal of creative activity in the classroom. The precept seemed interwoven throughout her work. Song improvisations were developed through singing conversations. Once melodies could be written, the children were gradually urged to harmonize them as well. Farnsworth also encouraged the creative principle as a means to vitalize the child's musical experience.

Gehrkens testified to this important aspect of progressivism in his *Music in the Grade Schools*. In opposition to the older theories of coercion and repression in educating children, Gehrkens pressed for the encouragement of initiative and expression. He did not confine creativity to the writing of melodies but suggested a number of other activities that could be used to foster creative expression, such as rhythmic interpretation and rhythm band work.

BEHAVIORISM AND CONNECTIONISM

Many factors that contributed to the doctrine of educational progressivism came from the psychologies of Watson, Thorndike and others. This section will only mention *Specific Learning*. *Curriculum expansion* and *tests and measurements* were of such consequence that the entire next chapter will be devoted to the development of those topics.

Specific Learning

This doctrine directed methods of teaching toward a refinement of functions rather than to the broader ideal of adaptation and adjustment. By emphasizing the formation of connections between stimuli and responses, the theory tended to feature a mechanistic view of life by translating all learning to a routine of habit formation and drill. There appeared to be no room for creative thinking.

Even though progressive music educators indicated a preference for the general method, there can be no doubt that drill for the specific purpose of establishing connections between stimulus and response was not an exception to the rule. Today many adults may recall only too vividly being told as children that, "practice makes perfect."

Progressives recognized that music reading was by no means the sum and substance of the total music program. There was an esthetic as well as a rational side to be considered. Too much attention to one aspect could easily destroy any hope of developing the other. Nevertheless, sight-reading was a part of the program and even though reading techniques were contributed to by such generalists as Dewey, Judd and others, specific learning received a share of attention.

According to *The Universal School Music Series*, "Constant individual practice in sight-singing is the surest way of assuring an attitude of independence in reading music."[3] In further support of this premise it is found that "The object of these drills is to make the response to musical symbols as nearly automatic as possible."[4]

A View of Philosophy

Educational practice has to be guided by explicit principles which can provide direction. The progressives were obliged to look to some kind of philosophy for guidance. In the beginning they had followed the best course psychology could prescribe and had anticipated that a philosophy would emerge. It was suggested in the last chapter that there was sufficient activity in the field of speculative thought to provide progressives with at least three popular philosophies from which to choose. It now remains to be seen which of them were selected.

Music educators believed that the school could no longer satisfy its responsibility by pouring facts into the minds of children. Traditionally the teacher was overly concerned with imparting concrete facts. Teachers who advocated a soft pedagogy tended toward the opposite extreme by removing every vestige of obstacle to the child's own way, which led to serious theoretical and practical consequences. The progressives seemed to call for a compromise position between the two extremes.

Of all the progressives Earhart seemed to be the one who most clearly enounced his philosophical foundations. While he does not appear to have stated anywhere that the universe received its momentum from God or from some Absolute, he frequently dis-

---

[3] Walter Damrosch *et al.* Universal School Music Series *Teacher's Book*. New York: Hinds, Hayden and Eldredge Inc., 1923, p. 8.

[4] Horatio Parker *et al.* The Progressive Music Series, Teachers Manual *Volume III*. Boston: Silver Burdett and Company, 1915.

cussed topics allied to the spiritual world. Conversely, his work dealt considerably with the intellect and with scientific knowledge —though there is not sufficient evidence to infer that he was a realist. He testified, particularly in *The Meaning and Teaching of Music*, to the dualism recognized by the evolutionary idealists.

According to Earhart the nineteenth century saw Western civilization gradually move from a position that maintained an equilibrium between natural and spiritual forces to one that effaced the spiritual and supported the natural. Science had been the moving force that brought about the new scheme of things. In spite of scientific advancement along many lines, man had to sacrifice certain values. This indicated that the type of progress was not as desirable as it had originally appeared.

Earhart accused science of so stressing man's physical being and his material goals as to sacrifice the thinking-feeling-willing being man could be. According to Earhart, the overemphasis of the external view led to sophistication and the acceptance of conventional forms, while simultaneously doing much to destroy creative vision.

Education could develop the individual with respect to the external view so that he might achieve a skill to fit him for industrialism. However, education must have a broader basis from which to work. It should not only develop the outer man but should address itself to the development of his inner being. Science had its place in education; but there were values that could not be measured by diagnostic tests because they were intangible and yet vital to the training of the whole man. Earhart affirmed both the internal and the external values, believing that the values of the inner man gave meaning to external life. One aspect could not be emphasized to the utter neglect of the other.

Earhart evidenced a preference for a broad view in education. While all of life could not be lived on an esthetic plane, it was equally unlikely that life could be complete if its focus were entirely directed toward that of rational utilitarianism. Therefore he asserted that a feeling as well as a knowing side, and an esthetic as well as a rational side, must be recognized. Considering both extremes, it would be incongruous to present to the child techniques of staff notation at the sacrifice of his love and appreciation of music for its own sake.

Although Earhart's *Meaning and Teaching of Music* did not

appear until 1935, these same views were reflected in *The Music Education Series*, which was published at least a decade earlier, with Earhart as principal author.

Farnsworth, in his book *Education through Music*, reflected similar thinking and provided clear definition of his position. A narrow conception of music education involved acceptance of but one of two essential elements in music teaching. On the one hand, there were those who emphasized the intellectual element and directed attention to the single goal of sight-singing. A teacher under pressure for results could have his students memorize the facts so well that few observers could detect a lack of understanding on the part of the students.

In contrast to this, there were those who advocated that the music pericd be taken up entirely with activities of emotional value to the pupils. Efforts were concentrated on songs that might imbue the children with love of home, friendship, country, and so forth. Farnsworth pointed out that each element alone represented a narrow conception of the subject.

Accordingly a combination of both elements had to be considered. Not only technical knowledge but also cultural training could be imparted through an understanding of both musical structure and interpretation.

Compatible with the progressive view, Coleman's work represented the progressive philosophy. She insisted that education must emphasize independence of thought and action. A complete music program must advocate not only technical skill but also wholesome direction of the emotions and appreciation of beauty.

Modern trends, as seen in 1919 by Gehrkens in his *Introduction to School Music Teaching*, indicated that attention should be directed beyond developing skillful performers toward helping children grow in the appreciation of music. Instead of emphasizing the skill of note-reading, the course should consist of a combination of intellectual and emotional training. This would include rote work, sight-singing, theory, music history, and listening.

In further support of the broad view, recognition must be given *The Progressive Music Series* with its prominent staff of authors, including Horatio Parker, Osbourne McConathy, Edward B. Birge, and W. Otto Miessner. *The Lyric Music Series*, as well as *The Eleanor Smith Music Course* and *The Universal School Music Series*, also deserve mention.

As suggested at the outset of this section, rather than philosophy leading the movement and providing a foundation upon which a platform could have been built, speculative thought emerged only as the essential character of the movement took form. Of those philosophies available, idealism, supported by naturalism, offered direction to progressivism. In other words, the theory of knowledge was derived from evolutionary idealism, the philosophy which not only supplanted F. W. Parker's *New Education* in the late nineteenth century but continued to provide the epistemology for the next major American platform.

CHAPTER
10
Music
Education
and
Determinism

THIS chapter will be devoted to the expansion of the music curriculum in the early twentieth century and to a review of tests and measurements as they applied to the study of music.

Music in a Period of Educational Expansion

Educators had once believed that through the study of the classics the mind could become so disciplined as to be able to cope with all of life's problems. According to Thorndike this premise was no longer acceptable. He maintained that all subject areas were educative if their content and method contributed to the particular goal of the individual. This concept did much to precipitate pressure for a widely expanded curriculum.

189

GROWTH OF MUSIC IN THE HIGH SCHOOL

Compulsory school attendance also contributed to the need for additional courses. By 1900 schools were forced to enroll numbers of students for whom the traditional curriculum had no meaning. If education were to serve the needs of an extremely heterogeneous school population, it must offer a curriculum compatible with the diversified character of the student body. Education gradually departed from its classical emphasis and began to instruct students in ways to earn a living.

As the schools absorbed the new vocational subjects that brought training to the working class, there was a brief lapse of interest in music. Very soon, however, music education recovered from its setback and made a more rapid advancement than ever before.

According to Birge this renewed interest was sparked by a program given at the Columbian Exposition in 1892. William T. Tomlins directed a children's chorus whose performance thrilled the audience. The concert did much to convince the public that such work should become a part of American education. The performance also opened up the question of enlarging the services of school music to include music theory and instrumental music. Both the high school and the grammar school were to be affected by this broadened interest.

In scientific study there was pure science, where an accumulation of facts from theoretic and abstract knowledge was the principal aim. There was also applied science, where the goal was the practical application of facts. Both were included in the high school curriculum. Pure science offered all children a general knowledge of its principles. For those who wished to study the subject with a view toward making it a career, applied science was also taught.

Similarly musical activities were divided into two parts. Since every child should appreciate music, appreciation would assume first place. But if high school was to fulfill everyone's needs, theory courses had to be made available for those students intending to make a career of music.

It was one thing to point out certain needs but another to have them gain recognition. Sciences were not introduced into the high schools until the colleges demanded them. Other subjects gained entrance into the curriculum in the same way. Realizing that a similar situation would be necessary if the complete complement of music subjects were ever to be received into the high school curriculum, music educators did what they could to encourage such a demand. The pioneer work began under discouraging conditions, but in spite of difficulties, considerable progress was eventually made.

In 1904 the National Education Association recognized music as part of the scholastic routine and approved it for credit. The amount of credit was to be the same as that granted to any other subject, with the following qualification: such courses as chorus and band, which called for no preparation, would receive only half of the regular credit. The NEA report received the approval of many institutions and leaders in education.

As a result of this action, certain events occurred to indicate that music was approaching full acceptance. The College Entrance Examination Board for New England and the Middle States added music to its list of accepted subjects in 1906, and in 1907 the first set of music examination papers was issued covering music appreciation, harmony, counterpoint, voice, piano, and violin.

Music education was on the march; its expansion and development were hardly less phenomenal than any other phase of the new curriculum. Up to the beginning of the twentieth century, chorus practice represented the only musical activity in most of the high schools, with only the slightest attention given to instrumental work and theory. The first two decades of the new century saw all this changed.

Once recognition was given by some of the College Entrance Examination Boards, music education broadened its earlier function of being merely a singing activity. Advancement may be noted in four distinct areas: (1) the beginnings of instrumental ensemble work, (2) the awarding of credit for applied music, (3) advances in the choral field, (4) courses in harmony and music appreciation.

Instrumental Music in the High School

Choral work was certainly the active representative of music education throughout the nineteenth century. Toward the end of that period, however, an instrumental ensemble of sorts was produced from time to time.

Edward Birge has offered some examples, pointing to a high school orchestra in Aurora, Illinois, organized as early as 1878 by

B. W. Merrill; another at Wichita, Kansas, in 1896 under the direction of Jessie Clark; and the substantial beginning of Will Earhart's instrumental work in 1898 at Richmond, Indiana.

The Middle West must be credited with the introduction of this particular phase of work, which, by about 1910, had spread to both the eastern and western sections of the country. At first the participating schools did not offer any kind of instrumental lessons. The organizations consisted of students prepared to participate in such groups as a result of outside study. The instrumentation was necessarily limited. Percussion instruments, certain woodwinds, and even violas and cellos were rarely available to those early school orchestras.

The attitude of administrators toward introducing these instrumental ensembles into the schools was far from negative, but there was much hesitation in the early days to grant any credit for participation and to permit rehearsal time to become an essential part of the school day. More often than not, the school orchestra practiced before or after school. The general acceptance of this activity, as we consider it today, did not begin until about 1915.

Richmond, Indiana, took the lead as early as 1912, when Will Earhart reported his high school orchestra membership at sixty-four players. He had almost a complete symphonic instrumentation, and his players received credit equal, hour for hour, to that received by any other school subject. A junior high school orchestra, organized to prepare students for eventual participation in the senior organization, boasted forty players. In the same way the high school provided a feeder service for a seventy-piece community symphony orchestra.

In the meantime another very important development occurred, namely, that of the band. This new instrumental venture began in the schools about 1910 as a result of an interest derived from the popularity of the town bands. Their parades and concerts, as well as the color of their uniforms, stimulated a desire among boys and girls to participate in similar organizations.

Two other important outcomes of this early pioneer work in the instrumental field must be mentioned. As early as 1905 it became apparent that a real effort had to be made to secure the more uncommon instruments as property of the schools. Until this was done, works of true symphonic caliber could never be performed. Supervisors therefore endeavored to solicit donations from local groups, use concert proceeds, and request allowances from school authorities in order to provide those instruments that parents seemed reluctant to buy.

With the eventual success of this procedure, it followed that lessons on these and other instruments had to be provided. At first special services of this kind were introduced on a part-time basis; as the instrumental program grew, regular teachers and supervisors were engaged to carry out this work on a full-time basis. Outstanding systems in those early days were Rochester, New York; Chicago, Illinois; Oakland, California; and Pittsburgh, Pennsylvania.

Applied Music in the High School

An endeavor was made at the beginning of the twentieth century to secure school certification for music instruction received from private teachers. Music educators argued that a musical child had as much right to study voice or an instrument as any other discipline in the curriculum. It was also determined that he should be granted credit, as long as competent judges could approve the work presented.

In this connection a circular entitled *Secondary Schools and Private Music Teachers* was sent out by the New England Advisory Board in Music. Upon request by any school committee within its jurisdiction, the Board would nominate adjudicators in music to examine pupils of private teachers. On the basis of the auditions, the judges would determine whether or not the student performers should be granted credit toward their school diplomas. In Massachusetts both Chelsea, in 1906, and Brookline, in 1907, adopted the plan. According to Earhart this credit for applied music study was a service that probably affected piano students more than any other instrumentalists.

Class Voice Instruction in the High School

Not to be outdone by the newly registered advances of the instrumental organizations, choral directors seriously appraised their situation. As a result of their evaluation, they found ways of expanding their services and upgrading their work to the degree that gains in that area became very apparent.

Class voice instruction was introduced to parallel the emphasis that instrumental lessons were then receiving. The development of this work did much to raise and support the standards of high school choruses. New emphasis was directed toward the development of better tone quality, greater technical efficiency, and more artistic performance. Important as these aims were, the idea that was uppermost in the minds of many music educators was the setting of more purposive goals in definite and challenging terms.

Harmony and Music Appreciation

Osbourne McConathy argued for including harmony in the curriculum. It was, he reasoned, as good a tool as any subject for developing the mind. Because of the professional preparation it could provide the more musical students, harmony ranked higher, according to McConathy, than other subject areas.

While the aim of the harmony course was not to turn out finished musicians, it could teach students to think musically and to hear tones in correct relationships; it could equip listeners to appreciate and understand music more fully and provide those who intended to pursue a musical career with solid training. In 1904 McConathy inaugurated a course in harmony in Chelsea, Massachusetts. Although harmony courses served a relatively small portion of the school population, they achieved real status in the curriculum.

Mention must also be made of music appreciation. The year 1910 was the time in educational history when listening lessons, at first confined to the high school, ceased to be a rarity. Impetus was supplied by C. M. Tremaine, of the National Bureau for the Advancement of Music, who advocated the so-called Music Memory Contest in an address before the Music Supervisors' National Conference in 1918. Originally initiated for the benefit of the school children and their parents, the contest grew to such proportions as to involve the entire community.

A list of twenty-five selections was handed out by those in charge weeks or months before the contest was to be held. Children were urged to procure the music and play it; phonograph shops stocked the records; theatre orchestras and church organists played the music; newspapers provided reprints of the contest rules and offered information that might be of use at the contest. As a result children, as well as adults, were surrounded by the music. At the contest itself young and old took part, with everyone deriving pleasure from the activity. According to Birge no project had ever been as successful in awakening community interest in music as this Music Memory Contest.

GROWTH OF MUSIC IN THE GRAMMAR SCHOOL

The changes in content and prospectus of the various subjects within the grammar school curriculum were also significant. The music course will serve to substantiate the validity of the statement. Supervisors attempted to broaden their concepts of exactly what should be included in a well-rounded music course.

Reading was emphasized only as it pointed directly toward and was embodied within the song. Materials were becoming better suited to the interests and capacities of the child. Melodies were chosen for their beauty rather than for the technicalities they might underscore. Poetry was acceptable only when it proved appropriate to the child's interests and the vocabulary was comprehensible to the age group for which it was intended. Action songs called for rhythmic movements of the hands and feet, the desired movements indicated by footnotes appended to the bottom of the page. William Tomlins directed attention to the need for the proper interpretation of the songs. He also provided a tone-building method that had great influence in the schoolroom.

At this point it might be said that under the best conditions at the turn of the century, music education included several activities. They were represented by the following: music reading, rhythmic motion, and voice training as it applied directly to Tomlins' idea of good tone quality, as well as a consideration of the proper interpretation of music.

In 1907 the Music Teachers National Association appointed a committee under the chairmanship of Ralph L. Baldwin to determine the aims of music courses in the grammar school. Up until that time there had been no fixed standards such as those already prescribed for the sciences and the modern languages. The committee set out to establish a set of requirements in music education that might be accomplished throughout the country. The way in which the classes would be directed to the desired goal was left to the discretion of the teacher.

Generally the report suggested that an acceptable music course, based upon eight years of grammar school training with a time allotment of sixty to ninety minutes per week, would have to satisfy three conditions. Children were to be instructed in the reading of the printed score; their affective and esthetic development was to be a major consideration; and their musical tastes were to be enlarged and improved.

The individual was to acquire a sufficient reading ability to sing at sight a melody or his part in a hymn tune of moderate difficulty by such composers as Dykes, Sullivan, or Barnby. The child was also to be required, at the completion of his training, to sing without words an eight-measure phrase in any major or minor key. Any time signature could be used, and the following problems were to be included: all time problems through the sixteenth note, syncopation, and all chromatic tones in ordinary use. He was further obliged to prove his knowledge of the two clefs and his understanding of keys and key signatures, including both major and minor modes, and to display a comprehension of common Italian terms of tempo and expression. In addition a biographical knowledge of noted composers since Bach was required, as well as an acquaintance with some of their representative works.

The requirements attracted wide notice and received generous criticism. Some thought undue prominence was given to the technical features, with insufficient emphasis on the esthetic side. Others just found the technical demands too severe. A year later Ralph Baldwin called for a greater balance between the esthetic and the intellectual aspects of music. While the report might have been rather rigid in its demands, at least there was a firm statement of expectations, which had never before been provided.

A similar report by C. H. Miller in 1920 did nothing to lower the technical requirements as originally set forth by Baldwin. From the kindergarten through the first half of the second grade, learning was generally confined to what could be elicited through imitative activities. From then on, problems of time and tune were carefully taught. Much time was set aside for the practice of sight-singing. Each year the work became progressively more difficult. In fourth grade two-part singing was introduced and was continued through fifth grade. The principal feature of the next two years was three-part singing, and in eighth grade it was four-part work.

Throughout grammar school training Miller emphasized the need for independent sight-singing, the development of good tone, and the rendering of all songs with proper phrasing and diction. At the completion of this course of study, it was expected that ninety percent of the students should be able to carry their part in a hymn tune and that half of the children should be able to sing more difficult music at sight.

Up to now music education had been more or less confined to singing. As in the case of other elementary school subjects, music endeavored to provide a maximum of enrichment. Of particular note was the addition of appreciation and instrumental work.

Music Appreciation in the Grammar School

This new offering took its place alongside other musical experiences in the grammar school curriculum. Edward Birge wrote in 1909 that advances had already been made. In the same paper he defined appreciation as the means of developing a taste for good music in preference to trash, and an enjoyment in hearing good music that transcended the mere study of form. Birge's paper indicates that the media for this study were the player-piano and the recording machine.

Listening to music, according to Birge, would enrich the child's life in the same way that his love for literature is enhanced when the teacher reads stories to him.

> . . . this reading of gems of literature to children is an indispensable part of their education. The child who has never been read to has been cheated out of a precious birthright, and this birthright ought soon to include music.[1]

It was recommended by Birge that for the primary grades music should suggest a story. In the middle grades the formal side should be pointed up. Binary and ternary forms might then be emphasized. Upper grammar school classes should become exposed to music rich in mood and color, which appealed to the romantic and idealistic tendencies of the preadolescent years. The music selected was to progress from simple harmonies and forms to chromatic harmony and more complex forms. Music appreciation, Birge warned, was not for entertainment but for study. Developing music listeners was a process that had to begin in the low grades and continue all the way through high school.

Lutkin testified that music appreciation had much in its favor. The music the students could sing was limited in kind and complexity; music appreciation exposed them to works beyond their own performance capabilities. The child might comprehend music

---

[1] Edward B. Birge. "The Language Method in Teaching Appreciation," Music Teachers National Association *Volume of Proceedings*, 1913, p. 166.

Early phonograph laboratory. From Thaddeus P. Giddings, Will Earhart, Ralph Baldwin, and Elbridge W. Newton, *Music Appreciation in the Schoolroom* of the *Music Education Series* (copyright 1926 by Ginn and Company, Boston), p. 19. Used with permission.

he would find impossible to perform. And, since the child's tastes were primarily unformed and unspoiled, with no prior prejudices to overcome, he should be receptive to the best in music.

Perhaps the greatest share of the credit for music appreciation in the public schools should go to the work of Mrs. Frances E. Clark, a music supervisor in Milwaukee. Her planned lessons in appreciation, which she designed for her own classes, led the Victor Talking Machine Company to found an educational department, with Mrs. Clark as director. Under her leadership records of great music suitable for classroom use were made available. Texts soon followed as guides to teachers. Of particular significance were *Listening Lessons in Music* by Agnes Fryberger and *Music Appreciation for Little Children* by Frances Clark, both of which were designed for use in the lower grades.

Instrumental Music in the Grammar School

Instrumental work in the grammar school developed in much the same way as it had in the high school. Ensembles were first to appear, followed by special instruction in the playing of instruments. According to Birge a grammar school orchestra appeared

198

Musician at work in the phonograph laboratory shown on the facing page, making recordings for *Music Appreciation in the Schoolroom*. This photograph appears on page 21 of that volume. The conductor was Dr. Henry Hadley.

in 1896 in New London, Connecticut, under the baton of Charles B. Jennings; in 1899 Hartford followed with a similar organization, directed by W. D. Monnier.

From all appearances orchestral work in the grades did not develop immediately as the result of a special need within its own unit of operation. High school directors indicated concern over the loss of players at each term's end. To assure the high school organizations a pool of candidates to step in and fill the gaps in the ensembles, instrumental groups were formed in the lower grades.

Once started, however, these new organizations soon developed sufficiently in size and strength to become independent units. In 1909 Los Angeles boasted of thirty such orchestras, and in 1915, Oakland, California, reported twenty-nine.

Just as in high school instrumental work, the grades soon felt the necessity of providing some kind of instrumental instruction to supplement these new ensemble groups. A great impetus for this venture was found in the Maidstone Movement. Originating in Maidstone, England, the idea was undertaken for the purpose of arousing a taste for orchestral music among children.

Albert G. Mitchell, a music supervisor of the Boston schools, was given a year's leave of absence to study class instruction in the violin at Maidstone. Apparently impressed with what he saw, he introduced a similar program in the Boston schools upon his return to this country. Between 1910 and 1920 his class methods and ideas found their way to all parts of the United States. Eventually they were applied to the teaching of all instruments of the band and orchestra as well as to piano class instruction.

By 1920 music educators had solidly established the boundaries of musical offerings. To improve what had been started, there was still much work to be done, and extensive campaigning to be carried out before the ideas of the program were accepted throughout the country. From information provided by a committee of the National Education Association and the Music Supervisors' National Conference in 1919, the following results were yielded by a study of 359 cities representing thirty-six states: a chorus in one form or other was offered in all schools; approximately two-thirds of the schools had a boys' and girls' glee club; 278 owned and loaned instruments; 88 maintained bands; 211 offered courses in theory, to include harmony; and 265 provided music appreciation as well as harmony. Almost half the schools reporting gave diploma credit for music courses maintained within the school, and somewhat less than one-third allowed credit for outside music study. Although the movement represented itself modestly, it was not insignificant.

Tests and Measurements

As early as 1897, J. M. Rice reported that he had gathered some objective evidence through testing in the area of spelling. His experiment pointed toward scientific measurement. He reported at a convention of school superintendents that children who spent forty minutes a day for eight years in the study of spelling were no better spellers than those who had received only ten minutes a day in the same study. The assemblage protested vigorously against Rice for presuming to measure the teaching of spelling by the children's ability to spell. This pioneer of the testing movement suffered denunciation for even suggesting that efficiency could be measured by the pupils' ability to do.

Perhaps the publication of Thorndike's *Hand-Writing Scale* in 1910 marked the real beginning in this country of a substantial series of tests used in the evaluation of the work of children. Once started, the movement grew by leaps and bounds with the appearance of a long list of tests that enabled teachers to measure the results of their instruction.

TESTS AND MEASUREMENTS IN MUSIC EDUCATION

Music educators were as interested in the area of tests and measurements as educators in any other subject area. According to a study by Flemming and Flagg in 1936, no less than fifty-seven tests were available for the purpose of determining either individual needs or the degree of individual accomplishment in the area of music.

There were tests in music to measure every conceivable phase of the subject: (1) tests for musical aptitude, (2) feeling and motor tests, (3) achievement tests, and (4) appreciation and performance tests.

Musical Aptitude Tests

One of the most outstanding names associated with tests and measurements in music was that of Carl Seashore. Assisted by his colleagues, he formulated the well-known musical aptitude tests referred to as *Measures of Musical Talent*. These included six phases: Sense of Pitch, Intensity Discrimination, Time Discrimination, Consonance Discrimination, Tonal Memory, and Rhythmic Discrimination.

In the test of the sense of pitch, the subject was asked to detect the difference in pitch ranging from an interval greater than a half-step to one of less than 1/100 of a scale step. The intensity discrimination test asked the subject to determine whether the second of a pair of sounds was louder or softer than the first. The time-discrimination test required the participant to judge from paired time intervals varying from 1 to 1.20 seconds whether the second was shorter or longer than the first. Consonance discrimination was evaluated on the basis of smoothness, purity, and blending, the student being asked whether the second pair of tones sounded better or worse than the first pair; the examination was then repeated in inverse order. To test tonal memory, fifty trials were offered, with each ten representing a degree of difficulty from two-tone patterns to six-tone patterns; in every instance the subject had to determine which tone was different from all others in the series. The last test, for rhythmic discrimination, required the subject to judge the differences in time, intensity, or both, from paired rhythmic patterns.

Music Feeling and Motor Tests

Another great name in musical measurement was Jacob Kwalwasser, who is known for his work in the category of music feeling and motor tests. His *Melodic Sensitivity Test* was designed to evaluate those responses upon which an appreciative attitude toward music could be developed. Thirty-five melodic fragments of two measures each were given. It was up to the subject to distinguish the good melodic progressions from the bad. The *Harmonic Sensitivity Test*, which employed a similar method, measured the subject's capacity to discriminate between good and bad harmonic progressions.

The Tapping Test: A Measure of Motility was devised by M. Ream to determine the motor fitness of students before they were offered instrumental training. The subject was asked to tap on a telegraph key as fast as he could for a period of five consecutive seconds. Twenty five-second trials made up the test. The motility rate was determined by the number of taps recorded on the Veeder counter during the examination.

Music Achievement Tests

A number of tests have been devised to measure achievement in music. The *Mosher Test* included seven parts. Test I drew out musical information represented by marks of expression, note values, as well as elementary theory and notation, history, measure, and scansion. The second phase stressed sight-singing, though no singing was required. The subject indicated his aptitude by recognizing melodic sequences through scale, chord, and chromatic patterns, answering, for example, "This chord is in the key of B-flat major. The name of the chord is ————." The next test endeavored to gauge the child's ability to discriminate note values in reference to a given time signature: incomplete measures were given, and the subjects were required to complete them correctly according to the dictates of the time signature. Sight-singing ability was appraised in Test IV; well-known airs were given, and by silent reading the children had to determine the title of the song. In Test V eight tonal patterns were played to include both major and minor modes, and the children were asked to write them from dictation. For Test VI, which dealt with rhythmic patterns, the examiner played an exercise on a neutral pitch, and the children were required to write it. The last test combined the elements of time and tune, with the examiner playing melodies that the subjects were required to identify by writing both pitch and rhythm.

The *Kwalwasser-Ruch Test of Musical Accomplishment* measured knowledge of music in grades four through twelve. Representative courses of study in music were carefully studied; from the findings ten separate tests were formulated to include: knowledge of musical meters and symbols, recognition of syllable names from notation, detection of pitch errors in the notation of a familiar melody, detection of time errors in the notation of a familiar melody, knowledge of the pitch or letter names of bass and treble clef, knowledge of time signatures, knowledge of key signatures, knowledge of note values, knowledge of rest values, and recognition of familiar melodies from notation. Other tests, similar in design and purpose, were the *Torgerson-Fahnestock Tests* and the *Kwalwasser Test of Musical Information and Appreciation.*

Music Appreciation and Performance Tests

Other tests measured appreciation and performance. Perhaps the first of these was the one constructed by S. A. Courtis, entitled *The Courtis-Standard Research Tests—Recognition of Characteristic Rhythms.* The test, required the subject to determine from the music played what activity was suggested. The multiple-choice answers might be "on foot, by boat, on skates, and on horseback," with the appropriate choice to be underlined.

Another Courtis test, *Recognition of Mood from Melody,* was similar to the one just described. From the music played, the subject was requested to select from a series of choices the thought most likely expressed by the music. For example, for the first selection played, the following choices were available: (1) going to a circus, (2) becoming a missionary, (3) becoming a policeman, or (4) becoming a soldier.

The frequently used *Kwalwasser-Dykema Music Tests* were based on the thesis that the traits of tonal memory, quality discrimination, intensity discrimination, feeling for tonal movement, time discrimination, rhythm discrimination, pitch discrimination, melodic taste, pitch imagery, and rhythm imagery were indicative of both musical achievement and talent. The tests were ten in number, one being assigned to the measurement of each of the above elements.

Esther A. Gaw's *Sight-Singing Test*, which was designed for individual testing, was made up of six parts. In Parts I and II the subject was provided with some short exercises, which included only tonic skips. He had to find his own note from the pitch pipe and sing the notation according to correct syllable name and accurate pitch. Parts III through V made a similar demand, but with the added element of time. The last portion of the test, Part VI, included elements of both time and tune in the exercises. After having sung it once correctly in that way, the candidate was required to repeat it a second time, replacing the syllables with the words of a given text. This test was devised and used as a criterion in sectioning classes in sight-singing at San Francisco State Teachers College.

CRITICISMS OF TESTS AND MEASUREMENTS

In closing this portion of the discussion, it must be said that a considerable amount of controversy accompanied the development of mental testing. However, as a consequence of the determinists' view, the doors were opened for an expansion of the curriculum, which, in turn, made possible the grouping of children according to ability, led to improved teaching methods, and aided in determining just what should be taught in order that the needs of both individual and society might be fulfilled. However, along with its assets certain liabilities must be delineated. Although certain specifics could then be measured with a degree of accuracy in the realm of arithmetic, spelling, and reading, there was still no scale provided to measure the more pertinent values of character and appreciation.

Testing provoked controversies too in the area of music education. According to Kwalwasser, one of the most energetic leaders in the field of musical measurement, tests could provide the basis of judging the possible success or failure of a candidate; they could lead to more efficient methods and scientific procedures in class instruction.

A more cautious note was sounded by Mursell and Glenn in 1931, when they pointed out to music educators the danger of taking an extremist view of testing in either direction. They held, however, that the movement should be supported in the hope that through continued experimentation real and definite values might be developed and scientifically validated.

PART
V

The Age of Experience and Experiment

CHAPTER
11
Experimentalism

The Need for a New Direction

BY 1920 THE FORCES that had precipitated the earlier progressive movement were almost spent. A new prosperity diminished concern for reform. Efficiency continued as the watchword; business prided itself on the methods it devised to regulate expense, time, and effort. School administration, and even classroom procedures, reflected this trend of the business world.

Science became almost a god and enjoyed unquestioned faith by the masses of people. Through the application of its principles to the processes of production and distribution of commodities, man dreamed of a life of comfort, wealth, and leisure in this new machine age.

As science came to overshadow religion, and with it conventional morality, youth began to defy accepted modes of behavior, and the bonds of restraint were broken with regard to sex. This trend away from established moral standards may have been partly due to the behaviorists, who oversimplified their psychology for the layman, emphasizing a materialistic and mechanistic conception of the mind. Fallacies were pointed out, and protests were raised, but the warnings went unheeded. It seemed that nothing could alter or impede the course of this exciting and prosperous era.

The urgency of war had created a certain social cohesion, but shortly after that crisis passed, there were unmistakable indications of disunity. Individuals became reluctant to accept discipline, and many of the traditions and conventions that had served in the past to hold society together were under attack. The worker proved more rebellious than ever, and syndicalists expected that union workers would take over industry if these conditions continued.

There were those who warned that man had easily accustomed himself to the use and products of machines but that he had not modified his thinking to coincide with the ways of a machine economy. Guy Stanton Ford did much to contrast the traditional characteristics of American civilization with the new machine age. He pointed out the necessity for "some conscious social purpose transcending the interests of the individual, of the locality, and at times even of the nation itself."[1] Others maintained that the new age of machines necessitated collective control in order to avoid unemployment.

Such warnings seemed to fall on deaf ears. Even when the deluge came in October, 1929, Americans did not blame the basic social and economic structure. Depressions had appeared throughout our economic history, and each time a recovery had followed. However, as the crisis deepened and dragged on into years, it became apparent that the Depression of the 1930s was quite different from any that had occurred before.

A search for formulas of recovery were necessarily of prime importance. Consequently the masses became willing to listen to new leaders. It was only natural that science was called upon to provide answers since the public had learned to rely upon its certainties. However, functionalism in biology and studies of relativity in the physical sciences were depriving the scientific image of some of its authority. New discoveries opened up more and more

---

[1] Merle Curti. *The Growth of American Thought.* New York: Harper & Row, Publishers, Second Edition, 1951, p. 709.

areas of unknowns rather than providing, as was expected, immediate and accurate answers to the problems of the day. A solution was not to be found easily.

Education could not remain complacent in the face of changes in so many phases of American life. New aims and values more compatible to the requirements of the times had to be established if education was to serve effectively. The new point of view to emerge was *experimentalism*, and it was John Dewey who provided the intellectual leadership.

Formative Aspects of Experimentalism

Pragmatism and experimentalism were by no means synonymous: the former implied a very definite philosophy; the latter indicated an educational platform or strategy, of which philosophy was but one of several factors. Aside from philosophical considerations, which will be discussed later, there were three areas that contributed heavily to the new educational theory: social psychology, gestalt psychology and, with regard to the arts, esthetics.

SOCIAL PSYCHOLOGY

The gradual growth of a collectivist attitude was becoming apparent in this country and abroad. The theory proposed a socialized state, with government accepting greater responsibilities for the public welfare.

In the United States the New Deal was probably the most widely accepted platform upon which a recovery could be founded. The government assumed a much more active role in economic affairs for the purpose of bringing about a better balance between producer and consumer. By this means the New Dealers anticipated a recovery as well as a reconstruction in the 1930s. In addition they hoped to safeguard personal liberties and individual opportunities. There were those from every walk of life who saw dangers in this idea of social and economic planning. No doubt their censure of the new direction did much to sustain an equilibrium between the individual and society.

There were movements in progress that emphasized a new system of disciplines dealing neither with the individual nor the social structure but rather with the interdependent relationships between them. Early in the twentieth century G. H. Mead and John Dewey began to consider individual psychology as a reflection of a group process. They theorized that self-development was not a process entirely of individual growth but a condition that must involve an awareness of and a relation to others. Mead pointed out the importance of language as a means of inducting the individual into the group. In this way the member could share sympathy and a sense of oneness with others.

Charles H. Cooley maintained that the social processes of the individual in the group could not be dissected to the point that one could be considered more important than the other. Individualism was no longer to retain a position of superiority; the individual must stand as an equal with society, with each having a responsibility to the other.

It will be remembered that the earlier progressive system was the result of protest and reaction. In an effort to protect the child from what appeared to be the subordination of the individual to the needs of the industrial age and from the dangers of mass methods, educators had emphasized a child-centered education. However, at the onset of the Depression, a movement within progressive circles pointed out that the stress upon individual growth represented an undesirable extreme. It was contended that individual growth without a continual reference to social issues might well have served a dominant economic class—the very end it had endeavored to avoid.

As a result of this charge, the Progressive Education Association designed a policy in 1933 entitled, "A Call to the Teachers of the Nation." Teachers were requested to "recognize the corporate and the interdependent character of the contemporary order, and transfer the democratic tradition from the individualistic to collectivist economic foundations."[2] The complicated industrial system made it impossible for the individual to control the conditions under which he worked. To save him from the complex forces that surrounded him, a means for his salvation rested in the cooperation of other individuals. As Ralph H. Gabriel put it, "Collectivism was made to serve the old democratic ideal of the free individual."[3]

[2] Progressive Education Yearbook, "Progressive Education: Its Philosophy and Challenge," Special Supplement, May 1941, p. 3.

[3] Ralph H. Gabriel. *The Course of American Democratic Thought*. New York: The Ronald Press Company, 1940, p. 416.

GESTALT PSYCHOLOGY

A decided reaction set in against behaviorism. Watson's work had represented a mechanistic view of life, deriving its analogies from responses of animals in artificial situations. All problems were simplified beyond justification as behavior was reduced to a sequence of reflexes. This psychology found no place for the creative activity of the human mind or for culture.

Gestalt psychology reflected more exactly the new trend of thought in this field. Formulated by Max Wertheimer and popularized by Kurt Koffka and Wolfgang Köhler, this doctrine was introduced into the United States through a paper read by R. M. Ogden at the Christmas meetings of the American Psychological Association in 1922. By 1933 gestalt psychology was established in this country, with its doctrines appearing in applied psychology, in education, as well as in anthropology and sociology.

Although similar in some respects to the experiments of Thorndike and his followers, the findings of the gestaltists indicated that a learner's trials were not entirely random. According to Köhler the behavior of the great apes suggested that an animal's trials did not represent mere blundering but offered an indication of insight into the problems solved. Where Thorndike's animals appeared blind to meanings and relations, where their behavior could have been characterized as mechanical, Köhler's animals seemed in constant search of solutions, which came in flashes of insight.

The gestaltist maintained that all learning came by way of insight. The learner directed attention to the relationship or *configuration* of the elements of a problem not as isolated phenomena but as they were arranged to effect a solution. This school of psychology emphasized insight, understanding, and thinking in solving problems, as well as the testing of perceived relations. It paralleled to a great degree Dewey's explanation of the thought process. In solving a problem, an hypothesis was proposed; in the course of solution, a trial-and-error procedure was carried on, which put each hypothesis to the test. Thinking continued as new elements of the problem were learned through errors. Finally the learner arrived at the hypothesis that squared with the situation.

Both the behaviorist and the gestaltist stressed activity. The former insisted that grooves must be worn into the nervous system, while the latter desired a revelation of the properties in the problem situation that would direct thought toward a solution by means of insight and understanding.

ESTHETICS

The New Deal created the Federal Arts Projects, which for six years afforded artists and scholars the opportunity for research in cultural fields. Until these studies had been made, many an American assumed that only Europe possessed a rich heritage of true folk art. Research projects, however, revealed such a mass of native American material as to demonstrate that the United States could also boast of such a legacy.

These findings precipitated a change in attitude among the artists of this country. As the fine arts of Europe represented the ultimate outgrowth of that civilization's folk art, the American artist now recognized that the same possibilities existed for him in this country.

This discovery may also have served as a means of enlightenment to art lovers. With an array of folk art available for study and evaluation, Americans could see art in settings for which it was created rather than in museums, isolated from its natural surroundings. Not only could spectators begin to understand art more easily in this way, but they would come to recognize that the artist had a function in society beyond that of merely providing decoration.

Dewey did a great deal toward introducing a functional concept in esthetics. He asserted that the growth of capitalism had powerfully supported the idea that the only place for art was in the museum. However, in such a setting specimens of fine art lost their functional validity by being placed under glass, completely cut off from the surroundings for which they were created.

Art, Dewey contended, flourished and developed as it was used to enhance everyday living. Ornaments and domestic utensils had been created in every civilization with such care that relics of older civilizations were collected for the museum. He further maintained that art has always existed in close connection with daily life and was not set apart for the initiated. Therefore, Dewey asserted that art could win greater acceptance if it were placed in a more directly human context. It could then serve in a far more functional way.

By no means did Dewey suggest that all functional items be accepted as art. An acceptable household utensil, for instance, would not necessarily qualify as art. On the other hand, Dewey maintained, decorative effects for the sake of decoration alone did not represent art but merely empty embellishment. Art, as true art, "is a union of the serviceable and the immediately enjoyable, of the instrumental and the consummatory."[4]

There was no real reason to believe that the new epoch made an integration of art in civilization impossible. As industry provided new products required by a technologically-oriented society, the individual became increasingly accustomed to the objects which gradually became a part of the world about him. As a result pictures, utensils, buildings, although different from those of the past, would eventually yield esthetic satisfaction. In this way art would become dynamic and coexistent with the everyday process of living.

Pragmatism

A general exposition of Dewey's educational position may best be presented through certain phases of his epistemology. For purposes of this study, the following discussion of pragmatism will be confined to three topics: (a) the individual and society, (b) life as growth, (c) the relation of discipline to interest.

THE INDIVIDUAL AND SOCIETY

Pragmatism established that society existed through a process of transmission. While each living organism, each member of a species, would eventually die, the species would continue on so long as it could adapt to an ever-changing environment. In the same way each individual was part of a society; and though the individual would die, the society would continue to exist. Therefore, it was essential that the characteristic life of the group be preserved through the initiation of new members into the beliefs and aspirations of its elders. By this means society, like any living species, would continually be renewed. Thus education was fundamentally a social phenomenon, for this process of social renewal worked through education.

[4] Dewey, John and others. *Art and Education.* Merian, Pa.: Barnes Foundation, Second Edition, 1947, p. 8.

It remained to find how this could best be done. Whereas a child could be trained to respond habitually to an environment that was entirely his own, he would derive values along the way that would develop selfhood to the utter disregard of others. In opposition to this, the pragmatist wanted to bring the individual into such a social environment that meanings and values would be derived as the result of a joint action. The child in the group would then begin to realize the emotional attitudes of the society. Through this experience his beliefs and ideas would take form as he recognized how they fit in the society of which he was a member. It became the responsibility of education to provide a simplified model of the society it represented. The school could then transmit the knowledge of the past that might serve to enrich or better a future society.

It has been said that the government was seeking ways of achieving a social cohesion that would unite its individual members and inspire them to work not only for themselves but also for the national good. According to Dewey the democratic concept must permit each member to participate on equal terms with all others. The institutions that represented the general life and culture of their members must readjust according to the changes wrought by society. Education should lead the individual toward a definite interest in social relationships and control. It must also point out how changes could be made by means other than chaotic eruption.

Apparently the primary aim of education was directed toward social efficiency. This did not mean that the individual was to become lost in the crowd. It was just as firmly established that all must be afforded an opportunity for the development of their individual capacities. In other words, an equilibrium between the two extremes had to be achieved.

Great stress was placed upon individual differences. The pragmatist proceeded from the hypothesis that each individual developed in accordance with his own natural ability. Natural powers varied with different individuals, and it was up to the educator to guide the pupil toward the fulfillment of those powers. However, the child had to be made to realize that he must give back to society in the same measure as he had received.

The philosophy of pragmatism has been accused of neglecting spiritual and moral values by disparaging inner experiences. Careful study reveals that Dewey was very concerned with character-building and moral development. However, his means for accomplishing those values and for evaluating their successful achievement varied considerably from more traditional views. The priority could no longer be represented by the mere development of ideas that may have proved congenial to the individual.

The pragmatist asserted that the moral fiber of a man had to be measured by the results he effected or the changes he induced. It was of no consequence what he might think unless his thinking precipitated activity that could benefit society. The moral man received from society in proportion to what he was willing to contribute. Education, therefore, was not to be concerned with the projection of precepts but was to serve as a catalyst in developing within each individual the capacity for shared experience. The school became a miniature community, in which students developed their power to achieve this kind of morality.

Life as Growth

The spectacular gains made in the field of science were represented more by the discovery of unknowns than by the ascertainment of solutions. In a similar way pragmatists maintained that there was no real end to education, that it represented a continual power to develop. From this hypothesis two educational principles were drawn. (1) Education was a process of continual growth. (2) Education was a process of perpetual reorganization, reconstruction, and transformation.

Education: A Process of Continual Growth

The infant was seen as an organism born with the ability for intellectual growth, a growth relying chiefly upon what the individual did on his own rather than what could be done for him. In learning an action, the individual was obliged to vary the factors or organize them into different combinations according to the situation that arose. Through this exercise the child not only accumulated knowledge but learned how to learn.

The educational implication drawn from this was that the individual must be constantly motivated with the desire for further growth. A child's curiosity should constantly be aroused by new stimuli, which would spark a continual responsiveness to his surrounding environment. Once a situation precipitated an interest, the child should be permitted to pursue that avenue with an open mind. However, this was only the first step.

An inclination to follow a certain activity was not considered an end in itself but only a sign of possible growth. Attention had then to be given to the proper development of the selected pursuit. If the child drew from the experience only a specific skill or an efficient means of performing a given act, he only learned to adjust or conform to a single situation, which might never recur. The educational value would have to be considered incomplete unless the individual was made to understand that his new ability could be used to effect subsequent changes in other situations.

Education: A Process of Reorganization, Reconstruction, and Transformation

The second point reflected the kind of knowledge that must be offered. Society, like a species, continued only as long as it was capable of readapting to an ever-changing environment. Therefore, the school had to teach the individual not only how to adjust to his present environment but how to deal with subsequent changes.

Dewey asserted that essentials must be first, refinements second. By essentials he meant those elements that were most fundamental to society and represented experiences in which the largest groups might share. Refinements suggested technical skills that would become of value to those who would select more specialized fields.

Although facts were essential items in solving a problem, in themselves they represented nothing but bits and pieces. Knowledge and fact accumulation could not be considered the same thing. What was truly known was the result of an experience in which a hypothesis, made up of intellectual resources, had proven itself to be correct. The known could not be represented by a particular but rather by a value that had derived meaning in an activity that modified or solved something between the individual and his environment.

Activity did not constitute experience unless the person undergoing the activity suffered or enjoyed a consequence. It was this union of activity and consequence that pointed the way to a recognition of meaning. Therefore, mind was not an isolated faculty into which facts could be poured but a term given to all human activities that terminated in real and significant changes.

Instead of being the result of the faculty of reason, thinking was a matter of problem solving and a process of investigation. Four steps were involved in this process: (1) a problem arose; (2) a tentative hypothesis was developed on the basis of existing conditions; (3) the hypothesis was tested through action; (4) acceptable patterns or solutions were retained and the others discarded.

The educational conclusion that followed was that learning took place best when situations or problems were derived from the activities of ordinary life rather than from ready-made subject matter. These experiences could not be developed by any definitely prescribed method. The student had to be placed in the center of a real situation and had to determine a solution through the employment of his own powers. The method was represented as a trial of ideas. Even when unsuccessful, the experience was worthwhile because learning could even be realized in failure, provided the endeavor was seriously carried out.

Efforts were directed toward the reorientation of the curriculum in terms of the more modern progressive thought. The project method, which had enjoyed such a vogue during the first three decades of the century, was re-evaluated. The older view used the techniques of projects and units as well as ability grouping to serve specific subject-matter ends. In opposition the new education maintained that the curriculum should be conceived on the basis of the entire range of experiences involved in the school program.

This new idea of the *experience* curriculum took its direction from the "activities movement" and its leading exponent, William Heard Kilpatrick. Schools that accepted this new philosophy tried to direct more attention to the well-rounded development of the child through an enriched activities program. Education was dealt with as a social process, with learning situations built around group activities and cooperative efforts.

In the earlier part of the century, students had either specialized in one field, which resulted in a narrow education, or jumped from one field to another, receiving nothing more than a smattering of everything. To correct these defects, the junior and senior high schools undertook a more well-rounded but unified program. Such terms as *coordinated units, fusion units, integrated units, correlated units,* as well as *broad fields* and *problems courses,* cut across the boundaries of the traditional subject areas in an effort to interrelate bodies of knowledge into more lifelike experiences. With so many devices as these—and there were more—it becomes impossible in this discourse to attempt definition. However, let it be said that all of these innovations indicated a movement toward *general education*, in which it was expected that the student might achieve not only a more integrated understanding of social development but a greater realization of his own role in a democratic society.

THE RELATIONSHIP OF DISCIPLINE TO INTEREST

The doctrine of interest played an important part in providing a solution to one of the problems of instruction. Interest, according to Dewey, connoted concern rather than the sugar-coating of material to which the pupil might otherwise be indifferent. Intelligence was not a gift but the result of activities so directed as to overcome obstacles and eventually lead to a desired goal.

Therefore, the teacher tried to select material that would provide an interest, involving the child's concern with the aim and purpose. Once this condition was established, the child would press toward the attainment of ends. Through concern or interest with the problem and its eventual solution, the child proceeded deliberately and considered his actions carefully. Along the way the very process he underwent developed discipline, a value that Dewey insisted was connected rather than opposed to interest.

A Summary of Principles

THE FORMATIVE ASPECTS OF EXPERIMENTALISM

There were three aspects that contributed heavily to the new educational theory: social psychology, gestalt psychology, and, in the area of the arts, esthetics.

Social Psychology

Early progressivism directed its efforts to the "child-centered" school, with techniques designed to bring about individual development. Experimentalism, on the other hand, focused its attention on social requirements as well. Emphasis upon both the individual and society was featured in order to protect the child from being exploited by the demands of industry.

Gestalt Psychology

Behaviorism was characterized as mechanical and completely ineffective with regard to the development of creative thought. The new psychology emphasized that all learning was achieved through insight. The learner therefore focused attention on the relationship of the elements of a problem as they were arranged to effect a solution. Gestalt psychology paralleled Dewey's explanation of thinking, emphasizing insight, understanding, thinking in solving problems, and the testing of perceived relations.

Esthetics

Dewey introduced a functional concept in art. He contended that art developed and flourished when it was used to enhance everyday living, that it could win a much wider acceptance if placed in a more directly human context.

EPISTEMOLOGY OF PRAGMATISM

The Individual and Society

The pragmatic view established that a relation of interdependence between society and the individual had to exist. On the one hand, education was to function primarily as a social phenomenon, working to preserve society by initiating the individual into the characteristic life of the group. In this way society would be continually renewed because the beliefs and aspirations of its older citizens would be transmitted through education to the new members.

On the other hand, it was asserted that each individual developed in accordance with his own natural ability. Education had to become concerned with each individual, directing and guiding him toward the fulfillment of his powers and striving to achieve equilibrium between the two extremes of individual and society. The individual, while enjoying the fruits of freedom, was to learn the necessity of a responsibility toward society.

Life as Growth

Education: A Process of Continual Growth   The aim of education was continual growth. The child had to be guided toward a responsiveness to his environment. In this way his curiosity could be aroused and his interests, beginning with mere inclinations, at first, could be pursued with an open mind.

Education: A Process of Reorganization and Reconstruction   Mind was not an isolated faculty into which facts could be poured but a term given to all human activities that terminated in real and significant changes. Learning took place best when situations or problems were derived from the activities of ordinary life. The student had to be placed in the center of a real situation and determine a solution through the employment of his own power. The method was basically a trial of ideas. Learning situations were built around group activities and cooperative efforts.

Relationship of Discipline to Interest

Interest was considered connected rather than opposed to discipline. By means of *interest* or *concern* the child proceeded carefully toward the solution of a problem, developing discipline through the process.

CHAPTER

12

Music
Education
and
Experimentalism

A Call for Revision

NEW AIMS AND VALUES began to affect education at the time of the great Depression of 1929. Caught up in the emerging spirit, music educators strove to pattern their work according to the principles provided by experimentalism. A great deal of attention was given to the revision of theories and practices. Courses and teaching procedures were submitted to a careful re-evaluation. Additions and deletions in approaches and techniques resulted.

Although music education included singing, listening, playing, and creative experiences as before, the content and methods reflected an entirely different attitude. Courses were organized on a new psychological and cultural basis in direct opposition to those that had formerly served subject-matter aims.

The pupils' attitude toward music was considered of far

greater concern than the skills they took away. Singing was first and always a pleasurable activity. However, reading was never discarded. It was expected that within the totality of the program, all aspects of music would be represented so that each child could take from his experiences all that his capacity would allow.

With this change of direction, the status of the music supervisor underwent changes, too. Heretofore, it had been his duty to set the pace and be responsible for the successful achievement of a carefully charted course of study. It had been his duty to visit classes and teachers, to see that all were meeting schedules demanded for the course of study, and that goals were being reached by the prescribed procedures.

However, such duties were found to be more undesirable than otherwise in light of the changes that were taking place. The term *music supervisor* gradually began to disappear. The music supervisors in the larger systems became known as *directors*, and their duties changed with their titles. Insofar as their connection with classroom teaching was concerned, they became resource people and consultants to the other members of the department. In other systems music supervisors were referred to as *special teachers* or *music educators*. This change doubtless reflected the fact that the construction of precise and detailed courses of study was no longer encouraged. The music course was to serve each specific class situation and every individual.

Integration, correlation, and the project method received an ever-increasing emphasis. In an effort to show the interconnectedness of things, education became akin to life, its activities associated with life's experience. The integration of subjects became a technique aimed at breaking down the partitions that separated the subject-matter areas and allowed the student to pursue practical and usable knowledge.

As a perusal of the Music Educators National Conference Yearbooks of the period will show, methods that motivated cycles of experience as a means of leading children toward the experimental aim were at first enthusiastically sanctioned by many music educators. Otto Miessner pointed out that as life situations were related one to the other, so the materials, activities, and methods included within the curriculum must also be interrelated if the children were to find them meaningful and real.

At the same time there were those new progressives who argued against the extreme use to which the method was occasionally put. Carried to its logical extreme, Miessner's principle could result in music's surrendering its status as an entity in the curriculum and becoming nothing more than a handmaiden to other areas. Among those who offered words of caution were Beattie, McConathy, Morgan, Kidd, and Pierce. These warnings did much to bring about an integration that permitted music to preserve its identity while still performing a service to the other areas of learning.

Psychology of the Individual

In the previous chapter three contributory aspects of experimentalism, beyond philosophy, were discussed: social psychology, gestalt psychology, and esthetics. Their effect upon music education was very important. Specific attention will now be given to the psychology of learning since its principles represented such a marked departure from the traditional concepts of the learning process.

It was apparent in the 1930s that a wealth of new psychological data had come to the fore, which proved highly significant to the educator. Many psychologists had revised their ideas pertaining to the learning process, opening the way for new viewpoints, developments, principles, and procedures.

For the most inclusive psychological data affecting music education, the best source seems to be *The Psychology of School Music Teaching* by Mursell and Glenn. Although a complete exposition of their findings would be impossible here, a few principles may serve to project a sounding, at least, of gestalt psychology.

Two doctrines, which were almost sacred commandments to the teacher, came under the fire of intense criticism. The first was "learning to do by doing," for its implication that learning took place only through mechanical repetition; the second was the contention that all learning proceeded from the simple to the complex.

Learning could not always depend upon drill and repetition. To say that a habit could be fixed as a result of strengthening the bonds between stimulus and response was no longer entirely acceptable.

In opposition to this older view, learning was looked upon as a process of transformation—of continually creating something new. The child who sought to learn discovered for himself better ways of meeting complex situations and overcoming problems. Therefore learning was found to depend upon interest and impulse. The child was only provided with experiences and tasks that were both meaningful and interesting. Drill, however, was not entirely discarded but was considered incidental to the situation—an aid that the child presumably would recognize as necessary in arriving at a particular end or accomplishment.

As to the second criticism, no authentic proof was found to support the time-honored proposition that learning proceeded from the simple to the complex, from the known to the unknown. The new gestalt psychology considered that learning occurred when the pupil was placed in the center of a problem to which he must find a real solution. The learning activity began with an interesting problem which the child could recognize as a meaningful whole. After the initial period, characterized by a crude and imperfect synthesis, the child gradually moved to a period of analysis. At that time, elements were singled out for particular study. This kind of work differed from the older periods of formal drill.

The particular feature that was isolated for specific study and attention was selected from a meaningful setting. The solution which was continually related to the preliminary synthesis, contributed to the ultimate, more perfect synthesis. Learning, then, proceeded from an imperfect synthesis, moved through a study phase, or period of analysis, which, in turn, led to a more perfect synthesis.

For this reason any attempt to teach the skills of music through a process of habit building could hardly be considered psychologically correct. Conversely the child's musical growth came from real and worthwhile situations in which he became actively engaged. He discovered through his tussle with the problems at hand knowledge that would further enhance his personal growth.

This type of learning, which proceeded from synthesis to analysis to synthesis, was not a process that could be termed explicit. Elements of notation or of technique were not set up as problems to be attacked directly, but rather to be dealt with as they emerged from a larger music project or experience, and were handled incidentally in relation to the whole.

Suppose the project was a song. Certain elements of notation might call for explanation before the more perfect rendition, or synthesis, of the music could be achieved. These problems were explained, but explanation was confined to the context. Mastery of the score was ultimately important for complete musical independence, and the child's attention had to be directed toward detail. However, Mursell and Glenn maintained that the best scientific evidence indicated that problems of the score should be incidental to music making and not receive major emphasis.

Upon the bases of these psychological findings, certain principles were projected upon which music instruction would soundly depend. From the broad viewpoint any favorable music program ought to offer three important kinds of musical experiences: listening, performing, and creating. Through these activities sound musical growth might take place. Singing activities were at the core of the entire program, followed by listening. Instrumental work, which included making and playing instruments, would hold a responsible place and embrace such related activities as improvisation, original composition, and toy orchestra. Rhythmic activities were also understood to be essential in the all-round musical development of the child. Ear-training was recognized as a vital phase of all musical experiences. With such a varied set of activities, the music program showed a real capacity for a wide field of musical projects.

Viewed from a more traditional and logical standpoint, such a broad interpretation could only offer a smattering of this and that; at best only the barest elemental skills could be imparted. However, none of these activities existed in isolation but were fused together into an effective force in pursuing the primary aim of music education—appreciation of music. Reading, for example, did not represent one isolated field, and listening another. It was asserted that while the child's attention at times was directed to problems of the score, he was constantly being led toward a greater appreciation of music. However, while the child was listening to music, it was conceivable that there were features of the lesson that would incidentally enhance the child's understanding of the score. There was no grade-by-grade course of study. The best that could be done for real musical growth was to supply each child with a sequence of real musical experiences that were within the scope of his capacity.

It was further contended that music education must not only be well correlated internally but also establish contact with other phases of schoolwork. Music ability did not stand by itself. It had been determined that outstanding musical ability was a manifestation of high general ability. Therefore, if music were to contribute to all-round growth, it could not confine its instruction to one narrow area but should develop its affinities to other pursuits. In this way music broadened its service to direct the child along the road to general culture.

Experimentalism in Music Education

For purposes of clarity, it is appropriate to pattern this discussion upon those experimental principles already established in the last chapter: that experimentalism (a) endeavored to achieve an interdependence between the individual and society, (b) looked upon life as growth, and (c) established that discipline was closely related to interest.

THE INDIVIDUAL AND SOCIETY

It has been established that Experimentalists strove to achieve an interdependence between the individual and society. Mursell supported this aim. His book *Music in American Schools* (1943) did a great deal to clarify the foundations of the new thought as it applied to music education

According to Mursell, the music teacher had to serve two masters, the social as well as the individual. He served society by directing musical experiences and activities so that individuals might be led into the beliefs and aspirations of the society as a whole. The instructor's second responsibility was to provide for the child's personal musical growth. Music would become "both subjective and objective, both mental and social."[1]

Concern for the Individual

Differences in individual musical ability naturally were recognized. In spite of varying capacities, there was such wide scope in the field of music that some elements at least could contribute toward the personal growth and fulfillment of every child. The highest aim was to develop an appreciation and understanding of music. This was recognized as a far greater goal than the acquisition of any specific skill.

A program was to be initiated, which would begin with general exploration and proceed, by means of a variety of rich musical activities and experiences, toward a widening of the individual's

[1] James L. Mursell. *Music in American Schools*. New York: Silver Burdett Company, 1943, p. 42.

cultural horizon. Even though skill was not first in importance, it was by no means set aside. Specific values, however, took into account the differences in nature ability between one child and another. A variety of approaches to problems was offered in order that each individual could follow what he found to be the best means of developing his skills and understanding.

Somewhere along the way every child should find *something* or even *many things* in music that would contribute to his greater happiness, whether it be the possibility of a career, a hobby, or an emotional stabilizer. The individual in a group could then be respected for his particular capacity and potential—instruction was based on his needs. From this angle there was an equal chance for the average, below average, and talented child to grow.

Concern for Society

Mursell offered three ways in which music might contribute toward the social aim. First, it had much to offer in the way of transmission, of which John Dewey had spoken. All good music symbolized or expressed certain ideals and aspirations of the civilization from which it had come. Therefore, the music class could bring children to a closer realization of the emotions and attitudes of their own culture as well as those of other civilizations. As the child, for example, participated in folk and social dances, which represented various countries of the world, he came to a closer understanding of the emotions and attitudes of his own culture as well as those of other nations.

Next, the very character of the music class, with its related performing units, offered group activities through which vital social experiences could result. Singing, instrumental work, dramatization, and singing games called for the interplay of children together.

Third, the music class provided valuable experiences in developing the ideals of democratic living. The success of any music group was measured by the opportunities for shared experiences, which overshadowed differences in economic and social status, and each individual's worth was evaluated by his contribution within the whole activity.

LIFE AS GROWTH

Under this same heading in the last chapter, the two following principles were discussed: (1) education was a process for con-

tinual growth; (2) education was a process of perpetual reorganization, reconstruction, and transformation. The validity of these
statements as applied to the field of music education will now be
considered.

Music Education: A Process for Continual Growth

According to Dewey the child should first be imbued with the desire
for further growth. To provide real momentum toward increased
musical growth, music must be a joyous experience for the child;
an enthusiasm for the subject must be cultivated through a
pleasant, ever-broadening experience in the art.

So that sound musical development could take place, a five-
fold program was initiated to include singing (rote singing and
voice culture), playing, rhythmic activities, listening (including
ear-training), and creative work. These activities contributed their
respective qualities to effect a strong force in developing perceptions, understandings, and skills in music.

Once an interest and enthusiasm was achieved, the first step
was completed. However, this could only be interpreted as a sign
of possible growth. Next came the problem of directing the proper
development of that pursuit, without ever losing sight of the principle that knowledge was of value to the child as he could use it to
effect subsequent changes.

Music Education as Reorganization,
Reconstruction, and Transformation

The Experimentalists considered mind to be a term assigned to all
human experiences that terminated in significant changes. Facts
were essential to the solution of a problem, but knowledge itself
could not be represented as an accumulation of facts, the known
could not be thought of as a particular fact but rather as a value
having meaning in an activity that modified or solved something
between the individual and his environment.

According to Mursell musical growth implied actual changes
in patterns of behavior. It was not sufficient that musical insights
and skills were developed unless they were expressed as live and
useful action, unless they became a part of everyday life, as when
the child attended concerts, listened to recordings, or played in a
musical ensemble. Music was a *doing* thing rather than a clutter of
facts stored in the mind and never used.

Learning in music was best accomplished when a situation

could foment an attitude of exploration and experimentation within the child. Placed in the center of a complex situation, the child discovered methods that would assist him in solving the problems the situation introduced.

Rather than teach music through a presentation of techniques, a reversal of procedure was emphatically prescribed. Effort was directed toward bringing the esthetic values of music to children, which, in turn, led them toward ever-increasing independence and insight and a mastery of its beauty, structure, and techniques. This type of knowledge was practical and useful, and it had meaning simply by having been learned through a genuine musical experience. Therefore, it became a part of the individual for use in subsequent activities.

It remains to be seen just what procedures could be used in order to achieve the aims set forth. According to Mursell the total number of school years were to be broken down into the more or less traditional manner—as primary, intermediate, junior high, and high school. Rather than paying particular notice to each individual grade, attention was centered upon the four major classifications stated immediately above. Since the first three dealt primarily with general music, they have been selected for further discussion.

The Primary School   During the early years every activity and experience centered around musical orientation. Through rote singing, rhythm bands, listening, creative activities, ear-training, free rhythmic movement, and improvement of the singing voice, the child could find stimulation in exploring the whole field of music. An interest might emerge that would lead toward musical independence. As interest appeared, discipline would follow; for it was the pressure of interest that motivated the pupil to undertake a task in music study and see it through to completion.

The Intermediate Years   The orientation established in the early grades would continue. By a diversity of musical experiences that demanded increasing esthetic insight, as well as a further development of technical skills, a greater and more genuine mastery might be achieved. Projects, mastery units, and the use of syllables (as long as they did not represent the end but rather one of several agencies) could be used. In other words, no specific method or technique was established as the only means by which the aims and goals could be accomplished. Above all, the whole process had to represent to every child an avenue for musical growth according to his capacity.

Specifics, or the elements, could only be considered after interest had been established. Grades four through six represented the period devoted to this more definite emphasis upon skills. However, problems had to *emerge* from their own unique and particular settings. While the analysis of certain technical difficulties were necessary, the work had to be done in such a way as not to disturb the general musical environment.

The Junior High School   The junior high program devoted its time to a consolidation of those technical problems already experienced in the intermediate grades. However, they would be offered in new contexts that demanded a firmer understanding even though they continued in an atmosphere of truly interesting and exciting musical experiences. Mursell also called it a period in which the child gathered a "musical momentum"—the years when capacities might be mobilized for real independent activity in whatever phase of musical opportunity he might choose in high school.

THE RELATIONSHIP OF DISCIPLINE TO INTEREST

The platform of experimentalism maintained that discipline was connected rather than opposed to interest. Mursell pointed out that the popular misconception of this premise resulted when interest was equated with whim.

Education had to provide material that would enlist the child's interest or concern so that he would find purpose in any given activity. This element of interest became the nucleus of real mental growth. Once it was properly established, a very constructive outcome could eventually result. Arbitrary imposition of discipline from external forces could stunt the intellectual growth of the child; but the child might react positively to the necessary disciplines that emerged naturally in the pursuit of his interest.

The aim of the *New Music Horizons* was to *stimulate* within the child a desire to follow through on the activities offered. However specific a consideration of technique might have been, it was not to be taught apart from a truly musical situation. Every consideration was given to provide beautiful materials, which would have appeal and interest.

A More Contemporary Psychological View

Until recently psychologists were primarily concerned with the development of procedures that would make specific learning more effective. However, this emphasis has since been criticized by some as being too narrow. Developmental psychologists, as well as mental hygienists and social psychologists, have pointed to other values as being worthy of greater concern.

They deemed it unwise to continue making distinctions in the general school program between those subjects responsible for imparting knowledge and those that built character. The important thing was the whole curriculum, both regular and extra. The value of each subject should be determined according to its capacity to contribute to the broader concept of personality development.

THE DEVELOPMENTAL APPROACH

For years music educators were in disagreement with one another as to which aspect of music should receive the greatest emphasis. Some preferred to point up its esthetic values by devoting most of the time to rote or listening experiences. Others believed that the study of the printed score should represent the primary concern.

Mursell, in his book *Education for Musical Growth*, maintained that music education could not consist of a storehouse of facts for which the child was to be responsible. Rather it was the development of musicality that formed the foundation of the subject upon which skills might later be built. In any case there must always be something for all and not just a few.

Skills and technique were to be presented incidentally so as never to obscure the genuine musical values. Further, no grade-by-grade breakdown of musical knowledge could be accepted as desirable. Until recently the readiness program had usually taken up the greater part of the elementary years. This kind of training was discontinued in the upper grades and the finer techniques emphasized. According to the new view the emphasis upon musicality would continue throughout all grades with esthetic experience given constant priority.

All experiences, activities, and learnings were organized so as to lead toward musical growth and responsiveness. The problem of teaching became centered upon the development of an emotional response to music; imbued with a high degree of musicality, the child found meaning and understanding in the technical aspects that followed. Presented in this way, music could affect the entire personality of the child.

When musicality was uppermost, the child could have the same quality of experience as the artist, though on a smaller scale. And what began as simple and elemental gradually grew to a more profound understanding of the esthetic qualities of the art.

Formerly, the piano student, for example, might have been directed in his early studies to a sonatina or two, after which to a Haydn sonata, later to a representative work of Mozart, and then to Beethoven. It is possible for a few students with diligence to achieve the technical aspects of such rapid progress. However, it is unlikely that they would acquire artistic concepts, simply because their artistic maturity would not grow at the rate that their technical skills were being forced. Their concept of music would center around the exhibition of technical skill, but the essence of the music, the beauty, would be undeveloped.

Still, in keeping with the example, when teachers were confronted with the idea that there were other aspects of value—such as style, ear-training, improvisation, sight-reading—the cry commonly heard was "no time." As a result their students, more often than not, missed many experiences which would have contributed to an all-round musical responsiveness. As a consequence, when it came time for these same students to teach, their aim very naturally followed the pattern encountered in their own training. They thought of themselves as drill masters rather than as guides who would develop the inner perceptions of the art of music in their students.

At the opposite extreme, developmentalism could have been criticized because of the many avenues of approach it supplied. Within the music class it was conceivable that activities might include rhythm band, singing, listening, performing on melody flutes, experimenting with music through the use of water glasses, and so on. However, rather than constituting a smattering of seemingly useless activities, all of these were contributors to the promotion of musical responsiveness which progressed in a clear and logical manner.

As poetry does not deal primarily with the projection of facts or profound literal content but imparts a feeling, so must music. Just as poetry uses words, music uses sound and rhythm as its tools to achieve or express an emotion. Therefore, a musical performance does not fulfill its purpose by merely providing a technically perfect rendition of a composition unless it also successfully conveys poetic or emotional feeling. Music education should turn from its emphasis on skills and proceed to develop within its constituents that musical responsiveness which is basic to the entire endeavor. Intellectual understanding and skill, though indeed important, are branches from the main stem—the art of music.

According to Mursell, "Musical growth, like all mental growth, is a process in which essential means are clarified, deepened, and broadened."[2] Throughout this process of development the child must be led toward meanings and emotional values of which, at first, he is only dimly aware. Each experience, whether with the rhythm band or singing a song, must give the child a greater and greater awareness of the inner expressive values of tone and rhythm. With every activity he must be brought closer to the full realization of the poetic possibilities music should impart.

It was not sufficient that music represent an ability to sing a song or play an instrument. Its purpose was to assist in the opening up of a richer life through new contacts and avocations; it was to provide a service within society, a chance of giving, and an opportunity for expression. The end value was not the mastery of specifics but the development of a truly musical person.

Music textbooks reflected this new approach, subordinating skills to serve musicality and the emotive functions of music.

According to Mursell there were five broad areas distinctly concerned with the manifestation of developmental aims. These were growth in musical awareness, initiative, discrimination, insight, and skill. These specific areas were in reality so thoroughly interwoven with each other that partitioning them into separate units is impossible. Skill might aid discrimination, musical awareness might serve musical initiative, and all five together could contribute a share toward the development of real musical growth. To neglect one was to weaken all the others.

Musical Awareness

The child was to be introduced to music in such a way that he would enjoy it and be motivated to explore it further. Activities were so selected and developed as to spark awareness of all the

[2] James L. Mursell, *Education for Musical Growth*. Boston: Ginn and Company, 1948, p. 50.

musical possibilities in the individual's relationship to himself and to the world about him. The total experience involved something that would affect his entire inner being, aiding him in the organization of his feelings and the judgment of values. Through its proper study children were encouraged to recognize music as an asset in opening up a richer life through new contacts, avocations, service within society, and an opportunity for expression. Music was presented broadly, to include its esthetic content, its skills and its history.

According to many music texts, numerous invitations were provided to interest the child in the free and happy participation of music. Such experiences were not confined to the primary years but continued at all levels. In this way the individual could gradually develop meanings and emotional values. Each activity, whether with rhythmic expression, dancing, dramatics, singing, listening, or creating through instrumental work, helped to yield awareness of the expressive values of music. If, for example, listening became the consideration, the form or structure of a specific composition was not of consequence initially. Rather, it was asserted that the child should be given the opportunity to gain a rich and exciting experience with a wide range of different types of music. Gradually, grasp of detail would increase as growth continued. No given sequence was proposed, no exact, proper time for this or that theoretical problem. Above all, the child's enthusiasm was never to be permitted to wane through discouragement or feelings of inadequacy.

Musical Initiative

Once the individual discovered the possibilities inherent in both the study and enjoyment of music, his enthusiasm was to be kept continually alive. Skills were not allowed to predominate but were played down until the child's musical experience reached a point when technical aspects could take on real meaning.

Musical initiative was a product of musical growth. As the study of music became more appealing, a momentum would result and be expressed in the individual's effort, through the pursuit of activities that he selected on his own.

There were many kinds of initiative that could be promoted so that in any given class there would be something for all; for instance: attending concerts, reading materials dealing with music and musical events, establishing new practice methods or pursuing some new phase of music study. Every experience was to be guided in such a way as to suggest activities worthy of accomplishment and to impart to the pupil a confidence for achieving them independently and with real satisfaction.

Many texts emphasized a varied musical program. This was intended to lead the child toward an awareness of the possibilities the subject contained. Individuals were also urged and inspired to make some choices of their own and to carry them through on their own initiative.

Musical Discrimination

By participating in performance groups or by listening to a great deal of music, the individual would become sensitive to the values contained in musical performance and in the compositions themselves. A preference for good music was thought to increase with experience.

The emotional content and meaning embodied in the music became of the utmost significance. It was then the inner essence of the music that would be emphasized first and foremost. A fine performance would be judged on how clearly the expressive values of the work were projected.

The theoretical and technical aspects of the music were but the means to an end. No composition could be considered great music because the composer merely exhibited a definite skill in the manipulation of the rules of harmony. The success of any original musical production would be judged on the meaning it conveyed. An achievement of this kind could not be realized without a refined understanding of theoretical principles. However, those elements were only the agents through which the emotional idea was projected. To stress theory as the prime consideration was to put the cart before the horse.

Accepting this as a controlling factor, musical selections for children were chosen for their intrinsic value, their appeal and interest. Skills were always to have a place because no music could be composed or performed without them. However, technique was considered as but the means by which an artistic expression could be achieved. Attention was primarily directed to the inner substance or the intrinsic meaning of the music.

Musical Insight

This topic stood for a homogeneity of two faculties which had often been treated separately, namely, the ability to identify and understand the elements of tonal-rhythmic patterns of music, and the capacity to recognize the expressive values that those particulars could impart. This was not the first time that these two precepts had been identified as areas worthy of emphasis in any intensively conceived music course. However, Mursell's view that the two processes were no longer to be dealt with separately was unique. The structural aspects and the expressive values of the music were in themselves only isolated entities without meaning until they could be united in such a way that each would complement the other.

Music notation was looked upon as a set of symbols conveying meaning. It was what those signs *said* rather than what each note represented in name or value that was of consequence. The study of music reading, therefore, had to be considered a process that would develop musical insight rather than skill alone.

Mursell pointed out a kinship between music and language reading. From the acquisition of language reading alone the reader could derive no value. It was the *comprehension* of what he read that was of real worth. In the same way the development of real musical insight increased the child's ability in musical expression.

When a song was read or sung by rote, attention could not always be focused on the intellectual problems provided by the score. Of equal importance was the musical content, which generated the beauty of the song. The individual had to be led to recognize the expressive values as they could be seen through the particular movement of the melody, the phrase development, and the rhythmic flow.

With children it was considered futile to expect precision at the outset of any developmental sequence. Real systematic study presupposed maturity. Therefore, the child was to be drawn toward musical insight in an unsystematic and incidental fashion. The child was immature and could only learn by moving from the concrete to the abstract, from the crude and imperfect to the consummate. The whole process was to be determined on the basis of genuine musical growth. The essential point was that notation should always be taught in real and varied musical settings.

Music reading, according to the texts of the period, was understood to be the same as musical understanding. The child was to be so guided that he would not merely see the singular elements of the score but actually derive the *music* implied in the notation. Music reading was developed by gradually connecting experiences of eye, ear, and muscle. It was the general shape of the tune that became significant.

The child was led to note the contour of the melodic line by curves on the blackboard or by letting him represent the ups and downs of the tune through physical movement. While these methods could be considered crude, they had their function in leading the child to musical meaning.

Gradually, as growth continued, the individual would be able to grasp finer details. When he was ready, more of the standard notation could be presented. At all times, however, the essence of the music was of infinitely greater importance than the detail.

Musical Skill

From a psychological point of view, Mursell argued that a skill did not imply dexterity alone but also denoted an ability to derive a desired musical effect by means of the voice or an instrument. Skill, or technique, could never be considered as an end in itself but rather could be judged according to the assistance it provided in the attainment of some desired goal or purpose. He considered two basic problems in connection with this topic of skill, namely, control and the action pattern.

Control, Mursell maintained, was revealed through a recognition of the musical intention of the whole composition. Once the individual realized the musical effect he must eventually achieve, he could plot out a course of action that would lead him toward that effect. The musical effect represented the control, determining the action patterns that were to be called into play to attain the desired result. Technique, therefore, could not be defined as a mechanical skill. Rather, it had to be accepted as a capacity to express beauty through a recognition of the beauty to be expressed.

The action pattern referred to the physical movements that came into play in the act of singing or playing. In the learning process these patterns would become more and more efficient. However, this would not be accomplished through long servitude to exercises and drills. Musical responsiveness remained the primary aim. Skill was attained as a result of a gradual growth sequence, which began with the unrefined and advanced to the culturally matured product. When the need for the development of a specific action-pattern was discovered, the problem was isolated, for the sake of analysis, and then synthesized into the whole or the actual musical context. Analysis began in its simplest form, at the most casual suggestions, and gradually became more exacting. A fine technique was not represented by great agility, but by an ability to comprehend and express beauty in music to the degree the child's capacities would permit.

The specific ability of music reading did not suggest a particular facility in dealing only with problems of time and tune. The symbolism was of little value unless a meaning could be derived from the notation. Without musical insight the individual would be incapable of recognizing any significant expression from the musical score though it was imperative that reading be taught, the skill itself could not monopolize the entire course of instruction. Placed on a proper psychological basis, it could render a real service so long as other values that contributed to a genuine musical development were not slighted.

This concept regarding the development of music reading was recognized by many of the newer music texts. While specifics were not ignored, the child was guided in his activities to derive genuine meaning and understanding from the music. Any drill that required the naming of notes or dealt with individual time elements was to be an exception to the rule and was to be used only in certain isolated phases of analysis. At such times particulars were to be quickly returned to their real context and synthesized into the whole.

Aside from the fact that the design of these texts was founded upon developmental psychology, it appears that the general aim and spirit was congenial to, and in close affinity with, experimentalism. This statement finds support through the emphasis given to both social and individual development, the promotion of correct emotional attitudes, and the enhancing of interest, discipline, and character building.

CHAPTER
13
Music Education
in
Contemporary
America

Soon after World War II educators became concerned that the curriculum had not kept pace with the great advances in mathematics and science of the twentieth century. The public was stirred into an awareness of the crisis when Russian educational efforts, crowned by Sputnik's success in 1957, presented a real challenge to American practices.

Education had been fundamentally considered as a social phenomenon by Dewey's educational philosophy. While the individual was not forgotten, the child had to derive values and meanings through joint action with others—only in this way was it considered possible for the process of social renewal to continue.

Experimentalism also emphasized character-building. Inner or spiritual values were of little consequence because morality was believed to be accomplished by the entire organism rather than by a mind directing a body through reason and thought. Man's moral fiber was measured only by the results he effected. Good thoughts in themselves were of little consequence if they did not precipitate good actions. Citizenship was valued according to the contribution the individual could bring to society.

Learning was considered more satisfactory if taken from the activities of ordinary life rather than from ready-made subject matter. Fusion units, integrated units, broad fields, and problems courses were designed to cut across the traditional subject areas in an attempt to interrelate bodies of knowledge into more lifelike experiences.

There was no general educational formula because there were no final or fixed values. The world was in a state of constant change. Hence, the best thing was to help the individual achieve a more integrated understanding of social development and a greater recognition of his role in the democratic society.

Values such as citizenship, character, personality, social development, as well as a decided emphasis upon the problem-solving attitude, were interpreted as fundamental educational aims; each subject in the curriculum became an *instrument* for the development of these objectives. The effectiveness of any area in the

A class of pre-teens. Courtesy Dalcroze School of Music, New York.

A creative project. Each student (ages eleven to thirteen) makes up a variation on a theme for his own instrument. Finally the students depict their instruments in suitable dance movements, sing, and play together their combined variations—in this case on "Happy Birthday." Courtesy Dalcroze School of Music.

school program was judged according to its adequacy in accomplishing the objectives of the experimental platform. The substance contained within any subject was only a secondary consideration. Of prime consequence was the development of broad educational values.

At the same time there was a growing dissatisfaction among music educators with those principles and procedures that had gained some favor during the war years. Some music activities were planned to engender social ends, others were designed to render a specific service in the personality development of the child. However, teachers gradually voiced serious doubts as to the musical value derived from any of these endeavors. Among the seven objectives proposed by the Commission on Reorganization of

241

A class of three- to four-year-olds. Courtesy Dalcroze School of Music.

Secondary Education in 1918 were civic education and character development. These objectives functioned to unify subject areas and prevent an overemphasis upon specialization in any one field. Teachers, however, seriously questioned the value of this unification because an evaluation of any program only revealed a series of unrelated experiences. There was no sequence to permit the child to follow any specific direction. As a result the benefits derived were of a peripheral nature rather than of real musical values. Courses in the curriculum served purposes for which they were never really suited.

Preface to a New Departure

THE INITIATION OF APPRAISAL

A deep concern was particularly evident in 1959 for an appraisal of teaching practices and an examination of fresh approaches that might more effectively impart to students the substance of the sciences. The National Science Foundation provided administrative and financial aid to several curriculum projects to include writing new mathematics textbooks, producing films for sophomore biology courses, and establishing methods for teaching geometry in the early grades. Distinguished scholars in the fields of mathematics and science contributed to the creation of new courses and materials.

An outstanding event was the Woods Hole Conference held in September of 1959 and convened through the efforts of the Education Committee of the National Academy of Sciences and supported not only by that organization but also by the United States Office of Education, the Air Force, and the Rand Corporation.

Among the thirty-five participants in the ten-day conference were educators, historians, physicists, biologists, psychologists, and mathematicians. All came together to examine ways and means of improving education. Such an assembly marked the beginning of what has now become a trend—a unity of efforts between teachers, leaders in fields related to education, and those distinguished in their respective field of specialization in the cause of elementary and secondary education. One of the most important results of that conference was the assertion that the substance of a course can only be understood in terms of its structure.

There were similar conferences in the field of music education. Supported by the Office of Education through the Cooperative Research Program, the Seminar on Music Education held at Yale University from June 17 through June 28, 1963 was one of the most important of these efforts. Attending the meetings were thirty-one scholars, teachers, and musicians. As in the Woods Hole Conference, outstanding people outside the field of music education were included and asked to contribute so that teaching methods and subject matter could become relevant to contemporary needs.

The participants at the Yale Seminar found the music curriculum inadequate both in character and content when compared to the music developments of the twentieth century. Not only new materials but new teaching methods were considered necessary if the child's capacity to express himself musically or to respond to music could ever be adequately realized.

Appropriate musical understanding, according to the findings of the seminar, could only be achieved through a knowledge of the *structure* of music. Fundamental to such training is the study of the elements to include melody, harmony, rhythm, and form. The individual must participate in a wide variety of activities, to include performance, bodily movement, creativity, listening, and ear-training. In that way his experience, relative to the stage of his training, can be as complete as that of a professional musician.

Another very important conference that had an impact on music education was the Tanglewood Symposium convened by the Music Educators National Conference in the summer of 1967, in cooperation with the Theodore Presser Foundation, the Berkshire Music Center, and the Boston University School of Fine and Applied Arts. The conference, attended by scientists, labor leaders, musicians, sociologists, educators, and representatives of corporations, foundations, and government, dealt with critical issues germane to the topic "Music in American Society" to discuss, among others, the role of the arts in a technological society, the status of the arts, and forces which could offer new directions. From the issues which provided the rationale for the Symposium, certain outcomes were anticipated. Among them were: a clarification of the unique function of music education, and the preparation of publications which would not only clarify the new objectives but assist music educators and others to evolve effective music programs.

Elementary music instruction was found to be separated so unsystematically into a number of activities that one experience had little or no relevance to the other. It was recommended that a new music program be established for the elementary school that would emphasize the substance and structure of music through the skills of singing, playing, reading, listening, moving, and creating. The need for quality teaching by competent music specialists instead of classroom teachers was emphasized.

General music in the junior high school was pointed to as often being of poor quality. It was recommended that junior high school courses be revised and upgraded in order that both the intellectual and emotive aspects of music be well represented. Appropriate skills, knowledge, and understanding of music could then be properly developed. A shift of emphasis from the use of traditional music literature to that of contemporary composition was earnestly prescribed. It was further recommended that music educators give due recognition to the music of both Africa and Asia. All three conferences had some things in common. New curriculums were to be made relevant to contemporary needs by tapping the great resources of scholars, teachers, and professionals in education and in related fields. Subject matter was reviewed and appraised in terms of its contemporary content. Of primary concern were the processes involved in imparting the substance of subject matter to students. It would appear that all three conferences pointed to the importance of structure as the basis for a proper understanding of any subject.

THE ADOPTION OF FOREIGN INNOVATIONS

In search of possible solutions, some teachers turned to systems from Europe and Asia, which emphasized musical content, structure, and sequence. Methods developed in Germany by Carl Orff and in Hungary by Zoltan Kodály have enjoyed some favor in this country in recent years. In the area of string instruction, the method advanced by the Japanese teacher Shinichi Suzuki has been viewed with some interest.

Carl Orff

The primary attraction of the Orff method, which made its entrance upon the American scene about 1958, may well have been its focus upon the basic substance and structure of music. Accord-

Children in music class using Carl Orff instruments. Photograph: Stan Levy. Courtesy Third Street Music Settlement, New York.

ing to Orff's system, musicality is cultivated by dealing directly with the elements of rhythm, melody, harmony, form, and dynamics.

The sequence suggested by the five volumes of the *Orff-Schulwerk* seems to recall the recapitulation theory which considered it effective for children to re-enact the various stages of the history of man. Beginning with melody and rhythm, the most basic elements, Orff constructs his program according to the way in which music developed in the history of Western civilization. Beginning with the most elemental structures, including the pentatonic scale and the simplest rhythm patterns, he guides the child to the diatonic scales, to more complex rhythms, and then to harmony—an element which developed later in the history of music. In the same way he deals at first with the musical phrase and then moves to the canon, the rondo, and then the larger musical forms. The process becomes one of moving from the most primal music to an understanding of the more culturally advanced art forms.

Rhythmic perception probably receives the primary emphasis. It is developed through its natural evolution of speech, rhythm, and movement. Speech patterns taken from jingles, chants, and nursery rhymes provide a natural way of inculcating rhythmic perception. The training is further enhanced by bodily movements —clapping, patschen (slapping the thighs with the palm of the hands), stamping, finger-snapping, or combinations of these.

The rhythms and movements thus established are then transferred to melodic patterns, using a complete set of instruments, which Orff has especially designed for this purpose. By this means children can create primitive ensemble music. When this work has been established and children can derive satisfying experiences in extemporizing and invention, musical notation is introduced. Among the positive contributions of the method is the awakening of the creative spirit through the rich experience provided in improvisation, an art almost forgotten in Western civilization.

Zoltán Kodály

Another system designed beyond the borders of this continent after World War II and founded upon the premise that the appreciation of music must be developed through an understanding of its structural content was Zoltán Kodály's. His method reflects a revival of several systems popular in years past not only in Europe but in this country as well. Curwen's tonic *sol-fa* system, which maintains a place in Kodály's work, was not without influence in the United States in the nineteenth century. Not only the principle of the movable *do* associated with Rousseau but that of figure notation invented by E. M. Chevé, a system of indicating the degrees of the scale by numbers, have been used in this country since the time of Lowell Mason.

The hand signs, originated by John Curwen in 1870 and used in the United States at the turn of the century, have become, in somewhat modified form, an important means of teaching the melodic elements of music. Another contribution from abroad was the use of time names, as developed by Aimé Paris in 1829, altered later in that century by Luther Whiting Mason and again at a still later date by Kodály.

In an effort to develop the plan according to a sequence the child would find most natural, Kodály bases musical education upon folk music, more readily accepted by children than art music. In this Hungarian system the emphasis is on sight-singing and dictation achieved through a careful study of the structural elements of music, including rhythm, melody, texture, and form. Improvisation becomes an important aspect throughout.

Zoltán Kodály in 1939. Hungarian National Office for Tourism.

Rhythm is emphasized first as children are led to recognize the pulse of a familiar song by reproducing it through movement. The melodic elements are gradually introduced, beginning with the descending minor third; from there other tones are added to complete the pentatonic scale. From that framework children move to diatonicism and the entire twelve-tone range of the octave. Hand signs are used as notes, and intervals are discussed. A cappella singing is fundamental in the process of ear-training, an important feature of every lesson.

Children are guided toward an understanding of harmony by improvising polyphonic exercises, associating appropriate chords to given tunes, and improvising rhythmic ostinatos. The basic elements of form are introduced first by experiencing repetition, similarity, number of phrases, or question and answer. Later the analysis of folksongs leads to the more complicated forms used in art music. The system constantly calls for action and involvement.

While such a system might be called rigid, it must be remembered that the Hungarian government is not only interested in music for all children but has established the Primary School of Music and Singing for those who indicate special musical competence; according to Frigyes Sandor there are approximately a hundred of these special schools located throughout Hungary. In the regular primary schools a system of this kind has to be carried on with extreme caution in order not to discourage the pupils by proceeding at a pace that could prove too rapid for their music capabilities.

While there are music educators in this country who have become interested in Kodály's work, they have recognized that some modification is necessary if the method is to prove suitable to the requirements of American education. Recently interesting adaptations have been produced through the work of Arpad Darazs and Stephen Jay in their book entitled *Sight and Sound* and by Mary Helen Richards in the *Threshold to Music Series*.

Some teachers have discovered similarities in the work of Orff and Kodály. This has precipitated endeavors to work the two methods together, as in *Music Making in the Elementary School* by Gerald Burakoff and Lawrence Wheeler.

Shinichi Suzuki

The violin teaching methods of Shinichi Suzuki, developed shortly after World War II in Japan, have recently received some attention in this country. The "Saino-Kyoiku" or "Talent Education" movement does not concern itself primarily with training artists. Its basic aim is to give children a unique opportunity to develop their musical potential.

Basing his thesis upon the premise that education begins the instant the child is born, Suzuki has patterned his methods on the way individuals learn their mother tongue. As a child responds to his early environment by learning to speak before he can read, it is possible for him to play an instrument before he can deal directly with the printed score. Capitalizing on this concept, Suzuki developed his method according to the rote-note process. Not everyone can achieve the same degree of perfection, but in each field of endeavor, everyone can learn to the limit of his natural capacity.

In the Talent Education program, children begin their study of the violin early—it is not unusual for some to begin at age three. Assistance from a parent is an indispensable requirement. The

Shinichi Suzuki with a young American student. Photograph: Louis Ouzer. Courtesy Sheldon Soffer Management, New York.

Two of Suzuki's youngest students. Photograph: Kazuyo Kageyama. Courtesy Sheldon Soffer Management.

mother or father receives a minimum of instruction first. During this period—usually a few months—the child simply watches and listens to the parent. After this stimulus, along with the further motivation of preliminary rhythmic and bowing-preparation exercises, the child is ready to begin playing the violin.

Most students receive three private lessons a month, each of which may be limited to about fifteen minutes, or whatever time might be considered suitable for the age of the individual. The parent attends each lesson in order to assist the child properly during practice periods at home.

Motivation is achieved primarily through cooperation rather than competition. The fourth lesson each month is designed for students of all levels to play together. At this time the older pupils can inspire and assist the beginners.

At first everything is done by rote. The child begins by listening to recordings of violin pieces, particularly "Twinkle, Twinkle, Little Star, with Variations"—the first piece to be learned. While finger patterns, bowing, and rhythmic figures must be dealt with, listening to recordings at first, and then working out the problems contained in each piece becomes the established process for adding new ones to the child's repertory. Each piece is learned from memory, and no finished selection is ever abandoned. Even when the individual can deal appropriately with the printed score, notation is not used at the lessons.

There is no designated age level at which children are expected to transfer from the rote experience to reading the printed score.

According to Suzuki, when the child begins the Seitz concerto, Volume IV, music reading is taught by means of associating the notes with a piece already committed to memory. In other words, the individual visualizes what he has already learned.

As the pupil progresses, skill development is carried on according to the problems presented in the musical context of the ten manuals prepared by Suzuki. While the emphasis is focused .on the Baroque masters, there are representative works of Beethoven, Mozart, and Weber, as well.

The methods of Suzuki embrace certain principles by no means antagonistic to American pedagogy. As with all systems there áre some teachers who find Talent Education a means of kindling interest in playing the violin; there are some who accept the general principles, adapting them to the particular needs of their students, and some who maintain that other systems are more effective.

The National Talent Education Concert, an annual event, in the Tokyo Sports Palace features as many as 2000 young violinists trained by Shinichi Suzuki or by teachers using his method. Courtesy Sheldon Soffer Management.

A new emphasis in this country on the substance and structure of knowledge was apparent, and new directions were being explored. But before any significant reform could be effected, a new or revised educational platform had first to be established. Patterns of education must still find definition in the epistemology of a specific philosophy. Otherwise the acceptance or rejection of principles and procedures becomes a guessing game among individuals, and the resulting educational effort lacks cohesion and meaning. A considerable amount of activity in this area can be noted.

Revisions in the Experimental Platform

Experimentalism as the guiding force in education was challenged. At its door the educational revolution laid a considerable amount of blame for deficiencies in principles and procedures. As might be expected, they have not been restated in the form that was generally accepted earlier in the century.

EDUCATION: A PROCESS FOR CONTINUAL GROWTH

The educational reform movement examined the principles that proved ineffective and corrected or revised them according to the requirements of the times. Accepting Dewey's broadly generalized statement that education represents a continual power to grow, each subject takes on importance when it serves that end. Since the concept of growth is the general aim, every course must determine its own unique function as well as its basic structure. On the basis of its appraisal, it can be judged as a valid or inadequate adjunct to the educational process. This kind of objective evaluation has become markedly evident in many of the disciplines incorporated in the curriculum.

THE RELATIONSHIP OF DISCIPLINE TO INTEREST

For a good many years music teachers have been urged to make the music period a pleasurable experience on the premise that if a high level of interest were not maintained, no learning would take place. This point was misconceived in the experimental platform.

According to McMurray, the words *like* and *interest* have been used interchangeably and incorrectly. The pragmatist maintains that *interest* can refer to pleasure on the positive side and fear on the negative side; in other words, learning must be accompanied by an emotional force—pleasant or unpleasant. Since effort is required in any learning situation, pleasure is hardly the best motivation. The kind of situation that is more likely to prompt action and effort contains an irritant—a challenge to be overcome—included in some material that is already familiar. Being confronted with a point of conflict is not pleasant, but it can be effectively used to spark action.

Education: a Process of Reorganization and Reconstruction

Education is a process of reorganization and reconstruction; meaning is achieved through the union of activity and consequence. A *known*, therefore, has value and meaning in the solution of a problem between the individual and the environment. In this framework technical knowledge is no longer to be avoided. Music theory, for example, can be of great benefit to the individual so long as it affects his tastes and choices and heightens his perception of the esthetic values contained in music. A child can *discover* through the study of musical structure the reasons for his preferences for one type of music over another. This is precisely the type of functional knowledge that pragmatism has meant to project.

These changes in educational thought have had their effect upon teaching principles and procedures. The most fundamental maneuver common to all projects specifically directed to conform to the educational reformation has been to re-examine each subject and ascertain its real nature and structure. Once those elements that give the subject its unity and uniqueness have been determined, aims appropriate to the discipline can be established. How music has responded to this educational revolution will now be considered.

The Uniqueness of Music

In essence mathematics represents abstract or relational thinking. Science can best be recognized through objective thought. In the arts *Man Feeling* becomes the focus, and the basic element is *subjectivity,* communication in terms of emotive experiences rather than by symbols.

It remains to determine how to justify the place of music in the curriculum. There is no room for any subject if its contribution is not dynamic enough to warrant time for it. The mass of knowledge has increased and continues to accumulate at a phenomenal rate. Even after sorting out the greatest specifics, no subject can really be completely represented. Nevertheless, the child must be provided with as many mental acquisitions as possible if he is to adapt to an ever-changing environment.

Music has its place in the curriculum, first, because it is an essential part of the individual's environment. It has had a place in the life of man from the beginning. Whether in primitive or highly sophisticated culture, the life of man has been accompanied by music. If a complete environment is to be presented to the child, music must be included.

Secondly, each generation must be inducted into the heritage of the past if society can be guaranteed any kind of continuity. For social change to progress smoothly and with some hope of improvement, knowledge of the past is essential. Before the social machinery can function more effectively with each passing generation, it is necessary that a knowledge of the known prepare for any adventure into the unknown.

The heritage of music can offer insight into the civilizations that have produced it. Art is not an isolated entity created apart from the world: it reflects the society and the times in which it was composed.

Thirdly, music can touch man's feelings in a way that language seldom does. As esthetic stimulation and personal expression, music is an important part of life, communicating beauty and contributing to the development of individual values. Images of what is beautiful, right, and good are imparted through the arts. It is important, too, that the individual's critical judgment be developed to the degree that he achieves a preference for the best in music, as the best cannot only give him the greatest satisfaction, but have an influence upon his patterns of behavior.

Through the arts the individual can learn to understand himself in the same way that he learns through science to understand the universe. Those who are capable of perceiving the beauty of serious art recognize values they could find through no other medium. Their environment is expanded, and they are assisted toward a richer and more rewarding life.

The Aim of Music Education

A new rationale has been taking form. At a time when attention in education is focused heavily upon content, music educators have warned against a return to procedures that call for a strenuous emphasis upon syllabification, time values, chromatics, and key signatures. Music must stress a generative rather than a vocational program. Terminal learning has no place in the new scheme of things. While participation in performance groups can be a worthy enterprise, the majority of students will not become musicians. There must be something for all.

Spokesmen for the field seem generally agreed that the aim of music education centers upon the development of *musicality* or musical responsiveness. This general objective is based upon the concept that the basic task is to promote response to music in terms of its melodic, rhythmic, and harmonic properties. In this way criteria for the improvement of taste and discrimination are established.

How a person reacts to the subjective experience provided by music is a personal thing between the listener and the work performed. However, beyond the affective domain, there is an intellectual or cognitive aspect. This element is revealed in the student's ability to *perceive* the basic structure of the music in such a way that he can defend his musical preferences by knowledgeable testimony. Theoretical problems regarding time and tune, then, have their place, but only as they assist the student in perceiving the musical content of any work.

Charles Gary emphasizes this point in his preface to a recent and important Music Educators National Conference publication. Music education has either stressed sight-reading skills or gone to the opposite extreme and tried to provide unbounded enjoyment in the hope that the child will be inspired to pursue the study more seriously. Neither direction has met with appreciable success in developing an understanding of music. A real knowledge of music can only be achieved if intellectual comprehension goes hand in hand with technical competence and emotional response.

According to Bergethon and Boardman, both musical expression and responsiveness can be successfully developed only if the individual is led to an understanding of the concepts contained in the structure of music: skill, knowledge, and insight are fundamental to an authentic musical response.

Further support of this is found in recent music texts. The general philosophy expressed in these new publications holds that experience in music should be directed chiefly toward esthetic growth. However, they maintain, a knowledge of musical literature, an understanding of the organization of music, and a development of performance skill and response are pursuits that lead to the achievement of musicality.

The ability to use music to express feelings and reactions can only be accomplished through an understanding of the basic elements of music. Little can be done directly to enhance an individual's emotional response to music, but a great deal can be accomplished toward refining his esthetic perceptions and intellectual grasp. These objectives, which are specific and precise, in turn serve the larger, affective functions of music.

Music Education and the Concept-Centered Approach

For some time it was generally accepted that the *whole method* of learning was superior to the *part method*. Large units of study were presented in all subject areas in an effort to capitalize on a psychological principle that promised to lead to more effective learning. Music teachers, organizing units of study according to the best techniques provided, produced endeavors with such titles as "Music from Latin-America," "Evolution of Jazz," and "Contemporary Music." Each topic contained several activities including singing, listening, rhythms, and creative activities to assist in the proper development of each unit.

In many respects the efforts proved disappointing. An evaluation of this kind of general music program could produce nothing more tangible than the fact that though many *experiences* had been provided, little or no relationship existed between one and the other. The benefits were of a superficial nature and could not be measured in terms of real musical values. The large unit provided a great deal of material and a wide area for exploration. However, the focus became so broad that only by assuming a maturity that did not and could not exist in a child might such units hope to achieve satisfactory results.

Gradually it became clear that the fault lay not so much with the method as with its interpretation. Effective wholes represent a complete unity within themselves. One concept or idea must lead logically into another; and, more important, the structure of the whole must be presented in such a way that the child recognizes the direction he is taking. He must also notice the relationships between one learning activity and another.

The unit need not be a large topic. A *whole* can be a single item of subject matter so long as it represents a functional and meaningful totality that can be connected and integrated with other wholes.

Subject matter has become of prime consequence. The problem is to explore the nature and structure of the field of knowledge under study and determine the substance from which will emerge the elements to be taught. A coherent course of study can then be systematically constructed around a theoretical framework of sound principles, where scope and sequence make possible a meaningful discipline.

The Nature and Structure of Knowledge

According to Jerome Bruner the substance of any subject is represented by its underlying principles. A principle represents but a portion of the subject. Standing alone it carries little meaning. However, placed in its proper context with all other elements of a particular field of knowledge, its function becomes clear. In the same way each subject finds its general definition through its content. Structure is described by the elements or principles which together constitute a given subject area. To learn structure is to recognize how the elements of a particular area are related. In the case of music, the elements are melody, rhythm, harmony, form, expression, and style. The elements constituting the design of a given subject can best be determined by those who are thoroughly competent in any given discipline.

Robert Gagné supports this view by maintaining that an individual can learn any content so long as he has first acquired the prerequisites. The ordering and specifying of the material is a condition of learning.

Structure refers to the parts of an object or thing as well as to the ways they are interrelated. The curriculum, for example, can be generally defined by means of its subject areas. While each field of knowledge can be more minutely analyzed, it is the group of subjects taken together that comprise curriculum.

About structure it must be understood that the whole is not necessarily the sum of its parts. Elements do not confer properties on the compound simply by virtue of their presence in it. It is the way in which those elements are organized together that makes each of them a vital contributing factor to the over-all structure.

A larger whole can only be understood in terms of its constituent elements and the relationships joining these units together. In teaching, the constituents go unexplained because they represent irreducible elements that exist only for the purpose of explaining the whole.

A problem arises, however, in identifying the constituent elements that effectively represent a given field of knowledge. In order to determine the substances inherent in a subject, the content must be reduced to its simplest elements, and must include the connections between the elements.

Gagné carries this further in a way that leads particularly well into the nature and function of the concept. He maintains that all subject areas included in the curriculum contain hierarchical organizations, or structures. These can be broken down into progressively simpler learning prerequisites. In any given subject the first and largest units to be considered are the principles, or constituent elements. These, in turn, demand prerequisite concepts. The child cannot be expected to learn the principles of music, for example, unless he first acquires the necessary concepts. One by one the concepts can be linked together in a chain to make possible the understanding of a principle. Learning the whole structure of the subject entails mastery of the entire set of principles that form the hierarchical organization of the field of knowledge.

Principles, which provide insight into the expressive organization of music, must constitute the basis of the music curriculum. The structure of music is fundamentally involved with melody, rhythm, and harmony along with its stylistic, expressive, and formal organization. Within each of these constituent elements are musical concepts that can lead to musical understanding.

Since each field of knowledge tends to cope with its subject matter by means of different conceptual frames, it seems reasonable to adhere to the writings of those who have specifically translated these educational principles into terms appropriate to music education.

Musical Concepts

Asahel Woodruff indicates that the concept has become the prime focus for teaching. According to psychologists the cognitive processes figure dominantly in nearly everything man learns and achieves. Through experience the individual acquires knowledge and understanding, which his mind retains and organizes. The individual's entire behavior is directly affected by the quantity and quality of this knowledge. Concepts, which together comprise this mass of knowledge, are mental images of real things that the individual has experienced. The senses become the only means through which concepts can be properly acquired.

Similarly Gary argues that the concept specifies what the mind retains as a result of a learning experience. This may be defined only in very general terms. Through the impact of an educational experience, the child may derive a specific bit of knowledge that will later provide the key to an understanding of a broader concept.

It has already been said that the principles contained in music are found to be melody, rhythm, harmony, as well as stylistic, expressive, and formal organization. Within these constants are musical concepts that can lead to musical understanding. Included in the list provided by Bergethon and Boardman are the concepts contained in *rhythmic organization*, to include meter, note lengths, pulse, and accent; *melody*, to include pitch, intervals, clefs, lines and spaces, and tonality; *harmony*, texture and multiple sounds produced together; *style*, the methods, types, and mediums of writing from one period, composer, or culture to another; *expression*, tone color, dynamics, tempos, and the organization of melody, rhythm, and harmony to project the affective side of music; and concepts of *formal organization*, such as the phrase, motive, and repetition-contrast. Similar elements are reflected in many of the most contemporary school-music series.

Each of these concepts is an entity having an internal organization that sets it apart as a complete unit. Like a cell in the human body, it has a function to perform and a meaning in the total structure of the system. For greater insight into its makeup, the unit can be broken down into parts and analyzed still more precisely. On the other hand, its meaning can be further enhanced by studying its relatedness to other wholes.

Any subject can be taught to any child, regardless of his age, if the teacher realizes that the child, at each stage of his development, has his own characteristic way of learning, that to teach him effectively, the structure of the field of knowledge must be presented in a way the child can understand. The individual can find a subject comprehensible only by understanding its fundamentals.

The teaching of concepts must therefore follow a process compatible with the most authoritative tenets governing the learning process. Woodruff and Mursell have done a good deal toward the establishment of principles and procedures that may contribute to the teaching of the complexities of musical organization. Mursell has emphasized that all situations must above all be compelling. Both writers have testified to the need for a good deal of concrete experience and an abundance of appropriate material for practical application. Represented here are three characteristics of good context that can be influential in the learning of concepts.

Motivation

The child can only become interested in music if music proves interesting, and can only wish to participate in music if music invites participation. Opportunity must be provided for individuals to explore a variety of musical literature in order to discover the value of music as a desirable mode of expression. From there a momentum may be set up that will enlist the active participation of the child and direct his efforts purposefully toward further expansion of his musical knowledge. His skills and understandings are achieved through the medium of the literature provided. The most appropriate setting that can be established, therefore, is a repertoire of music of the highest quality.

A notable advance in this area of music material is very apparent in current texts. The range of selection is decidedly broader than ever before, with a great variety in the type of music provided.

Excellent examples of folk and art music have been made available for every grade level. Best of all, there has been special recognition of each great art period. The nineteenth century no longer receives the major portion of attention: songs of the Renaissance, Baroque, Classic, and Romantic periods all find a place in these new books. Fine poetry and excellent pictures testify to an integration of the arts. Music of the twentieth century is generously represented.

A wider classification in regard to media provides further proof of an expanding awareness of what constitutes a balanced and interesting repertoire. Vocal music includes examples of the solo, several types of small ensembles, and choruses. The instrumental literature embraces selections for solo instruments, ensembles of many kinds, as well as a fine representation of band and orchestral music. Real effort seems to have been made to provide a desirable musical setting for outstanding material through which effective learning may take place.

Concrete Experience

Objects or things must be experienced in concrete settings if the resulting concepts are to be assimilated into organically unified wholes instead of remaining as mere fragments. Verbal explanations are to be avoided until the individual has first achieved an initial impression of the object or thing through sensory experience. Therefore, a knowledge of music must come from listening and actively participating in the making of it. Bruner's three modes of learning, to include the enactive, iconic and symbolic, only serve to support Pestalozzi's basic principle of "the thing before the sign."

Initially the experience must be perceptual. From stimuli gathered from the specific studied, bits of meaning are transmitted to the brain through the sense organs. This process continues until all the meaningful parts of the referent have been absorbed, from which a true mental image may eventually be constructed.

Once the fragments, or parts, of the subject have been perceived, the mind must then organize them into a whole that represents as nearly as possible the specific under consideration. This is primarily a conceptual process.

The individual recollects the image he originally observed, mentally explores each particular, and gradually reconstructs the parts in such a way as to satisfy himself that his image is in agreement with what he originally perceived. Verbal discussion can stimulate the gaining of an accurate perception, but it can never become a substitute for concrete experience.

Teaching a concept properly requires that the referent be visible, discernible, or self-evident at the outset. It is defined, and through a process of exploration and examination, its particulars are exposed to view. The process moves from the whole to the part and back again to the whole.

For example, at a certain point in the teaching of music, building the major scale can be explained, verbally, in a rather short space of time. This kind of instruction, however, does not square with concept teaching. From *Exploring Music*, Book IV, a learning situation, directed toward the concept of tonality, is based completely upon concrete experience.

The child is first led to sing songs in the key of C. The letter names of the scale are pointed up in a song, and the appropriate melody bells are selected to construct the scale. Further experience is given in the key of F under a similar procedure. The individual recognizes, as he builds the new scale with the bells, that some alteration is necessary if it is to sound right. Other activities offer even more opportunity to deal with scale construction in order that the child can recognize how one scale varies in structure from another.

Differences between whole steps and half steps are pointed up in musical situations. When the child can make a distinction between the two, he is led to discover the appropriate sequence of steps that make up the scale. Then, he is invited to build other scales, beginning on notes of his own choosing. Gradually he learns to recognize the scale as something more than just a word or a definition. Understanding is derived from meaningful experiences.

The child is led to investigate, to inquire, and then to discover for himself concepts of tone, melody, rhythm, and the other aspects vital to genuine musical understanding. The concept is developed as the individual listens to music, as he performs, analyzes, and discusses it. All sorts of activities should be used to make the child's mental images clearer. Listening, singing, bodily movements, and the use of simple instruments all have important services to perform in reinforcing the development of each particular.

A very definite and renewed interest has become apparent in using bodily movement to help children discover musical concepts. Creative experimentation is gaining favor as a means of leading children toward insights into tone color, dynamics, imitation, contrast, pulse, phrase line, and other important factors.

If concepts are to be presented in effective learning situations, the music program must provide a setting that will contribute to the recognition and understanding of the complexities of musical organization. Learning cannot be successful if teaching focuses too much upon the abstract.

The effective presentation of any structural element in music must rely upon a concrete context. Knowledge, however, is valuable only as it can be used in new and different situations. In other words, concepts become worthwhile when they are sufficiently understood to become instruments for dynamic and useful purposes.

Application

Concrete experiences cannot be limited or restricted in their applications. To be properly understood, a concept must be used frequently. The learner must be a participant and apply his new knowledge usefully and in such a way that it can be thoroughly tested and readjusted. Drill and repetition can become dull and can seriously hamper the learning process if exercises are too limited in scope. If experiences are to be dynamic and compelling, the application must be carried out in a variety of ways.

Emphasis upon specifics is a very important principle of the educational reformation. However, there is no valid argument, psychologically or educationally, that even hints at a return to procedures that strive for a refinement of function in one area before other areas are investigated.

The primary objective in music education is *musicality*. Attention is therefore directed to the expressive qualities of the music, as well as to those concepts of musical organization that make it expressive. By itself no element of a theoretical nature has value. Conversely, any concept can be of the utmost importance only when it functions with other elements to help the individual recognize the potential of music as a means of expression.

The teaching of note values can be considered essential so long as it is not confined to a reading experience. The study of form can be a valid enterprise when analysis does not become the prime objective. Each musical concept has application in all areas of music.

The knowledge of key, for example, can be applied to the area of music reading. However, activities in listening, creating, playing, and singing are all available contexts in which that concept can be advantageously developed. Furthermore the individual can derive a far greater understanding of a specific when it is placed in a variety of contexts. In this phase of the operation, the child can see each part in relation to all others and note its unique function within the total structural scheme. He can put the pieces together into a unified and meaningful whole.

Included in the programs of the new music series are the skills of listening, singing, reading, creating, playing, and moving. The plan is recommended for two reasons. First, the child is permitted to explore different ways of enjoying music. He not only recognizes the means of expression most suitable to him, but his understandings of musical concepts become greater through the experiences provided by each skill.

Materials are carefully selected and graded; appropriate contexts that are within the grasp of children are abundant.

New Implications of Sequence

Learning cannot simply rely upon the effectiveness with which each separate concept is taught. It must also depend upon the arrangement of those units into an orderly and meaningful sequence.

Current texts in music education reveal that a great deal of attention has been given to the order in which concepts are to be presented. A study of these new books will generally indicate, however, that the term *sequence* does not imply the laborious refinement of one topic before another can be treated.

The study of growth patterns can provide certain determining factors that are of particular consequence in the arrangement of a proper sequence. The child grows physically, emotionally, and intellectually; any order of presentation established upon an acceptable approach must take these three elements into consideration.

PHYSICAL GROWTH

Very young children in the early primary grades are just beginning to develop muscular coordination. As they mature, a greater refinement of their physical control will become evident. It is a waste of time to insist upon certain coordinative refinements which will come about naturally through maturation without a great deal of drill or practice.

Therefore, to require complete mastery of one essential before a new one can be taken up has nothing to recommend it. On the other hand, to postpone certain experiences in movement, instrumental work, and singing would be unfortunate, when they can be of particular value from the very beginning. It must be accepted that learning, which involves physical participation, must gradually move from the crude to the exact coordinated movement.

Music texts have now been designed with this in mind. Only physical demands that suit the level of the child's muscular coordination at any given point in his development are incorporated. For example materials may call first for activities using simple percussion and easy melody instruments and then for experiences that require progressively greater coordination. Rhythmic and tonal requirements move from simple to more complex patterns.

EMOTIONAL GROWTH

The child's emotional development is another factor for consideration in determining an appropriate sequence. In his early years the individual is primarily concerned with himself. The outer world has significance only as it distinctly affects him within the narrow limits of his budding experiences.

As he matures, his environment gradually broadens, and he begins to prefer activities that involve others. Beyond recognizing the benefits of working with a group, his imagination begins to carry him to the next step of development. The narrow world of childhood becomes inadequate. He tries to broaden his horizons to include the past and even indicates some concern for the future. Emotional growth, then, proceeds from the immediate to the more remote.

It becomes apparent that publishers of classroom music texts have carefully considered the emotional growth of the child in the plotting of sequence. Modern publications emphasize songs of the home, school, and community in the early texts. Later, music that points up historical sequence, exploration, and distant lands finds a place of considerable importance.

INTELLECTUAL GROWTH

As with the physical and emotional makeup of the child, his mental capacities, which are present at birth, grow and mature in a gradual but continuous process. Just as nature does not ordain that a child move his arms with the perfect coordination of a mature adult before he can begin to use his legs, no intellectual concept should be thoroughly refined before another concept can be explored.

Mental growth can only be achieved by means of specific learnings. However, this does not mean that, upon the completion of one concept, another is built on top of it, and so on ad infinitum. This kind of sequence represents the type of spoon-feeding where one morsel must be thoroughly masticated and completely digested before another bite is offered. Such a procedure was tried in music education, as with other subject areas, and it failed.

While the structure of music can be broken down into parts, those elements are not sufficient in themselves but are vital specifics in the generic understanding of music. In this way the core of musical concepts must be treated together, with no one element given more emphasis than another. It is the totality that is important.

Musical understanding can be developed through a recognition of its expressive qualities; this becomes the objective, the thread connecting sequential musical experiences. The learnings that make up these units are determined from knowledge that represents music's basic structure. Specific concepts relating to the organization of melody, rhythm, harmony, form, style, and expression become the core of specifics required to bring about an understanding of music. All learning proceeds together, contributing a share to an understanding of the main objective of musical understanding.

This is referred to as a cyclical development, or spiral curriculum, a kind of order and arrangement not unique to music. It has been recently used in a number of other subject areas. The same elements of knowledge are used repeatedly, each time studied in greater depth or breadth. From crude and imperfect notions each succeeding application leads to finer insights.

Each concept has a relationship to the central idea and contributes to a progressively clearer insight into the prime over-all objective. Sequence, then, can imply a step-by-step process as experiences containing the structural elements of the subject render increasingly intelligible the originally established core of meaning.

Today publishers of music series are very explicit about the musical accomplishments contained in each of their books. Growth charts often accompany these series in order that the teacher may have some idea of what to expect from the child's previous training and what further learning should be developed for the benefit of future experiences. In this way teaching can be organized more satisfactorily than it has been in the past. Evaluations can also become more precise. Specifics are presented together where one element can interrelate with others. The individual can see the position of one whole as it stands beside another and the structure of all units as together they build the unity and completeness of the study area.

CHAPTER
14

Portents
of
the
Future

IN SPITE OF THE educational principles derived from Pestalozzi, Froebel, Spencer, Herbart, Parker, and Dewey, American education has found it difficult, if not impossible, to break entirely away from the traditions of the old classical curriculum. Mental discipline often reigns supreme, and the educational establishment continues to measure pupil growth on the basis of the "faculty of memory." Objective examinations report the results of what is remembered rather than how knowledge can be used to its greatest effectiveness.

According to Gideonse, Western civilization has made a distinct separation of reason and emotion. Historically education dealt with a purely intellectual program; the responsibility for providing meaning and fostering value judgments was left to the church, family, and other social institutions. To maintain a purely objective kind of education today is to assume that society is the same as it was many years ago.

Our society is marked by a single-minded preoccupation with the accumulation of material things and with a constant search for ways to raise the standard of living by increasing productivity. The means to this end has been through specialization and a division of labor. Emphasis has therefore been placed upon objectivity and the development of the outer man to the neglect of the subjective aspects of the inner man. Social cohesion fails in our society as each man is increasingly concerned only for himself.

In the area of value training, the function of both family and church seems to be decreasingly effective as society moves more and more toward secularism. The church seems hesitant in its leadership, and parents appear unable to pass on traditional values and mores to the young.

While these institutions are vulnerable to criticism, education must be held equally accountable. Educational institutions still jealously guard their empire of objectivity, their dominion of reason, at a time when matters beyond the intellectual are in desperate need of attention.

Educators and students alike are demanding change. A new education must be dynamically different. It must deal with all aspects of life in new and exciting ways. To serve up Aristotle once again will kindle fires of student rebellion and stifle a genuine pursuit of knowledge for years to come. Education cannot continue to be primarily concerned with imparting a massive collection of facts and with the granting of diplomas and degrees on the basis of the student's recollection of those materials at examinations. It is the whole man that must be considered—not just the intellectual or cognitive side but the affective as well.

According to Benjamin S. Bloom, the affective domain, which deals with interest, attitudes, values, appreciation, and adjustment, is of profound significance if a complete educational experience is to be provided. Objectives that represent the cognitive domain, through the development of intellectual abilities and skills, remain important, but they must be set in proper balance and perspective.

Changing Attitudes toward the Arts

A few years ago it might have seemed absurd to predict any significant change in disposition regarding the service of the arts to the curriculum. An assessment of the early period of the recent educational revolution would reveal that the acquisition of scientific knowledge was of first concern. Science and subjects closely related to it were given such unprecedented emphasis that music and its sister arts appeared to be driven to a position of complete irrelevance.

Recently, however, there has been an unmistakable change in attitude toward the arts since the educational reformation has had time to assess its position and formulate its doctrine more completely. While science is of extreme importance in a technological society, it cannot provide the formula for developing man's capacity to appreciate and to feel. Since the time of the ancient Greeks, it has been a general educational proposition that the arts must maintain a place of importance along with other areas of study. To distort the balance is to prevent the student from complete self-realization.

Educators seem convinced that a balanced curriculum must eventually be provided. Music and the arts, therefore, will have a definite and respectable place in modern education. In 1959 the American Association of School Administrators indicated its concern over the imbalance in education and endorsed a balanced curriculum wherein the fine arts could be accepted on a basis of equality with other areas.

Dr. Sterling M. McMurrin, a former U.S. Commissioner of Education, emphasized that the arts and humanities have just as important a contribution to make in education as the sciences. Dr. James B. Conant recommended that the junior high school include required courses in both music and art. In a study by the University of Kansas, it was found that musical students held a greater share of class offices, generally achieved higher grades, showed greater accomplishment in individual sports, and indicated broader ranges of interests than those classified as nonmusicians. Recently, Dr. James E. Allen, Jr., former Undersecretary of Health, Education and Welfare and United States Commissioner of Education, urged that the arts be recognized as "indispensable to the development of a completely literate individual."[1]

According to Gideonse, "It is time to consider the full and systematic development of the so-called 'fads and frills' as an

---

[1] The University of the State of New York. *Re-encounter with the Performing Arts*. Albany: The State Education Dept., Division of the Humanities and the Arts, 1968, pp. 4–5.

essential part of a free and democratic society."[2] Samuel Gould, former Chancellor of the State University of the State of New York, argued that the arts are essential to the curriculum to compensate for the overemphasis recently given to science and technology. Through an intensive and coordinated effort the objective *and* the subjective aspects of education must be brought together in equal balance.

An entirely new dimension has emerged. Within the past few years a renewed interest in expanding the service of music has become evident. Research has revealed that the arts have an important function in the development of perception, intellect, and the emotions. Courses specifically designed for those who are not performers as a balance to technical studies have been initiated in addition to the more traditional musical offerings.

According to the National Education Association, there is a trend toward more rather than less music in the public schools. In a NEA study made between the school years of 1956–1957 and 1961–1962, five times as many schools reported an increase in the time given to music as reported a decrease. During the same period of time, fifty percent of the secondary schools reporting indicated an increase in the enrollment of music courses with only six percent noting a decrease. From another source it was found that while academic demands on school children had increased markedly, a greater percentage of students had been participating in choral and instrumental programs in the schools.

A recent study of 12,000 school systems showed that in comparison with all other special facilities in school construction, including science, home economics and language, music-room facilities made the most spectacular gains. In 1962, 35 percent of newly completed secondary schools provided facilities for music as compared with 75.1 percent in 1964. Of those secondary schools being built in 1965, 81 percent included music facilities. An important growth of this same kind was noticeable in elementary schools. Of those completed in 1964, 13.7 percent provided adequate rooms for the study of music, as compared with 7.2 percent in 1962. In 1965, twenty percent of the buildings under construction made adequate provision for the study of music. Also indicative of growth and interest in the area of music is the increase in per-

---

[2] Harry D. Gideonse. *Against the Running Tide.* New York: Twayne Publishers, Inc., 1967, p. 41.

sonnel. Over the six-year period extending from 1960 to 1966, the Music Educators National Conference increased its membership by approximately 53 percent.

The Contemporary Music Project for Creativity in Music Education (CMP) was initiated in 1963 through a grant by the Ford Foundation to the Music Educators National Conference as an expansion of the "Young Composers Project" begun in 1959. The grant (to include an additional gift in 1966) totaled $1,630,000. Procedures and policies of the CMP are determined by a committee of educators, composers and outstanding persons active in related areas. The aim of this project has been to bring professionals together for the improvement of music education at all levels from the elementary grades to the university.

The Federal government has demonstrated its endorsement of art and music education through generous financial provisions granted in "The Elementary and Secondary Education Act," Public Law 89–10, approved April 11, 1965. Opportunities that can challenge the imagination are made available through the five titles included in this act. The degree of success this law is capable of achieving now rests in the hands of teachers and scholars, who must determine the most productive, dynamic, and beneficial ways to use this assistance. It is clear that music has become a respectable, valid entity in the new curriculum.

It must be recognized that there are different ways of deriving benefit from music. There are a considerable number of students who require a thorough foundation in the fundamentals of musicianship. Therefore, at least one course in music theory should be provided in every high school. Those same students, in company with many others, prefer the opportunity to develop their instrumental or vocal ensemble techniques. Concert and stage bands, orchestras, choruses, as well as madrigal and chamber ensembles, should be made available. For those who are interested in music for purposes of recreation—guitar, accordion, folk-singing, and barbershop ensembles can perform a service. Experimental groups in non-Western and ethnic music also have an important place. Still another segment of the student body finds satisfaction in responding to great works performed by others; courses in music history and literature are important to their musical growth.

Even if the general music program can be sufficiently broad to include a wide variety of skill activities, the endeavor does not become entirely valid if the sequence terminates at the end of the eighth or ninth grade. There is a need to expand the music program, particularly in the high school.

MUSIC FOR THE TALENTED

The definition of the talented student used in this section considers both the academically talented as well as those who are especially gifted musically. Concern has recently been expressed over the lack of opportunity for suitable musical training offered to talented students. The notable absence of this aspect of their training has been due to the general notion that the arts do not fulfill the requirements of an academic discipline. Whether or not high schools choose to provide the student with opportunity in this area, college admissions practices have continued to discriminate against those with a genuine interest in the arts.

While music is a fine art, it is also a discipline: it communicates in terms of feeling or emotion, but it has distinct intellectual aspects. Both the intellectual and the emotive must be treated simultaneously; any time this duality is not maintained, the music program must be considered inadequate.

According to Schwab an academic discipline must include two major aspects: the structure or content that defines the subject and the way in which those elements function within the totality of the discipline. The content of music is defined through the constituent elements of melody, rhythm, harmony, form, style, and expression. The organic unity of those elements is established through reading, singing, playing, creating, listening, and moving. By these activities the method of inquiry into the function of the elements is consistent with the subject itself.

There is a growing realization that music and the other arts have a unique contribution to make to the student's growth. The academically talented student has intellectual abilities that will permit him to develop profound insights into the complexities of music if existing programs can be tailored to his requirements. The individual's potential indicates that his responsiveness to music should surpass that of the average student in quality. It remains for the instructor to augment and enrich existing courses with additional substance and activity.

In an effort to assist teachers in designing effective programs for these highly gifted students, Hartshorn, Housewright, and Tipton, through the sponsorship of the National Education Association, have prepared a publication that provides some guidelines on planning special programs for the academically talented. Although the fundamental service of music is in the communication of feeling, that kind of response by the academically talented can evoke intellectual study which, in turn, can foster even greater emotional response.

The musically *gifted* student is one who ranks among the top two to three percent of all students in musical ability. The musically *talented* individual can be found among the upper 20 to 25 percent of all students. These individuals must also be provided with challenging musical experiences commensurate to their talent and ability. They must have the same opportunity to prepare for the college of their choice as their classmates who select other careers.

Harmony, Theory, and Music Literature

Courses in harmony, theory, and music literature are not new. They took their place with other subject areas years ago during the curriculum expansion that occurred at the turn of the century.

The aptitudes and interests of each individual must be considered, and unless a curriculum is sufficiently flexible to tend to the needs of every student, it falls short of its real responsibility. All children cannot be cast into the same academic mold. For the academically talented and those particularly gifted in the arts who would benefit from specialized music classes, electives in theory, harmony, and music literature should be made available. In his first report on the American high school, Conant recommended that a well-constituted sequence of music courses should be available for students.

Music courses, however, are due some careful re-examination if they are to fulfill the requirements of these special students and justify the new faith invested in them. Music theory must break away from its traditional position of emphasizing the eighteenth-century chorale style and adopt a far more comprehensive approach. It should include the activities of listening, singing, playing, and writing. The involvement of all these aspects provides a relationship between the score and the principle under consideration. In this way musical meaning is developed in a musical context. Theoretical concepts cannot be treated in isolation. They must be related to music history and music literature. The student must be urged to create original music in order to develop insights into the styles and techniques of both past and present.

Music history and literature courses cannot continue to assign prime importance to biographical information on composers. Frequently such material has represented the fundamental substance of such courses. Instead music history should emerge from the study of the style and technique of one composer as opposed to another. Musical facts can find relevance and significance only when they come alive through directed listening activities. Listening is the most important part of any successful course in music history. Only thus can the individual become aware of the esthetic principles of music that are the instruments by which the expressive qualities of the art can be perceived.

A lack of good music courses seriously handicaps those students who, upon completion of high school, intend to pursue the study of music at a college or conservatory. It also limits the possibilities of future growth for other students whose interests in music are of a quality which can lead to a fine avocation.

Performing Groups

Performance groups must, of course, continue. They are ideal activities for further expanding the student's general musicianship and for providing a continuance of a specialized musical momentum built up from the grades. The choir, band, and orchestra absorb those who look to music as an avocation as well as the specialist. These performing organizations have a very important function to fulfill so long as they are not the only means of teaching an appreciation and understanding of music.

Performing organizations are no longer viewed by the more progressive music educators as organized solely for the purpose of performance, but rather as a distinct part of the educational process. Each rehearsal is devoted not only to problems of skill and of ensemble playing, but to the further development of concepts incorporated within musical content, structure, and style. The music is chosen for the teaching value it contains as well as for its effectiveness in a concert. The objectives of a rehearsal have been broadened: not only will the participants learn the techniques of ensemble playing and improve their vocal or instrumental skills, but they will have opportunities for directed listening, analysis, and demonstration. Through such exercises as these, they will achieve a finer understanding of the structure and the art of music.

Some performing groups have already extended their service by providing opportunities for musical growth to the general student body. Special assembly programs are presented with each one being uniquely different in nature than the other. Concerts devoted to the works of individual composers or representative of specific music periods are provided. Members of the performing groups acquaint the student audience with the form and style of the works and discuss any other musical elements that might prove pertinent and helpful. While extramusical performances within the community remain desirable, they are considered by-products of the program rather than the influential factors they once were.

There are music directors who are not only improving the quality of the music performed, but are also indicating a much broader view of the literature to be used and the periods to be represented. Contemporary music, which has all but left tonality in favor of serial techniques based upon the principles of Schoenberg and Webern is performed more often. While it is impossible at this time to tell what music will best represent this period, students must hear and perform contemporary works in order to develop some criteria for judging it. Music directors must become aware that today's music should take its place in the standard repertoire.

Stage bands have recently gained in favor. Most schools that include this kind of activity insist that members of the bands participate also in the regular performing groups so as not to become overspecialized in one aspect of music. However, there is value in this kind of ensemble. Valid experiences are provided in improvisation, as well as in technical development. In 1966 a study reported 11,000 school stage bands in the United States.

String programs are on the increase in the schools and, as a result, school orchestras are frequently found in even the smaller systems. Schools in the United States support about 68,000 large performance groups, including 50,000 concert and marching bands and 7000 orchestras. Thousands of small instrumental ensembles have been recently reported. Youth symphony orchestras number in excess of 340, most of them having been organized since 1960. School-music programs, along with other amateur performing groups, have so grown in number that instrumental sales in the last twenty years have increased approximately 400 percent.

Performing groups organized on a systemwide basis have served a very useful purpose. All-city bands, choirs, and symphony orchestras provide experiences for specially talented children. There is evidence that some systems are expanding their summer programs, as well as their Saturday morning music classes, and there is growing recognition of the importance of performing in small ensembles as a means of developing musicianship.

MUSIC FOR THE MAJORITY

According to the Yale Seminar on Music Education and the Tanglewood Symposium, the category of services must not be confined to the musically talented. Opportunities should be provided for the nonmusic major to assist him in responding to music and in finding his own means of musical expression.

It would appear that every normal child is born with a receptivity to, if not an actual aptitude for, music. Almost from infancy children respond to music by moving or dancing to rhythms or by creating their own melodies and by indicating interest in the sounds produced by musical instruments. But at some point this responsiveness is stifled in many because of the way in which music is presented to them.

A total music program must include music that can hold a child's attention even beyond the schoolroom. For years teachers have accepted the theory in principle if not in fact. Allemandes, gigues, polonaises, mazurkas, minuets, gavottes, and waltzes are generally a part of every school's record library. Dance music must then be acceptable; but is such music good only when it is old?

Youth Music

Because they are original, jazz, blues, rock, soul, and folk music must be construed as art forms. From their wide acceptance these styles must indeed reflect the tempo and spirit of the times—a basic requirement of any art form. It is not unusual to find numerous examples of dance music included in the opera and symphony, as other nations have absorbed popular music into the larger art forms. Our refusal to accept seriously a distinct expression of American music only serves to strengthen the argument that the function of art in this country is badly misunderstood. It appears that Americans, more often than not, consider art to be a very exclusive commodity to be kept under glass, revered for its age, and worshiped for its monetary value rather than for what it communicates.

According to the Tanglewood Declaration, youth music of

today is recognized as a very legitimate aspect of any music education program. The longer it is rejected or ignored, the further off is the day when music education can hope to render any substantive service to that large number of students who are as yet untouched by the music programs in the schools.

The Youth Music Institute, held at the Madison campus of the University of Wisconsin during the summer of 1969 brought educators into contact with the music of youth and with the young people who compose it, perform it, and enjoy it. The communication gap was bridged for the moment as educators and students discussed popular teenage music and its potential role in music education programs.

It would be unfortunate if students are continually obliged to seek musical training outside the school when it is the responsibility of music teachers to provide a sound comprehensive music program inside the school.

Just how can the music teacher be of genuine service in the area of youth music? Reports indicate that students are well aware of many ways in which teachers could be of assistance. First of all, young people want the schools to acknowledge their music as a respectable art form. From their comments, they do not ask that it replace the classics or other expressions of twentieth-century composition—only that it be included as a part of the music course.

In the realm of performance, the essence and spirit of the whole movement demands freedom. Therefore, the need is for practice space rather than for teacher direction. Students requested help as they needed it in music theory, arranging, and the development of instrumental skills. Their recommendations are both reasonable and within the realm of possibility, if music educators will but give them serious attention.

Social Instruments

Instruction in instruments of a nonorchestral kind, such as the guitar, and the electric organ, is finding a more significant place in current music programs. Opportunities in these areas should be expanded as consistent with the goal of assisting the pupil to find his own means of musical expression and his own response to music.

Both the guitar and the electric organ have had a phenomenal growth in popularity over the last few years. According to John

Wilson, between 1950 and 1965 the sale of console organs increased from 10,000 to 126,500. In the same period, guitar sales rose from 220,000 instruments a year to 1,500,000.

All of the services mentioned above became especially practical in the light of a movement toward more flexible scheduling. Some schools have extended their daily class periods from six to as many as nine. Others have been experimenting with such devices as modules and individual demand scheduling. All of these can be interpreted as containing new promise and greater possibilities for the expansion of music education.

Non-Western Music

There is a fundamental need to point up the qualities of American music that have been absorbed from non-Western cultures. By identifying rich and significant ethnic contributions to the culture of this nation, citizens of Asian and African descent can more readily achieve their long sought self-respect in American society. Caucasians will be encouraged to understand and respect these minority groups when they recognize that cultures beyond the Western perimeter, when judged in their own right, are just as significant as those of the West. Efforts in this regard should be concentrated upon children whose environmental experiences have yet not driven them to prejudice and intolerance.

The opportunity now exists for establishing music in a position of pre-eminence among the arts by doing something concrete to justify the often made, but never proven, claim that music is the one truly universal language. A total music program must involve the study of great current movements in music in order that all concepts of beauty can be recognized. Experiencing non-Western music leads the individual to a familiarity with the melodic beauty of monophonic texture, a greater awareness of sounds, an awakening to the creative possibilities of improvisation, and a recognition of new possibilities through a greater variety of scales and microtonal intervals.

Preschool Education

Little children are more responsive intellectually to life than older children because their capacity to respond has not been paralyzed by the imposition of verbal symbols. They are capable of learning more at an earlier age than was ever thought possible. Based upon available data provided by Benjamin S. Bloom, in terms of intelligence measures at age seventeen, about 50 percent of development takes place between conception and age four and about 17 percent between the ages of four and six. The Wann study found that very young children could manage certain steps in the reasoning process in order to form concepts. This strongly suggests that the nursery school and kindergarten can have a profound effect upon the educational growth pattern of children.

While music has always been a part of nursery school and kindergarten activities, it has generally been presented with a series of unrelated experiences instead of as a structured discipline. Presently, however, there are innovative techniques and sensory-motor approaches being developed that can make the most difficult subjects possible for even the youngest to comprehend. It remains for teachers to overcome the old fear of imposing learning disciplines at an early age.

Music, as other subjects, must be presented within a cognitive

A group of preschool children discovering the elements of music at the Cleveland Institute of Music.

framework, so that the child can discover the structure that leads to meaning and understanding. Verbal symbols must give way to the young child's nonsymbolic way of knowing. A multiple sensory approach must be used to include not only the visual and tactile but the auditory and kinesthetic as well.

Preschool programs have a definite service not only to the middle-class child but to the ghetto youngster as well. They can provide an excellent foundation for further growth. Music can be of particular assistance in helping children learn how to learn because so much of that training can take place initially through sensory-motor experiences.

The Unity of Knowledge

At the present time concern with the design of new curriculum projects has focused on the single subject. Educators in each subject area have been far more interested in determining its nature and singularities than in seeking out interrelationships with other fields. According to Bennett Reimer this type of effort might well be the most practical first step. After the essential character of each subject has been thoroughly defined, some very substantial relationships between areas may be discovered and found to represent something far more profound than the superficial similarities that are sometimes more apparent than real.

THE CREATIVE DIMENSION

No educational program can point up the relevance of knowledge so long as each discipline is treated in isolation. Presently the curriculum appears as a mass of cells, each partitioned from another in such a way that the full value of skills and knowledge can never be realized. Hopefully, a catalyst can be found to produce a reaction that will bring all subjects together in one common purpose, where the subjective and objective aspects of the curriculum can each lend support to the other.

As Dewey has pointed out, education is a process of reorganization, reconstruction, and transformation, which must teach the individual not only how to adjust to his environment but also how to deal with subsequent changes. If man is to continue successfully through a constant process of self-renewal, all aspects of his training must become relevant.

Specific knowledge has a place; but an effective system of education cannot rely exclusively on the development of memory, nor can learning be considered complete with the mastery of formal content alone. The reproduction of fact confines meaning to something fixed and unchangeable. Facts in and of themselves, constitute a series of disconnected ideas, having no meaning or vitality of their own.

It is not quantity of information that will be sought in a new educational platform—knowledge has increased at such an unbelievable rate that it would be impossible to teach all the facts of every subject, even if it were desirable.

Education must emphasize, increasingly, the process of learning how to learn. The new aim will be for a quality education where ideas may be few but vital and important. These ideas must be set and reset into as many different combinations as possible. Then the individual can recognize not only the interrelatedness of the disciplines that contribute to those ideas but also the ways in which the ideas relate to his life. Education must become a process in which the student is taught how to *use* knowledge instead of a collection of mere facts, with no guidance in combining them into comprehensible structures and patterns.

Men such as Torrance, Guilford, Getzels, and Jackson have pointed out that the processes of acquisition, impression, and learning skills have received far too much attention, to the utter disregard of production, expression and creation. In their studies of the creative dimension, they have become convinced that the development of independent thought must counterbalance fact accumulation.

Presently some of the best students exhibit the least creativity. This is not because they are incapable of independent thought but because a content-centered curriculum tends to establish the need to compete for grades. Finding themselves pressured into this kind of situation, individuals learn to take the safest course, to become conformists. In this way initiative is stunted because students are not motivated to think but only to memorize. Rather than awakening to the unity of knowledge and achieving an understanding of the relevance of subject matter by combining parts into meaningful patterns through the creative process, they passively devour facts peculiar to each particular subject area without recognizing any relationship of one idea to the other.

In recent years the pressures upon students for fact accumulation have far outweighed the development of creative thinking. While not disparaging the importance of substance or information, the Creative Dimension points up the need for balancing specific knowledge with independent thought. Such a process calls for rearranging facts into new and more meaningful entities. It represents a step into the unknown where discovery, imagination, and experimentation are possible.

HUMANITIES

According to Goodlad this single-subject concentration leads to an evasion of some very important problems in the school program, particularly with regard to scope and sequence. He points to the desirability of cutting across the boundaries established between one course and another in order that the student can recognize the relationship of facts and ideas. Broad subjects, such as humanities courses, are distinctly recommended.

A growing number of educators and laymen are concerned about the student unrest spreading across the colleges and downward into the secondary schools. While there are many theories as to its causes, many agree on the need for helping young people find values that lend meaning to their lives. Structures for humanities courses represent a variety of opinions as to how this help can best be rendered. Some courses integrate music and art with an established literature or English course by means of team teaching. In some courses history and social studies represent the core of the program. In other instances the humanities course can include all the aforementioned areas with the addition of some philosophy and psychology. However, all of them have in common the aim of confronting the student with value.

Courses of this kind are being initiated as a means of tying together all aspects of the curriculum. The humanities provide a central point toward which all areas can contribute. This is unique at a time when subject areas are organized into isolated cells in such a way that the full value of skills and knowledge can never be made use of unless some catalyst brings them into reaction with one another. Humanities need not take the place of any subject but may serve to bring into focus the value of all subjects. Each field of knowledge can become an important part of such a program. Opting for values is not a guessing game. It is a study, in which solutions are found through the use of specific knowledge. The knowledge derived can give direction to life.

The Arts and Humanities Branch of the Federal Office of Education, established in 1964, has developed programs to promote the arts and humanities in education. According to Miller's report a few state departments already publish materials for use in humanities courses. Many of these departments have indicated that schools are showing an ever-increasing interest in this area of instruction. There is a distinct awareness of the educational possibilities the humanities can contribute. Professional music magazines and conference sessions have done a great deal to point up the need for such programs.

Of Principles, Processes, and Methods

Today we are bombarded by all sorts of new ideas. This is not unique. The same thing has happened in American education from almost the beginning. Innovations are constantly being developed by creative music educators, and the enthusiasm of these teachers urges them to lobby for their particular modus operandi and seek support and discipleship. Their points of view, devices, and techniques can be introduced frequently into most programs so long as the basic underlying pattern is not unduly disturbed. On the one hand, it is not only desirable but necessary to experiment with new ideas in order that a particular process can become enriched. On the other hand, an entire program cannot be completely reconstructed annually if even just passable results are to be realized.

However, changes in the basic educational fabric, woven from the principles of philosophy and psychology, do not come about quite so rapidly as some might expect. Educational platforms, each in their turn, take a much slower pace in their ascendancy, and their decline can be equally gradual.

In a very similar way, some methods can sometimes achieve a momentum that permits them to enjoy unusual popularity for a considerable length of time. Principles, processes, and methods of real consequence do not change, like clothes, with the season. In support of this position, extracts of articles published just prior to the time this book went to press have been included in the following pages in order to show how principles, processes and methods, discussed in these last two chapters, continue their ascendancy.

By approximately 1963 both the conceptual process and the discovery method were acknowledged in American educational thinking. Asahel D. Woodruff in discussing the conceptual process[1] indicates that it still represents a vigorous portion of the main stream of music education in the United States.

Man's conceptual structure constitutes so much of him that to speak of man in any complete sense is to speak largely of his thoughts and feelings.

Conceptual development is not, therefore, simply one of several possible things of interest to an educator; it is rather the essence of the concerns of an educator.

Because conceptual functioning is equivalent to human functioning, it is impossible to understand conceptual development without knowing how fully behavior is tied to one's conceptual patterns. With the possible exception of reflex responses, there is some kind of conceptual component involved in every act whether it be simple visceral response to some external signal or a prolonged act of creative deduction and invention.

Concepts are the directive factors in most of these acts. . . . When concepts are recognized and verbalized, they provide the capacity for critical analysis and *deliberate and conscious decision making.*

The concepts in any person's repertoire are as highly differentiated as are his responses to the countless different things he responds to. This is because they are generated by his interactions with those objects and events. . . . Hence, the conceptual patterns we possess are literal reflections of the properties of the environmental referents we interact with. The greater the accuracy of this reflection, the more effective the behavior of the person can be.

. . . Learning of the kind that affects behavior is a *by-product* of goal-seeking behavior. It does not occur as a separate process detached from the environmental situation it is

[1] Asahel D. Woodruff, "How Music Concepts are Developed. . . ." *Music Educators Journal,* Vol. 56, No. 6 (February 1970), pp. 51–54. By permission of the *Music Educators Journal* and the author.

More and more children are being taught basic music concepts in groups, larger classes, and laboratories with visual aids and electronic equipment. Here, Paul Sheftel, author of *Exploring Keyboard Fundamentals* (Holt, Rinehart and Winston, 1970) instructs a class using electronic pianos and one master control unit. At the flick of a switch the teacher may work with one, several, or twenty-four students. For private instruction and practice the instructor and student hear each others' voices, instruments, and audio aids through their headphones, communicate through their individual microphones. For supervised practice the teacher can monitor the student without disturbing him while a group of students, hearing each others' instruments, play together as an ensemble. This new approach often means that, with one or two hours' laboratory work a week, outside practice is not required. Photograph by Wesley Balz courtesy of *House Beautiful* Magazine and the Baldwin Electropiano Laboratory.

expected to effect. People rarely set out to *learn* something. They set out to *get* something they want. Learning occurs incidentally on the way. There can be no such thing as learning detached from an act of adjustive (or goal-seeking) behavior.

. . . Before we can name any objective worth pursuing, our attention has to turn from the outlines and taxonomies of musical knowledge to the musical life of a person outside of school. This question has to be answered: If we have succeeded in making a person musically alive and literate, what musical behaviors will he then be engaging in? In other words, what are the behaviors of a musically literate person? It is these behaviors that we should be trying to develop in school by a direct behavioral approach.

It may be useful now to turn to three subordinate problems, all relevant to any instructional unit. . . . [Man] is preeminently a storer and user of experiential memories. By means of them he is able to bring the past to the service of the present and to project his wants into the future in the form of long-range goals and ideals. In spite of the noisy and pervasive function of speech, the process of storing and using experiential memories is basically a nonverbal one. . . . First, conceptual behavior of notable effectiveness goes on at the subliminal level and therefore at the nonverbalized level in all people, and it goes on in both people and higher animals without language capacities. The place of language is *adjunctive* to conceptual behavior, not central. Conceptual behavior is basically adjustive in nature, not communicative.

. . . The second problem that must be solved before attempting to devise instructional units concerns the affective side of learning. The notion that feelings operate independently of knowledge is of long standing, but it is false. . . . Unfortunately, the division between affect and conception has been further fortified by the wide acceptance of the two-domain concept, putting the affective domain on one continuum and the cognitive domain on another.

The human being is an affective organism. Affect is always present in his behavior, just as the perception of meaning is always present. Both affect and meaning exist as two sides of every experience. Meaning makes the person aware of possible alternatives. Affect dictates the choice between them. One cannot form a concept without an affective component, and he cannot have an affective experience without a conceptual component. The result of this duality is that our appreciations and motives are acquired simultaneously with our conceptual patterns, and operate through those conceptual patterns. We learn to like those objectives and conditions that are emotionally rewarding to us as we experience them.

. . . The third problem concerns creativity. The phrase refers to an original idea or product that works. Both originality and workability are properties of concepts and of the things people make or do because of their concepts.

. . . We can make things that work if our store of percepts is accurate, and if we have acquired the necessary technical competencies for putting our original ideas into workable physical form. . . . An applied type of summary might go somewhat as follows:

(a) Concepts are individually constructed covert memories of the musical substances we have encountered in the past and of the way things have gone with us in those past encounters.

(b) Our conceptual memories are as numerous and varied as the array of substances we have encountered, and they grow in completeness and accuracy only with repeated encounters that bring to our attention the critical properties of those substances and processes.

(c) The concepts that govern our behaviors are those that were acquired in episodes in which we were trying to fulfill our wants under the typical conditions of everyday behavior. This is as true of musical behavior as of eating, sleeping, and playing behaviors.

(d) Our affective preferences and tastes (our values) grow out of our satisfaction or annoyance with our experiences with things, concurrent with our understandings of them. In any learning situation, students are experiencing both meanings and feelings simultaneously, and their concepts and value patterns reflect those meanings and feelings.

(e) The most powerful way to help students acquire rewarding musical behavior patterns is to engage them in the very musical behaviors believed to constitute a desirable repertoire of out-of-school behaviors and to see that those behaviors carry the learning of important concepts and competencies along with them.

(f) Since all behavioral acts are adjustmental acts in that they are parts of the pursuit of things people want, we are most likely to succeed in enticing students into rewarding musical behaviors by helping them become aware of satisfying things that can be had through musical activities and then by helping them pursue those satisfactions.

(g) The experiences students have will be most effective if they are genuine personal encounters with music, rather than verbal substitutes for those encounters. This implies, of course, that the student, not the teacher, is the active party in the encounter.

(h) We can cultivate creativity by providing copiously for encounters with musical objects and events under satisfying circumstances, and with great freedom for interpretation and self-expression, and by helping students acquire the technical skills and the discrimination abilities they will require when they try to express their musical ideas, whether in the form of composition, performance, description, criticism, or appreciation.

In support of the discovery method Charles B. Fowler states:[2] "The discovery or nonverbal awareness method is a deliberate attempt to institutionalize self-discovery, to make it a definite part of the educational process in the classroom. In teaching the concept of dynamics, for example, the teacher plans the teaching situation so that students are provoked into finding out for themselves the necessity for dynamics, according to the discovery process."

Discovery is the act of obtaining knowledge for oneself by the use of one's own mind. The student is no longer a bench-bound listener confined to rote accumulation, memorization, and regurgitation. Instead, he is provided with an opportunity to exercise creative options, imagination, and self-mastery. Students find discovery a stimulating and rewarding way to learn because instead of being provided with all the

[2] Charles B. Fowler, "Discovery: One of the Best Ways to Teach a Musical Concept," *Music Educators Journal*, Vol. 57, No. 2 (October 1970), pp. 25–30. By permission of the *Music Educators Journal* and the author.

COMPARATIVE METHODS—CHART 1
Three Approaches to Teaching a Musical Concept
Through Performance

*Concept To Be Taught: Dynamic contrasts provide a source
of variety and expressive meaning in music.*
Material: "Evening Prayer" by Engelbert Humperdinck

1. *Lecture* Teacher points out the signs for dynamics in the printed score and demonstrates how these are to be performed. Signs for crescendo, diminuendo, very soft, ritard, and other dynamic indications are shown, and the names attached. Students practice the music until they perform it correctly according to the composer's markings.

2. *Socratic* *Teacher:* How many have noticed that some music is louder or softer than other music? Does anyone see a place in this music where it should be sung very softly? *Child:* Right at the beginning. *Teacher:* Is there a sign there that says "sing very softly"? *Child:* The music says "pp." *Teacher:* That's correct. Is there a sign that says "get louder"? *Child:* poco cresc. *Teacher:* Right. What kind of a sign tells us that we should sing loudly? *Child:* "mf." *Teacher:* Can you draw the sign on the board that tells us to grow gradually louder? *Child* draws   . When the students' attention has been drawn to all the signs, the piece is performed with the proper dynamics and tempo.

3. *Discovery* Students learn a piece of music from a score that contains no dynamic markings. The teacher invites the students to experiment with the way they sing the song, in order to make it more beautiful, or to communicate its message more effectively. Students invent their own tempo, dynamics, and phrasing, appropriate to the text. They may invent signs to indicate their preferences. They can compare their version with the composer's original markings or with edited scores, and try to understand why the composer used dynamics in the way he did.

Chart from Charles B. Fowler, "Discovery: One of the Best Ways to Teach a Musical Concept," Music Educators Journal Vol. 57, No. 2 (October 1970) p. 25. Used by permission.

answers, they are invited to conquer their own ignorance. They win their own possession of knowledge.

Using the discovery approach the teacher seeks to set up circumstances in which the student himself finds the concept being taught. The discovery, or nonverbal awareness approach, returns to the original sequence of the creative process. It recognizes that awareness of a new concept gives impetus to inventing a name for it. The abstraction exists first; a verbal designation is assigned later. Names are affixed to entities. The distinction between idea (concept) and word remains clear. Words are vehicles for concepts, but not substitutes for them. They are merely labels.

. . . In this approach the teacher sets up an environment of materials, and challenges the student to use them in a particular way that forces the student to encounter and solve a problem. In the process the desired generalization—in this case, a musical concept—is revealed. Neither the teacher nor the students verbalize the concept. The teacher knows that a student understands the concept not when he can tell it, but when he can show it, or perform it. Discovery permits students the personal exhilaration of making the concept their own.

. . . Making education a functioning part of the human being is one of the basic aims of any successful methodology. If students can and do use what they supposedly have learned, we know that the material is relevant, and we know that we have been effective teachers. If what has been taught has become an intrinsic part of the student, he will be able to transfer his knowledge, unaided, to a different set of circumstances.

The work of Gagné has had a considerable effect upon contemporary education. Robert L. Lathrop, in support of Gagné's thinking, writes:[3]

The role of the music educator is primarily as a facilitator of student learning. In this role his principal competencies should be described in terms of his abilities to organize effective music learning experiences, to motivate students to want

[3] Robert L. Lathrop, "The Psychology of Music and Music Education," *Music Educators Journal*, Vol. 56, No. 6 (February 1970), pp. 47–48; 141–145. By permission of the *Music Educators Journal* and the author.

to make music a part of their lives, and to serve as a diagnostician and critic of student musical efforts. Of course, in order to assist students to learn music, the music educator must have a good command of his content discipline. Equally important, however, is his understanding of how children learn. It is in this domain that a closer tie with the field of educational psychology could prove beneficial.

Musicians, Psychologists, and Music Educators

The interest of the musician in music is largely contained in its utility as a means of expressing one's self, in much the same way as a written work serves the author or a painting serves the artist. It is an attempt on the part of a performer to communicate an idea, a feeling, a mood. A psychologist, on the other hand, although he may be interested in music as an expression, is more likely to be interested in the response of the person experiencing a musical stimulus. In particular, the psychologist would like to know what variables in a musical stimulus determine the type of listener response.

The music educator falls squarely between these two groups, the psychologists and the performing musicians, with clear and obvious responsibilities to understand music both as a stimulus and as a response.

. . . The point of education is not teaching but learning. While we in education pay a great deal of attention to what is done by teachers, we might well be more attentive to the behavioral changes occurring in the learner. . . . People are annoyingly fickle about what they will learn—almost as if they had minds of their own!

. . . Learning is a construct (an explanation) used to account for predictable changes in behavior presumed to be based on experience rather than maturation. A person has learned a skill or concept when he is able to use the skill or concept (such as up-down, fast-slow, loud-soft) voluntarily and appropriately, as the result of contact with his environment (as opposed to reflexes and motor skills that are involuntary or the result of physiological or neurological development). Historically, certain psychologists have attempted to explain all learning behavior in terms of one general principle or theory (stimulus-response, association, gestalt, conditioning, or some other). However, contemporary thinking about learning distinguishes types of learning processes and accepts the possibility that different types of learning may be based on different principles.

One difficulty in thinking about learning in music is that musical performance involves an intricate interaction of cognitive and of motor skills. Most of the studies in music education have not distinguished these two aspects of learning but have been concerned with the efficacy of gross methods of teaching students. Such questions as whole or part learning, massed or distributive practice, and a number of others probably cannot be answered with any generality in the area of music until we either break the complex phenomena down into more basic units or settle for less generalizability than we expect in laboratory experiments.

In his book, *The Conditions of Learning* (Holt, Rinehart & Winston, 1965), Robert Gagné argues convincingly that the phenomenon we call learning can be subdivided into at least eight distinct levels or types of learning, ranging from what psychologists have typically called classical or Pavlovian conditioning to the highest level, which Gagné describes as problem solving. [The eight levels of learning include signal learning, stimulus-response learning, chaining, verbal association, multiple discrimination, concept learning, principle learning and problem solving.]

. . . If we accept Gagné's subdivisions, we should vary our instructional procedure depending on the type of learning we are dealing with. . . . In any complex behavior we may recognize two, three, or four types of learning taking place more or less simultaneously. It is important that we not be so preoccupied with what we as teachers want to happen that we fail to recognize and facilitate the learning processes actually being used by learners.

The name of Piaget has commanded much attention these past years as a result of his educational writing. Testifying to the fact that his ideas continue to have an impact upon music education an article entitled, "Percept and Concept: Implications of Piaget," by Marilyn Pflederer Zimmerman is relevant.[4]

[4] Marilyn Pflederer Zimmerman, "Percept and Concept: Implications of Piaget," *Music Educators Journal*, Vol. 56, No. 6 (February 1970), pp. 49–50; 147–148. By permission of the *Music Educators Journal* and the author.

Curriculum reformers stress that the structural elements and unifying concepts of music need to be translated into terms children at various age levels can understand and assimilate. . . .

Insights into the development of children's thought patterns have been provided by the monumental research of Jean Piaget. Piaget views concept development in terms of conservation, which refers to an individual's ability to retain the invariant qualities of a particular stimulus when the stimulus field has been changed.

For Piaget, conservation can be traced through a successive growth from the child's perceptually dominated view of reality to a conceptual view. The use of conservation principles allows the child to think away visual qualities and concentrate on the logical relationships involved. When the child sees that the total amount of a quantity remains the same even when divided into smaller units, he is demonstrating conservation. Conservation is justified by the properties of reversibility and compensation. Only when the child is able to return to the initial state of a given material by an inverse operation, does he arrive at conservation of that material.

Inherent in the Piagetian idea of conservation is the very real relationship that exists between perception and concept formation. A concept is a clear and complete thought about something acquired through sensory perception. The interdependence of percept and concept is especially evident in musical learning. It seems almost a truism to say that musical learning begins with perception of music. From our various perceptions of music, we develop musical concepts that permit us to think about what we have heard and that provide us with a basis for communicating our musical ideas through performance and at the symbolic level of notation.

. . . Young children and older beginners in music have a tendency to fixate their perception on a dominant or biasing aspect of the music. Piaget refers to this perceptual fixation as "centration." The tendency to "center" upon the dominant, to overestimate the immediate, makes one ignore other facets of the stimulus situation, and systematic distortions in perception result. For this reason, perceptual thought suffers from instabilities conceptual thinking is later able to overcome. In musical learning, centration can result in an inaccurate and incomplete survey of the total musical configuration, be it vocal or instrumental. For example, the tone color of a trumpet may so capture the focal point of a child's perception that any other information about the music is excluded from his ears. As children are able to decenter their perception, that is, to explore other aspects of what they are hearing, they receive more complete and undistorted information about the music, information they can derive musical concepts from. Thus, the musical learning process moves back and forth through three phases, from the perception of tonal–rhythmic relationships to the mediation of these relationships into meaningful concepts to the representation of these relationships at the symbolic level. . . .

Results [of a research project at Northwestern University] show that even young children are capable of comprehending fairly complex musical concepts. Teachers may be doing students a disservice by teaching them music too slowly . . . concepts such as inversion, mode, and rhythm pattern can be taught to children at ages lower than previously imagined. . . . Children should have the opportunity to create and experiment with music in a very active way, so that by their own creation and experimentation, they may learn that such aspects of music as tonal pattern, rhythm, tempo, and intervals are equally as plastic but immutable as clay. . . .

There needs to be a better match between the music curriculum and children's age levels. Music educators should organize the elementary music curriculum into a sequence of learnings, based upon knowledge of the intellectual and musical capabilities of children at various ages. . . . In too many instances, the curriculum has been a haphazard mixture of facts and songs that do not challenge and stimulate either the musical or intellectual growth of children. . . .

More emphasis should be placed on active experimentation with rhythm and meter in the elementary schools. After a systematic study of variation technique, the variation of musical patterns and themes should be incorporated into the classroom. . . . From the beginning, children should be taught the proper musical terminology and vocabulary. More instruction should be given in musical mode, inversion, and rhythm pattern. A system of notation to clarify the aural stimulus can and should be used as early as age seven. . . .

Over the years a considerable amount of attention has been directed to methods from abroad which include particularly those of Suzuki, Kodály, Orff, and Dalcroze. Alfred Garson considers:[5]

"What is the future of the Suzuki method?

The Talent Education Institute in Matsumoto, Japan, was completed in 1967 and is now in operation. . . . In Japan, Dr. Maseaki Honda, the director of Talent Education and by profession a pediatrician, has no doubt been able to advise and aid Dr. Suzuki in his experiments and the evolution of his theories. An Early Childhood Development Association has been established to apply the Suzuki Talent Education ideals to subjects other than music. The association plans to build a center to which educators from all over the world can come for research and observation.

Suzuki violin and cello methods have already been published. It is probably only a matter of time before similar methods are published for the viola and double bass, since smaller instruments are now being manufactured. The Suzuki method will probably also be adapted to other instruments. In fact, Zen-on Publishing Company of Tokyo is planning to publish the Suzuki String Group Method and the Suzuki Piano Method. I have heard tapes of some of his young pupils playing Bach partitas and Beethoven sonatas after only one or two years of study.

With an array of miniature instruments, perhaps one day we will be able to listen to symphony orchestras of ten-year-old children performing works by children and being conducted by children. There will be chamber groups and recitals, where the soloists are accompanied by children playing on miniature pianos. The scope is limitless, but I will pause here before being accused of indulging in "music-fiction." The Suzuki method can also be applied to other subjects. There is no reason, for instance, why preschoolers who can read should not be taught typing on miniature typewriters. We have to come down to the level of the child's physical and mental needs. The

[5] Alfred Garson, "Learning with Suzuki: Seven Questions Answered," *Music Educators Journal*, Vol. 56, No. 6 (February 1970), pp. 64–66; 153. By permission of the *Music Educators Journal* and the author.

reason many of the so-called "latest" methods of education are ineffective is that they are too often devised for the adult mind. I shall never forget the day I observed Dr. Suzuki pausing for a while before entering a class of three- to six-year-old pupils. I asked him why he hesitated. He told me that it was not hesitation, but that he was preparing himself for the children by "descending mentally" to their age level. Many years ago Maria Montessori realized the importance of this mental attitude. To make it clearer, imagine yourself in a world where "adults" are twelve feet tall, where a snarling dog is sometimes bigger than you, where you have to climb up onto a chair because you cannot see out of the window. Miniature toys such as "doll houses" and "pedal cars" are so successful because they bring the adult world within the reach of the child. The time will come when school subjects are taught in a way that will enable children to work at their maximum capacity.

The Suzuki world is fascinating and limitless. It is a world full of unsolved questions. Dr. Suzuki himself may not have all the answers, but he has opened the doors to his new world and shown us the way. It is now up to us to explore it through research.

Denise Bacon, in an article entitled "Kodály and Orff: Report From Europe," delineates the potential of the methods originated by these two men.[6]

The Kodály and Orff concepts could create a musical revolution in this country that would lead to a musically literate child and eventually to a national audience for good music. I believe we should *not* throw out everything and start over again; we have much that is good that we should keep; but, we must keep open minds and try to use the best of many methods for whatever they can offer us. I happen to be more interested in these two methods than others for particular reasons: the Kodály because it leads to musical literacy and has proved successful with a whole nation; the Orff because it holds out the hope that each child may become a freer individual, better able to express himself and to relate to the world

[6] Denise Bacon, "Kodály and Orff: Report from Europe," *Music Educators Journal*, Vol. 55, No. 8 (April 1969), pp. 53–56. By permission of the *Music Educators Journal* and the author.

in which he has to live. The Kodály is disciplined, sequential, and truly musical; the Orff is free, not stereotyped and creative. I think our children need *both* discipline and creativity. Music must take its place as an academic discipline in the core of the curriculum. But it is up to all of us to do something to follow up; we need to get after parents, public school music teachers, principals, and superintendents, to say nothing of foundations, publishing companies, and the government to supply money for much needed research. We need to insist that public schools look into these methods, that they send teachers to be trained, and that they be willing to pay for such courses.

The Dalcroze method is not new to this country. It has enjoyed considerable popularity among some for a number of years. A recent article by Judith Willour points up the fact that it remains a method to consider.[7]

The primary characteristic distinguishing the Dalcroze eurhythmics method from other methods of teaching music is that it develops a feeling for and an awareness of music through *body movement*. In this system of rhythmic re-education, originated by the Swiss musician Emile Jacques-Dalcroze (1865–1950), the body is actually used as a musical instrument in interpreting the sounds.

Rhythmic sense, a musical ear, the voice, and muscular coordination are developed simultaneously through various body activities. Improvised piano music is used in the classes because it can be changed to fit the child's own rhythm. Later, the child learns to adapt his rhythm to that of the music. With improvised music, there is always change; repetition occurs only when the improviser desires it. Because the music is always changing and cannot, therefore, be learned by rote, the children are forced to listen constantly. Thus, listening is of primary importance from the very first lesson. . . .

As with any unusual approach in teaching, there are some difficulties to be overcome. One problem is that the music teacher may have little skill in movement. The teacher also

[7] Judith Willour, "Beginning with Delight, Leading to Wisdom: Dalcroze," *Music Educators Journal*, Vol. 56, No. 1 (April 1969), pp. 72–75. By permission of the *Music Educators Journal* and the author.

may not have enough experience at the keyboard to improvise. The ability to improvise at the piano should be a skill demanded of everyone who will teach music in public schools. A third problem that must be met in initiating eurhythmics classes is that of space. In order to have freedom of movement, there must be adequate room. These problems are not without solutions, and the benefit of exposing children to Dalcroze eurhythmics makes it worth working to eliminate the difficulties.

Because Dalcroze eurhythmics is a creative approach to music, each music educator can develop the concepts with variations. It can be treated as a pure subject or incorporated into an already existing music program. The aims of Dalcroze eurhythmic study are constant but the teaching methods can be very flexible. Music educators should incorporate some Dalcroze eurhythmics work in their general music program for kindergarten and primary grades and expose each child to as much of this type of training as possible.

Too often music is taught by drilling facts and theory into children rather than by arousing their interest so that they want to learn more about music. Certainly, music can and should at times be an academic discipline, especially in upper grades. However, enjoyment of music and a serious, academic study of it are not mutually exclusive. Emile Jacques-Dalcroze himself believed that the most important effect of music study should be an awakening of a love for the art in the pupil. Dalcroze eurhythmics is an example of an approach to music that is serious and yet at the same time can be thoroughly enjoyed by all participants. If more music were taught with this philosophy, our schools would produce many more music enthusiasts as well as serious musicians.

Much attention has recently been given to the question as to whether rock has a place in the school music program. The Music Educators Journal has devoted a considerable amount of space to the question as well as a good deal of conference time. The emphasis continues as indicated by Sidney Fox:[8]

[8] Sidney Fox, "From Rock to Bach," *Music Educators Journal*, Vol. 56, No. 9 (May 1970), pp. 52–55. By permission of the *Music Educators Journal* and Sidney Fox, Program Specialist, Music, Follett Education Corporation.

Today's rock should be compared with traditional music not to decide which is better, but to learn how man uses music to satisfy his ever-changing needs. The music educator must do a great deal of listening not only to get acquainted with the whole area of rock but also to be able to carefully select the rock that can be useful in teaching the elements, structures, and feeling of all music. Finding the connection between rock and great music means relating the melody, rhythm, harmony, form, timbre, and mood of each to the other. The music must be allowed to serve as an aural stimulus, its true function, unencumbered by the verbal or visual blocks presented by the teacher. Facts about the composer and the music are not music. The "vital" statistics are merely incidental, and should be used only after the sound of the music is experienced. Presenting challenging questions will allow the students, with the guidance of the teacher, to explore the music aurally. Following this with constant reinforcement will enable the student to perceive musical structure and to discover musical concepts from his own experience. The teacher will thus fulfill his real role as a guide or coach. The use of rock can be the key to opening the doors that have locked in both students and teachers, and it can broaden and enrich the lives of both.

Stuart Smith writes:[9]

Today's children are citizens of another culture. They are not merely immature, inexperienced members of ours, who, with proper guidance and encouragement, will carry on the musical traditions we have maintained. They have, instead, developed their own music, rock, which is really a whole multitude of musical forms synthesized from rock 'n' roll, the blues, jazz, gospel music, folk idioms of America and the British Isles, Indian classical music, Baroque and other European styles, electronic music, avant-garde forms, and still other sources. Even at an early age, children are aware of this music and can often sing some of the current tunes. Today's child, then, is not a *tabula rasa* on which we can inscribe whatever

[9] Stuart Smith, "Rock—Swim in it or Sink," *Music Educators Journal*, Vol. 56, No. 5 (January 1970), pp. 86–87; 141–142. By permission of the *Music Educators Journal* and the author.

music we wish, but comes to us as an already partially formed individual with his own musical tastes and attitudes.

. . . The musical culture of our young people is a mass culture transmitted by the mass media. We music educators are not in control of this music, so it is futile to attempt to suppress it or redirect our student's interests toward something we consider better. Nothing short of tyrannical control of the mass media could hope to accomplish either of these ends. But, more to the point, the desire to suppress or redirect is an elitist attitude inappropriate in our democratic pluralistic society. We cannot justly enforce a "prestige" culture to the exclusion of all others, nor can we train, at public expense, a musical elite expert in this supposedly superior culture while ignoring the needs of everyone else.

Rather, our aim has to be to help every child deal with his environment as he actually finds it. In music, this means using our training and experience to help the child find his way through the vast, uncharted regions of the mass-music culture. Moreover, the child's experience of this music is the only possible basis from which we can introduce him to the traditional musical heritage; it is his only frame of reference. We need not *embrace* popular music, however, or even treat it as a necessarily benign force (the racial and class hostilities expressed in hate-rock and psychedelic fantasies of acid-rock are clearly antithetical to society as presently constituted). But to ignore this music altogether and to maintain the arrogant posture that we alone are able to provide what is good and worthwhile in music can only increase our students' alienation from and disrespect for schools and other institutions.

Just as soon as one may become sufficiently aware of the need to incorporate rock into the music program, there are those spokesmen in the field who quickly remind the music educator that the question is not merely, Shall we teach either classical music *or* rock, but shall our programs represent an honest reflection of *all* aspects of music. John M. Eddins provides an article in support of two important musical trends:[10]

[10] John M. Eddins, "Two Trends in Teaching Music: The Comprehensive and the Cross-Cultural," *Music Educators Journal*, Vol. 56, No. 1 (September 1969), pp. 69–71. By permission of the *Music Educators Journal* and the author.

According to such educators as Jerome Bruner, the most comprehensive learning takes place when the learner is involved in a total process rather than in the piecemeal absorption of isolated facets of that process.

It follows that any serious student of music should develop structural, analytical, performance, and listening skills by composing, performing, and critically evaluating music in various styles, rather than by studying these skills as separate, self-contained "subjects." In this way, the acquisition of musical skills will be based on and integrated with the comprehension of musical processes, rather than be prerequisite to such comprehension. In combination with this, music educators should learn about all kinds of music—from the best practitioners of the art. This second principle, though seemingly obvious, has too often been neglected in practice in the past.

These educational principles are being implemented in many programs and schools throughout the country. One example of a successful program incorporating this approach is the institute for music educators conducted by New England Conservatory at the Berkshire Music Center, Lenox, Massachusetts. During the summer of 1968, two courses were offered, both meeting two hours daily for six weeks, and both carrying four graduate credits at the Conservatory.

. . . The class in contemporary composition, taught by Mr. Alper, composed a number of short exploratory works for various instruments and sonorities, beginning with simple organizations of "nonmusical" sounds, using voices, then sound-producing objects.

. . . By starting with current compositional techniques, the class quickly learned to handle musical materials without having to acquire a detailed technical proficiency in a specific medium. This generated a freedom of expression that, along with the stimulus of the class members' involvement in the performance of their own works, resulted in a total production of over eighty compositions during a period of six weeks— this from a class of only eight people, most of whom had previously composed little or no music!

. . . The second class consisted of a series of seminars presented by outstanding professional musicians.

. . . Each of the artists presented his materials in his own way, depending on how he could best understand and express his work. Yet their strikingly different modes of presentation all proved effective.

. . . The necessity for music educators to learn from performing artists was well illustrated in the seminars because some experiences common to several of the artists seemed to run counter to accepted educational theories. The elaborate improvisations in jazz, Indian music, and African music are all based on the instantaneous retrieval and appropriate rearrangement of prelearned pitch and rhythm patterns. These patterns are learned almost exclusively through rote repetition, and they represent patterned perceptual behavior rather than highly conceptualized abstractions.

. . . Perhaps music educators should deemphasize conceptualization as the immediate goal of musical learning and pay increased attention to perceptual experience and patterned behavior.

. . . The availability of these institutes is certainly an encouraging development for music educators, and more programs of this nature should be offered all over the nation.

According to Virginia Hagemann,[11] there remains still another facet that has not been tapped. "One area of contemporary music in the secondary schools that has been virtually untouched is electronic music composition. . . . The electronic music laboratory established in the Masterman School, a public school for gifted children in Philadelphia, Pennsylvania, is a clear example of the possibilities for electronic composition on the secondary school level.

An example of children's musical capacities is the work produced at the Masterman laboratory by students ranging from age eleven to thirteen. Andrew Rudin, director of Philadelphia Musical Academy's electronic music studio, observed: These students, given the opportunity of working in pure sound (much as a painter works directly with paint on canvas) and without the necessity of learning the elaborate symbol

[11] Virginia S. Hagemann, "Are Junior High Students Ready for Electronic Music?" *Music Educators Journal*, Vol. 56, No. 4 (December 1969), pp. 35–37. By permission of the *Music Educators Journal* and the author.

system of traditional notation, have produced music that is astonishing in its imagination and very unselfconscious in technique.

The argument against having a course in electronic composition at the secondary level because of the high cost of the equipment is equally invalid. Expensive equipment is not necessary to teach the fundamentals of electronic music composition. An adequate laboratory can be equipped for less than three hundred dollars.

. . . One of the main objectives of the course is to give the student the *freedom to create.*

. . . Although the importance of free, creative expression is stressed, the need for *specialized knowledge* is also recognized.

. . . Each student is actively involved in experimentation and discovery. He and he alone must decide what will be the most effective way to translate the musical elements into an expressive musical experience.

. . . The course focuses on the cooperative interaction of the group through the critical evaluation of student compositions. Group discussions, analyses, and constructive criticism of the relative merit of each completed work contribute to the development of musicality in each participant.

The disciplines taught in the laboratory are of prime importance in the development of musicality and the aesthetic potential of the individual. The adolescent need for independence will be satisfied by the creative freedom encouraged within the laboratory. The study of the basic concepts of electronic music will help the student gain a critical perspective of himself, of his social environment, and of the ways he can shape new goals of learning.

From "Strip the Mind of What Doesn't Work,"[12] an article that appeared in January, 1970 an interesting remark was contributed by Jack E. Schaeffer, Director of Music Education, Seattle (Washington) Public School when he said:

[12] Jack E. Schaeffer, "Improve the meager diet," from "Strip the Mind of What Doesn't Work," *Music Educators Journal*, Vol. 56, No. 5 (January 1970), p. 84. By permission of the *Music Educators Journal* and the author.

Our curriculum has been planned around the past three hundred years of European music. This is only a small part of the total music of the world. We should be doing a great deal more to interest the boys and girls in all kinds of music. So we've been experimenting, bringing into the picture a great deal more than the rather meager diet that has been considered the music program for all the years up until now. We are experimenting a great deal with drums and guitars—instruments the students can pick up and learn to play quickly—rather than putting all the emphasis on the violin and the string instruments and the brass and woodwinds. We need to get people who can change as the schools change, and we need the innovative equipment and materials to involve the eighty percent who are outside the traditional school music program.

Special interest is being directed toward non-Western music and teaching in underprivileged areas.

According to Henry Pleasants in his article "Afro-American Epoch–Emergence of a New Idiom,"[13] "The national MENC Convention in Chicago, with its emphasis on the new musics, is evidence of a new awareness on the part of music educators that more is afoot musically in our century than a conventional and traditional distinction between serious and popular music, that what we are experiencing, what we are faced with, may well be the most momentous development in Western musical evolution since the emergence of diatonic harmony from the idiomatic convulsions of the seventeenth century.

. . . Most music educators will concede, I think, that too many students are being schooled today for a profession in classical music that is not growing and that, in certain areas, is actually contracting.

. . . For the violinists there is demand, not as recitalists, but as orchestra players. But for the pianists and singers there lies ahead a corpse-strewn road leading, probably in nine out of ten cases, right back to the campus. Indeed, many of them will never leave the campus, at most exchanging one campus for another.

[13] Henry Pleasants, "Afro-American Epoch–Emergence of a New Idiom," *Music Educators Journal*, Vol. 57, No. 1 (September 1970), pp. 33–37. By permission of the *Music Educators Journal* and the author.

One may argue that the campus has become the refuge of serious or European music, playing the preservative role of the monastery in medieval Europe.

. . . There is a certain autometabolism implicit in the sequence of teaching others to teach others to teach others and so on. It brings with it the danger of withdrawal from society, insularity, complacency, and in the end, redundancy.

. . . While professional opportunity in the one idiom is declining, it is growing in the other. And it will grow faster as the public schools face up to the requirement of starting a young person's education in a kind of music he feels to be his own. There are great opportunities today for the composer-arranger, the film composer, the studio musician, the musical director, the record producer, the artist and repertoire man—and the educator! This is the challenge to music educators today.

Bennett Reimer's, "General Music for the Black Ghetto"[14] provided these ideas:

Should the general education of black ghetto children be different in kind from the general education of children who are not black and/or do not live in city ghettos? Are the aims of general education different for different segments of American society? Or are the aims constant with a variety of means used to achieve them?

. . . For some Negroes, good education is good for reasons having little if anything to do with race. A good music program, for such people, would be good on the basis of criteria having nothing to do with the color of the teachers teaching it or the children studying it.

. . . At the other end of the continuum are people for whom race is the determinant of all attitudes toward and expectations of the world. For such people good music education is good entirely on the basis of race-connected criteria.

. . . Between these two extremes are an infinite number of points at which musical aims and racial aims coexist in varying degrees of balance. Music educators of any color who con-

[14] Bennett Reimer, "General Music for the Black Ghetto," *Music Educators Journal*, Vol. 56, No. 5 (January 1970), pp. 94–96; 145–152. By permission of the *Music Educators Journal* and the author.

sider their primary obligation when teaching to be musical can promote musical aims for children at every point on the continuum up to but not including the extreme of black racism. The position being taken in this paper is that music education should indeed be guided by musical aims rather than racial aims, and that music educators, when acting as music educators . . . should be guided by the common aim of helping children share the art of music in its myriad manifestations. Racial considerations need not and cannot be ignored, but should be taken as opportunities for developing musical sensitivity applicable to any and all music. This is not to minimize in any way the importance of race-related concerns. It is to assert that musical experience is too valuable to be limited because of a person's race, that musical sharing can and should include levels of aesthetic meaning far below the surface of skin color, that the processes of musical teaching and learning are necessary in order to develop each child's ability to share musical pleasures (each child's "musical sensitivity"), and that music educators—as music educators—are first and foremost obligated to promote the aims of *musical* education.

A Final Word

Despite the multitude of facts elicited by psychologists regarding the process of learning, the one perfect way of succeeding with every pupil still eludes us. The existence of so many schools of educational psychology serves to underscore this fact, as each school seems to be constructed on the incompleteness of the other.

Years of argument between theorists has brought no agreement on one completely acceptable platform. Answers, however, do not lie in the past but must come through a constantly dynamic and energetic search for truth. It can be hoped that a philosophical millennium may one day be reached when, according to Morris Cohen,[15] ". . . the idealistic lamb shall lie down beside the realistic wolf, or perhaps when some pragmatic tiger shall so have swallowed up all opposition that complete peace shall reign thereafter."

[15] Morris, Cohen. "The Conception of Philosophy in Recent Discussion," *The Journal of Philosophy and Scientific Method*, Vol. VII (July 21, 1910), pp. 401–410.

Bibliography

Chapter 1

Birge, Edward B. *History of Public School Music*. Boston: Oliver Ditson Company, 1928, pp. 7, 11–12, 17–18.

Burton, Warren, and Clifton Johnson (eds.). *The District School As It Was*. New York: T. Y. Crowell Company, 1833, 1928.

Butts, R. Freeman. *A Cultural History of Education*. New York: Mc-Graw-Hill Book Company, Inc., 1947, pp. 210–211, 219, 257–258, 264–267, 271–272.

———, and Lawrence A. Cremin. *A History of Education in American Culture*. New York: Henry Holt and Company, 1953, pp. 118–119.

Chase, Gilbert. *America's Music from the Pilgrims to the Present*, 2d ed. New York: McGraw-Hill Book Company, Inc., 1966, pp. 52–54, 183–187.

Cubberley, Elwood P. *A Brief History of Education*. Boston: Houghton Mifflin Company, 1922, pp. 150, 153–154.

———. *Public Education in the United States*. Boston: Houghton Mifflin Company, 1947, pp. 12, 13, 26, 43, 77.

Curti, Merle. *The Growth of American Thought*, 2d ed. New York: Harper & Brothers, 1951, pp. 50, 60, 79–80.

Curwen, J. Spencer. *Studies in Worship-Music*. London: J. Curwen and Sons, 1880, p. 59.

Lang, Paul H. *Music in Western Civilization*. New York: W. W. Norton and Company, Inc., 1941, pp. 213, 259.

Laurie, Simon S. *Studies in the History of Educational Opinion from the Renaissance*. Cambridge: University Press, 1903, pp. 7–9.

Monroe, Paul. *A Textbook in the History of Education*. New York: The Macmillan Company, 1916, p. 369.

Reisner, Edward H. *The Evolution of the Common School*. New York: The Macmillan Company, 1930, pp. 37, 41, 44.

Roback. A. A. *History of American Psychology*. New York: Library Publishers, 1952, p. 32.

Scholes, Percy A. *The Puritans and Music in England and New England*. London: Oxford University Press, 1934, pp. 262–263.

Swan, M. S. *The New Harp of Columbia: A System of Musical Notation*. Nashville: W. T. Berry & Company, 1867.

Chapter 2

Anderson, Lewis Flint. *Pestalozzi*. New York: McGraw-Hill Book Company, Inc., 1931, pp. 6, 8, 40–41, 81–83, 102, 151–155, 169–173, 195, 201–204, 240–241.

Barnard, Henry (ed.). "Lowell Mason," *American Journal of Education*, Vol. IV (1857), p. 142.

Butts, R. Freeman. *A Cultural History of Education*. New York: McGraw-Hill Book Company, Inc., 1947, pp. 248–250, 435, 436.

———, and Lawrence A. Cremin. *A History of Education in American Culture*. New York: Henry Holt and Company, 1953, pp. 52–53.

Compayre, Gabriel. *The History of Pedagogy*. Boston: D.C. Heath and Company, 1896. pp. 425, 428–429.

Curti, Merle. *The Growth of American Thought*, 2d ed. New York: Harper & Brothers, 1951, pp. 105–157.

Graves, F. P. *Great Educators of Three Centuries*. New York: The Macmillan Company, 1912, pp. 52–64.

———. *A History of Education in Modern Times*. New York: The Macmillan Company, 1937, pp. 149–153.

Holman, H. *Pestalozzi*. London: Longmans, Green & Company, 1908, pp. 28, 143–144, 155–156, 160, 162, 169–170, 173, 175, 178–179, 181–182, 184–185, 224, 230–231, 238–239.

Laurie, Simon S. *Studies in the History of Educational Opinion from the Renaissance*. Cambridge: University Press, 1903, pp. 123–150.

Leitch, James. *Practical Educationists and Their Systems of Teaching*. Glasgow: James Maclehose, 1876, pp. 75–88.

Payne, Joseph. *"Pestalozzi: The Influence of His Principles and Practices on Elementary Education."* A lecture. New York: E. Steiger, 1877.

Pfeiffer, Michael Traugott, and Hans Georg Nägeli. *Gesangbildungslehre Nach Pestalozzischen Grundsätzen*. Zürich, 1810.

Wilds, Elmer H. *The Foundations of Modern Education*. New York: Farrar and Rinehart, 1936, pp. 324, 476.

Chapter 3

Alcott, William A. "William Channing Woodbridge," *The American Journal of Education*, Vol. V (June 1858), p. 63.

Anderson, Lewis Flint. *Pestalozzi*. New York: McGraw-Hill Book Company, Inc., 1931, pp. 172–173, 175.

Barnard, Henry (ed.). "Educational Labors of Lowell Mason," *The American Journal of Education*, Vol. IV (September 1857), pp. 142, 145.

Brayley, A. W. "The Inception of Public School Music in America," *The Musician*, Vol. X (November 1905), p. 484.

Dwight's Journal of Music. "Music in the Public School," Vol. XV (July 2, 1859), pp. 107, 110.

Fowle, William Bentley. "Vocal Music," *American Annals of Education*, Vol. V (May 1835), pp. 225–229.

Gehrkens, Karl W. "The Twentieth Century—A Singing Revival," Music Teachers National Association *Volume of Proceedings* (1922), pp. 179–184.

Mann, Horace (ed.). "Singing in Common Schools," *The Common School Journal*, Vol. III (June 1841), p. 190.

Mason, Daniel G. "A Glimpse of Lowell Mason from an Old Bundle of Letters," *The New Music Review*, Vol. XXVI (January 1927), pp. 49–51.

Mason, Lowell. *Manual of the Boston Academy of Music*. Boston: Carter, Hindee and Company, 1834, pp. iii, 10, 12, 18, 25–28; (1836 ed.) p. 26.

————. *The Normal Singer*. New York: Mason Brothers, 1856, p. ii.

————. *The Song Garden Series, Book I*. Boston: Oliver Ditson and Company, 1864, pp. iv, v.

————. *The Song Garden Series, Book II*. Boston: Oliver Ditson and Company, 1864, pp. 3, 21, 22.

————. *The Song Garden Series, Book III*. Boston: Oliver Ditson and Company, 1864, p. iii.

————, and Theodore F. Seward. *The Pestalozzian Music Teacher*. New York: C. H. Ditson and Company, 1871, pp. 7–12.

————, and George J. Webb. *The Primary School Song Book in Two Parts*. New York: Mason Brothers, 1846, pp. ii, 75, 79.

————. *The Song-Book of the School-Room*. New York: Mason Brothers, 1856, pp. ii, 36.

Miller, C. H. "Music in the Grade Schools of the United States," Music Teachers National Association *Volume of Proceedings* (1920), pp. 44–54.

Seward, Theodore F. "Educational Work of Dr. Lowell Mason," (n.d.), pp. 12–13.

Upham, J. P. "Annual Report of the School Committee of the City of Boston for 1858," *Dwight's Journal of Music*, Vol. XV (July 2, 1859), p. 105.

Chapter 4

Anderson, Lewis Flint. *Pestalozzi*. New York: McGraw-Hill Book Company, Inc., 1931, p. 8.

Bristow, George F. "Music in the Public Schools of New York," Music Teachers National Association *Volume of Proceedings* (1885), pp. 30–31.

Brown, O. B. "Teaching and Teaching Reforms—Music in Public Schools," Music Teachers National Association *Volume of Proceedings* (1889), p. 108.

Butts, R. Freeman. *A Cultural History of Education.* New York: McGraw-Hill Book Company, Inc., 1947, pp. 462–465, 518.

Notated in part from Cubberley, Elwood P. *Readings in the History of Education.* Boston: Houghton Mifflin Company, 1948, p. 659.

Curti, Merle. *The Growth of American Thought,* 2d ed. New York: Harper & Brothers, 1951, pp. 324, 508, 518.

Gabriel, Ralph H. *The Course of American Democratic Thought.* New York: The Ronald Press Company, 1940, pp. 143–145, 147–148, 150–157.

Good, H. G. *A History of American Education.* New York: The Macmillan Company, 1956, pp. 160, 316–318, 320–322.

Graves, Frank P. *A History of Education in Modern Times.* New York: The Macmillan Company, 1928, pp. 326, 330–332, 334–335.

Holman, H. *Pestalozzi.* London: Longmans Green & Company, 1908, p. 185.

Holt, Hosea E. "Better Teaching or a New Notation: Which?" National Education Association *Journal of Proceedings and Addresses* (1886), p. 5.

———. "Teaching and Teaching Reforms—Music in Public Schools," Music Teachers National Association *Volume of Proceedings* (1889), p. 113.

Jepson, B. "The Science of Music Versus Rote Practice in Public Schools," Music Teachers National Association *Volume of Proceedings* (1887), p. 176.

Mason, Luther W. *The National Music Teacher.* Boston: Ginn Brothers, 1872, p. 12.

———, et al. *The National Music Course, Book II.* Boston: Ginn Brothers, 1872, p. iv.

Noble, Stuart G. *A History of American Education,* rev. ed. New York: Rinehart and Company Inc., 1954, pp. 294–296, 301.

Spencer, Herbert. *Education.* New York: A. L. Burt Company (n.d.), pp. ix, 6–11, 16–211.

———. *Essays on Education.* New York: E. P. Dutton and Company, Inc. Reprinted 1949, pp. iii, x–xvi, 23–24, 56–60, 68–69, 80–83, 102, 104–105, 107–110, 119–120, 121–123, 126, 135, 149. Reprinted 1963, pp. 84–152.

Thut, I. N. *The Story of Education*. New York: McGraw-Hill Book Company, Inc., 1957, pp. 223, 243–244.

Wilds, Elmer H. *The Foundations of Modern Education*. New York: Farrar and Rinehart, Inc., 1936, p. 476.

Chapter 5

Baldwin, Ralph L. "The Aims of Music Courses in Grammar Schools," Music Educators National Association *Volume of Proceedings* (1907), p. 117.

———. "Report of Committee on Public Schools," Music Teachers National Association *Volume of Proceedings* (1907), p. 165.

Bicknell, Thomas W. "Music in Public Education," Music Teachers National Association *Volume of Proceedings* (1886), p. 178.

Birge, Edward B. *History of Public School Music in the United States*, New and Augmented Ed. Boston: Oliver Ditson Company, 1937, pp. 132–135.

Brown, O. B. "Teaching and Teaching Reforms—Music in Public Schools," Music Teachers National Association *Volume of Proceedings* (1889), pp. 109–110.

Currie, James. *The Principles and Practice of Common School Education*. Cincinnati: Robert Clarke and Company (1884), p. 265.

Dickey, Frances M. "History of Public School Music in the United States," Music Teachers National Association *Volume of Proceedings* (1913), p. 205.

Dwight's Journal of Music, "Music in Schools" (September 15, 1860), pp. 194–195. Condensed from an article in the *Rhode Island Schoolmaster*.

———. "Music in the Public Schools of Boston," Vol. XX (December 28, 1861), p. 307.

Flueckiger, S. L. "Why Lowell Mason Left the Boston Schools," *Music Educators Journal*, XXII (February 1936), pp. 20–21.

Gehrkens, Karl W. "The Twentieth Century—A Singing Revival," Music Teachers National Association *Volume of Proceedings*, (1922), pp. 179–184.

Graham, Percy. *Vocal Music in the Elementary Schools*, rev. ed. Boston: C. C. Birchard Company, 1950, p. 14.

Information imparted by Percy Graham through a lecture at Boston University College of Music, Boston, 1939.

Hohmann, Christian H. (trans.). *Practical Course of Instruction in Singing Prepared on School Principles*. Boston: Oliver Ditson and Company, 1856, pp. 4–5.

Holt, Hosea E. "Better Teaching or a New Notation: Which?" National Education Association *Journal of Proceedings and Addresses* (1886), p. 5.

———. "Conference on Public School Music and Popular Sight-Singing," Music Teachers National Association *Volume of Proceedings* (1897), p. 103.

———. "Music in Public Schools," Music Teachers National Association *Volume of Proceedings* (1883), pp. 43–46.

———. "Music Teaching from a Psychological Standpoint," Music Teachers National Association *Volume of Proceedings* (1886), p. 24.

———. The Normal Music Course *First Reader*. New York: Appleton Company, 1883.

———. The Normal Music Course *Introductory Third Reader*. New York: Silver Burdett and Company, 1887, p. v.

———. "Teaching and Teaching Reforms—Music in Public Schools," Music Teachers National Association *Volume of Proceedings* (1889), p. 114.

Jepson, B. "A Plea for the Elements of Music in Primary Grades," National Education Association *Journal of Proceedings and Addresses* (1885), p. 386.

———. "The Science of Music Versus Rote Practice in the Public School," Music Teachers National Association *Volume of Proceedings* (1887), pp. 174–187.

MacAllister, James. "Teaching and Teaching Reforms—Music in Public Schools," Music Teachers National Association *Volume of Proceedings* (1889), p. 125.

Mason, Luther W. *The National Music Course, Book II*. Boston: Ginn Brothers, 1872, p. iv.

———. The National Music Course *New Second Music Reader*. Boston: Ginn and Company, 1895, pp. 8, 23.

———. *The National Music Teacher*. Boston: Ginn Brothers, 1872, pp. 10, 12.

———. "Time-Names," *The School Music Journal*, Vol. I (June 1886), p. 164.

————, *et al.* Educational Music Course *Teachers' Edition.* Boston: Ginn and Company, 1898, pp. iv, xii.

Mathews, W. S. B. (ed.). "Luther Mason and School Music," *Music*, Vol. II (September 1892), pp. 474–482.

McConathy, Osbourne. "Evolution of Public School Music," Music Teachers National Association *Volume of Proceedings* (1922), pp. 161, 163, 170, 193.

McLaughlin, James M., and George A. Veazie. *The Introductory Music Reader.* Boston: Ginn and Company, 1895, pp. iii, iv.

National Music Course, The. *Catalogue and Announcements*, Common School Ed. Boston: Ginn and Company, 1891, p. 54.

Ripley, Frederic M., and Thomas Tapper. The Natural Music Course *The Music Primer.* New York: American Book Company, 1895, Section I; p. 3.

————. The Natural Music Course *New Harmonic First Reader.* New York: American Book Company, 1895, p. 3.

Seward, Theodore. "Music in the Public Schools of New York," Music Teachers National Association *Volume of Proceedings* (1885), pp. 42–44.

Silver, Edgar O. "Special Report on the Condition of Music Instruction in the Public Schools of the United States," National Education Association *Journal of Proceedings and Addresses* (1889), p. 691.

Spencer, Herbert. *Education.* New York: A. L. Burt Company (n.d.), pp. 65–79.

————. *Essays on Education.* New York: E. P. Dutton and Company, Inc., 1911. Introduction by Charles Eliot, pp. ix–xvi. Reprinted 1949, pp. 330, 325–329.

Stewart, Coe. "Music in Public Schools," Music Teachers National Association *Volume of Proceedings* (1883), pp. 40–41.

Tufts, John W. *Child Life in Song.* New York: Silver Burdett and Company, 1890.

————. The Normal Music Course *A Handbook of Vocal Music.* New York: Silver Burdett and Company, 1896, pp. v, 5, 6, 9–14, 19, 23, 25.

————. The Normal Music Course *Teachers' Manual.* New York: Silver Burdett and Company, 1898, p. 10.

———, and Hosea E. Holt. *Manual for the Use of Teachers*: To Accompany Readers and Charts of the Normal Music Course. New York: Appleton Company, 1883, p. 11.

———, ———. The Normal Music Course *First Reader*. New York: Appleton Company, 1883. New and revised edition. New York: Silver Rogers Company, 1887. Allied to this course were: Tufts, *Cecilian Series of Study and Song*, 1892, and Tufts and Holt, *The Common School Course*, 1892.

Upham, J. Baxter. "Music in Our Public Schools," *Dwight's Journal of Music*, XV (July 2, 1859), p. 110; XXXI (May 20, 1871), pp. 26–27.

Waterston, R. C. "Music in the Boston Public Schools," *Dwight's Journal of Music*, XXVIII (April 13, 1867), p. 11.

Chapter 6

Bowen, H. Courthope. *Froebel and Education through Self-Activity*. New York: Charles Scribner's Sons, 1906, p. 119.

Boyd, William. *The History of Western Education*. London: Adam & Charles Black, 1932, pp. 405–406.

Bristow, George F. "Music in the Public Schools of New York," Music Teachers National Association *Volume of Proceedings* (1885), p. 30.

Butts, R. Freeman, and Lawrence A. Cremin. *A History of Education in American Culture*. New York: Henry Holt and Company, 1953, pp. 324–330.

Dewey, John. "Criticism Wise and Otherwise on Modern Child Study," National Education Association *Journal of Proceedings and Addresses* (1897), pp. 867–868.

Froebel, Friedrich. *Education of Man*. (Translated and annotated by W. N. Hailmann) New York: D. Appleton-Century Company, 1887, pp. 1–2, 5, 14.

Garrett, Henry E. *Great Experiments in Psychology*. New York: Appleton-Century-Crofts, Inc., 1941, p. 318.

Good, H. G. *A History of American Education*. New York: The Macmillan Company, 1956, pp. 208–209, 337.

———. *A History of Western Education*, 2d ed. New York: The Macmillan Company, 1960, pp. 476, 479.

Hall, G. Stanley. *Adolescence, Volume I*. New York: D. Appleton and Company, 1915, pp. v–xi.

————. *Adolescence, Volume II.* New York: D. Appleton and Company, 1915, pp. 31–33, 58, 451–454.

————. "Child Study as a Basis for Psychology and Psychological Teaching," National Education Association *Journal of Proceedings and Addresses* (1893), pp. 717–718.

————. *The Forum*, XXIX (August 1900), pp. 687–702.

————. "The Ideal School as Based on Child Study," *The Forum*, XXXII (September 1901), pp. 24–39.

————. "Music Teaching from a Psychological Standpoint," Music Teachers National Association *Volume of Proceedings* (1886), pp. 12–17.

————. "The Psychology of Music and the Light It Throws Upon Musical Education," National Education Association *Journal of Proceedings and Addresses* (1908), pp. 848–854.

Harris, W. T. "Pedagogical and Psychological Observation," National Education Association *Journal of Proceedings and Addresses* (1890), pp. 108–113.

————. "Rational Psychology for Teachers," National Education Association *Journal of Proceedings and Addresses* (1898), p. 571.

Heidbreder, Edna. *Seven Psychologies.* New York: The Century Company, 1933, pp. 63–64.

Herbart, Frederick. *Outlines of Educational Doctrine.* (Translated by Alexis F. Lange and annotated by Charles DeGarmo.) New York: The Macmillan Company, 1904, p. 22.

Kandel, I. L. (ed.). *Twenty-Five Years of American Education.* New York: The Macmillan Company, 1924, pp. 61–62.

McMurry, Frank. "Herbartian Pedagogy for Normal Schools," National Education Association *Journal of Proceedings and Addresses* (1892), pp. 430–431.

Miller, C. H. "Music in the Grade Schools of the United States," Music Teachers National Association *Volume of Proceedings* (1920), pp. 44–54.

Misawa, Tadasu. *Modern Educators and Their Ideals.* New York: D. Appleton and Company, 1909, pp. 267–275.

Parker, Francis W. "The School of the Future," National Education Association *Journal of Proceedings and Addresses* (1891), pp. 82–89.

————. *Talks on Pedagogics*. New York: E. L. Kellogg and Company, 1894, pp. v, 18–21, 25, 113–116, 122, 128, 141–145, 226–228, 234, 348–350, 383.

Patridge, Lelia E. *Talks on Teaching*. New York: A. S. Barnes Company, 1883 (copyright transferred to Francis W. Parker, 1893), pp. 5–10, 17–19.

Pommer, W. H. "Methods versus Results," National Education Association *Journal of Proceedings and Addresses* (1904), pp. 696–699.

Quick, Robert Herbert. *Essays on Educational Reformers*. New York: D. Appleton and Company, 1900, pp. 411–412, 523.

Ragsdale, Clarence E. *Modern Psychologies and Education*. New York: The Macmillan Company, 1936, pp. 1–8, 114.

Rix, Frank R. "Some Features of Music Instruction in the Schools of New York City," National Education Association *Journal of Proceedings and Addresses* (1905), pp. 657–662.

Russell, E. H. "Observation and Experiment Essential in Pedagogical Inquiry," National Education Association *Journal of Proceedings and Addresses* (1889), pp. 275–285.

Chapter 7

Baldwin, Ralph L. "The Aims of Music Courses in Grammar Schools," Music Teachers National Association *Volume of Proceedings* (1907), pp. 93–100.

————. "School-Music—Has It Made Music Readers?" National Education Association *Journal of Proceedings and Addresses* (1903), pp. 705–708.

Bentley, Alys E. *The Song Series*. New York: A. S. Barnes and Company, 1907, p. 167.

————. The Song Series, *The Song Primer, Teachers' Book*. New York: A. S. Barnes and Company, 1907, p. 57.

————. The Song Series, *Book Two*. New York: A. S. Barnes and Company, 1910, pp. 163, 193.

Birge, Edward B. *History of Public School Music in the United States*. Boston: Oliver Ditson Company, 1928, p. 140.

Boyd, William. *The History of Western Civilization*, 6th ed. London: Adam & Charles Black, 1952, p. 349.

Butts, R. Freeman. *A Cultural History of Education*. New York: McGraw-Hill Book Company, Inc., 1947, pp. 502, 511–512.

Casterton, Elizabeth. "Correlation of Music with Other Branches of the School Curriculum," National Education Association *Journal of Proceedings and Addresses* (1905), pp. 637–643.

Cole, Samuel W. "The Real Purpose of Teaching Music in the Public Schools," National Education Association *Journal of Proceedings and Addresses* (1903), pp. 695–699.

Congdon, C. H. The Congdon Music Readers, *Music Reader Number Three*. Chicago: C. H. Congdon, 1913, p. 1.

———. "How Pupils Learn to Know and Do in Music," National Education Association *Journal of Proceedings and Addresses* (1895), pp. 778–785.

———. "Should Music in the Public Schools be Taught from the Song to the Exercise?" National Education Association *Journal of Proceedings and Addresses* (1900), pp. 538–540.

Curti, Merle. *The Growth of American Thought*, 2d ed. New York: Harper & Brothers, 1951, pp. 521–523.

Dann, Hollis E. The Hollis Dann Music Course, *Teachers' Manual*. New York: The American Book Company, 1912.

———. "An Anomalous Situation, With Suggestions for Improvement," National Education Association *Journal of Proceedings and Addresses* (1902), pp. 616–621.

DeJarnette, Reven S. *Hollis Dann*. Boston: C. C. Birchard, 1940, pp. 13–14, 31; Chap. X.

Fullerton, C. A. "The Opportunity and the Responsibility of Normal Schools in Public-School Music," National Education Association *Journal of Proceedings and Addresses* (1911), pp. 822–826.

Gaynor, Jessie L. "Child Song—Its Music," National Education Association *Journal of Proceedings and Addresses* (1908), pp. 857–859.

Gehrkens, Karl W. "The Twentieth Century—A Singing Revival," Music Teachers National Association *Volume of Proceedings* (1922), pp. 179–184.

Goedhart, Anna. "Educational Rhythm-Training," National Education Association *Journal of Proceedings and Addresses* (1908), pp. 859–862.

Graham, Percy. *Vocal Music in the Elementary Schools*, rev. ed. Boston: C. C. Birchard, 1950, p. iii.

Graves, F. P. *History of Education in Modern Times*. New York: The Macmillan Company, 1937, pp. 207–211.

Hayden, P. C. "Ultimate Object of Music Study in the Schools," National Education Association *Journal of Proceedings and Addresses* (1899), pp. 972–977.

Herbart, Frederick. *The Science of Education.* (Translated by H. M. Felkin.) Boston: Heath and Company, 1892, p. 1.

———. *Outlines of Educational Doctrine.* (Translated by Alexis F. Lange and annotated by Charles DeGarmo.) New York: The Macmillan Company, 1904, pp. 66–67.

Hodgon, W. A. "Rote-Singing and Its Proper Place in the Public School— Practice Versus Theory," National Education Association *Journal of Proceedings and Addresses* (1904), pp. 658–692.

Hofer, Marie Ruef. "What is Music and How Can We Help Children to Become Musical," National Education Association *Journal of Proceedings and Addresses* (1898), pp. 833–837.

Kelsey, David. "Music in the New Education," National Education Association *Journal of Proceedings and Addresses* (1894), p. 930.

Luckey, G. W. A. "Practical Results Obtained Through the Study of Children's Interests," National Education Association *Journal of Proceedings and Addresses* (1897), pp. 284–288.

Marshall, Leonard N. "Success in Public-School Music," National Education Association *Journal of Proceedings and Addresses* (1910), pp. 826–831.

McKenzie, Millicent. *Hegel's Educational Theory and Practice.* London: Swan, Sonnenshein & Company, Ltd., 1909, pp. 55–71.

McLaughlin, James M., and W. W. Gilchrist. *The New Educational Music Course.* Boston: Ginn and Company, 1904.

Parker, Francis W. *Talks on Pedagogics.* New York: E. L. Kellogg and Company, 1894, pp. 198–199, 200–201, 211–215.

Parr, Marie Burt. "Primary Music Methods," National Education Association *Journal of Proceedings and Addresses* (1904), pp. 681–685.

Pommer, W. H. "Methods Versus Results," National Education Association *Journal of Proceedings and Addresses* (1904), pp. 696–699.

Ripley, Frederic M., and Thomas Tapper. The Melodic Music Readers *Manual.* New York: The American Book Company, 1906, p. 8.

———. The Natural Music Course *New Harmonic First Reader.* New York: The American Book Company, 1903, p. 3.

Rix, Frank R. "Some Features of Music Instruction in the Schools of New York City," National Education Association *Journal of Proceedings and Addresses* (1905), pp. 657–662.

Rugg, Harold. *Culture and Education in America.* New York: Harcourt Brace and Company, 1931, pp. 147, 170; Chap. IX.

Smith, Eleanor. The Modern Music Series, *A Primer of Vocal Music.* Chicago: Scott, Foresman & Company, 1898, pp. 3–5.

————. The Modern Music Series *A Second Book of Vocal Music.* Chicago: Scott, Foresman & Company, 1893, p. 3.

————, and Richard Mueller. The Modern Music Series *The Third Book.* Chicago: Scott, Foresman & Company, 1898, p. 3.

Summaries of the Course in Methods. A series of Lessons prepared by the Institute of Music Pedagogy. Northampton: Alumni Association, n.d.

Tomlins, W. L. (ed.). The Laurel Music-Reader *Teachers' Edition.* Boston: C. C. Birchard and Company, 1914, p. ii.

Towers, John. "Teaching and Teaching Reforms—Music in Public Schools," Music Teachers National Association *Volume of Proceedings* (1889), p. 129.

Tufts, John, and Hosea Holt. *The New Normal Music Course.* New York: Silver Burdett, 1910.

White, William A. "Specific Musical Education Versus Culture Through Music—Which?" Music Teachers National Association *Volume of Proceedings* (1911), pp. 200–203.

Chapter 8

Bode, Boyd H. *Conflicting Psychologies of Learning.* New York: D. C. Heath and Company, 1929, pp. 313–340.

————. *Modern Educational Theories.* New York: The Macmillan Company, 1927, p. 178.

Boring, Edwin G. *A History of Experimental Psychology.* New York: The Century Company, 1929, pp. 520, 570–571, 653.

Boyd, William. *The History of Western Education,* 3d ed. London: A. & C. Black Ltd., 1932, pp. 404–406.

Brubacher, John S. *Modern Philosophies of Education,* 2d ed. New York: McGraw-Hill Book Company, Inc., 1950, pp. 309–310, 315–316.

Butler, J. Donald. *Four Philosophies and Their Practice in Education and Religion.* New York: Harper & Brothers, 1957, p. 493.

Butts, R. Freeman, and Lawrence A. Cremin. *A History of Education in American Culture.* New York: The Macmillan Company, 1956, pp. 333, 338–339, 444.

Cole, Lawrence E., and William F. Bruce. *Educational Psychology.* New York: World Book Company, 1950, pp. 408–409, 418–419, 514 (quotation by Charles H. Judd).

Cook, John W. "Progress of Education for the Year," National Education Association *Journal of Proceedings and Addresses* (1909), pp. 390–397.

Cooley, Edwin G. "The Adjustment of the School System to the Changed Conditions of the Twentieth Century," National Education Association *Journal of Proceedings and Addresses* (1909), pp. 404–410.

Croly, Herbert. *Progressive Democracy.* New York: The Macmillan Company, 1914, pp. 14–15; Chap. XIX.

Dewey, John. "The Primary Education Fetich," *The Forum* (1898), pp. 315–328.

Gabriel, Ralph Henry. *The Course of American Democratic Thought.* New York: The Ronald Press Company, 1940, p. 332.

Graves, F. P. *A History of Education in Modern Times.* New York: The Macmillan Company, 1937, pp. 200–201.

Heidbreder, Edna. *Seven Psychologies.* New York: The Century Company, 1933, pp. 209–214; Chap. VII.

Hook, Sidney. *Modern Education and Its Critics* (Pamphlet).

Huey, Edmund Burke. *The Psychology and Pedagogy of Reading.* New York: The Macmillan Company, 1913, pp. 306–307, 336–354.

Judd, Charles Hubbard. *Genetic Psychology for Teachers.* New York: D. Appleton and Company, 1907, pp. 76–79, 99–100, 106, 116–123, 134–145, 237–254.

Kandel, I. L. (ed.). *Twenty-Five Years of American Education.* New York: The Macmillan Company, 1924, pp. 62–63, 104, 106–110, 112–113, 157, 167–168.

McConathy, Osbourne, "Teaching Music Theory in the Public Schools," Music Teachers National Association *Volume of Proceedings* (1918), pp. 224–228.

McMurry, Frank M. *Elementary School Standards.* New York: World Book Company, 1914, pp. vii, 156.

———. "Herbartian Pedagogy for Normal Schools," National Education Association *Journal of Proceedings and Addresses* (1892), pp. 430–431.

Mencken, H. L. (ed.). *The American Mercury,* Vol. XXIV, No. 96 (December 1931), pp. 440–446.

Murphy, Gardner. *Historical Introduction to Modern Psychology.* New York: Harcourt Brace and Company, 1940, pp. 213–214.

New York Teachers' Monographs. November 1890, pp. 1–51.

Partridge, G. E. *Genetic Philosophy of Education.* New York: Sturgis and Walton Company, 1912, Chap. II.

Reisner, Edward H. *The Evolution of the Common School.* New York: The Macmillan Company, 1935, pp. 487–488, 491, 501, 537–538.

Russell, John Dale, and Charles H. Judd. *The American Educational System.* Boston: Houghton Mifflin Company, 1940, pp. 453–456.

Sargent, S. Stansfeld. *Basic Teachings of the Great Psychologists.* New York: Barnes and Noble, Inc., 1944, p. 5.

Wilds, E. H. *The Foundations of Modern Education.* New York: Farrar and Rinehart, 1936, pp. 507–513.

Chapter 9

Casterton, Elizabeth. "Correlation of Music with Other Branches of the School Curriculum," National Education Association *Journal of Proceedings and Addresses* (1905), pp. 637–643.

Coleman, Satis. *Creative Music for Children.* New York: Putnam Company, 1922, pp. 29, 33, 82, 122, 149, 153, 171, 184.

Curti, Merle. *The Growth of American Thought,* 2d ed. New York: Harper & Brothers, 1951, pp. 564–565.

Damrosch, Walter *et al.* The Universal School Music Series *Teachers Book I.* New York: Hinds, Hayden, and Eldredge, Inc., 1923, pp. vii, 2, 43–99.

Dykema, Peter. "The Relation of School and Community Music," Music Teachers National Association *Volume of Proceedings* (1920), pp. 77–88.

Earhart, Will. *The Meaning and Teaching of Music.* New York: Witmark Company, 1935, pp. 91–94, 96–100, 140, 211.

——. "The Project Method," *Music Supervisors Journal* (October 1939), p. 27.

Farnsworth, Charles H. *Education Through Music*. New York: American Book Company, 1909, pp. 7–8, 15, 32, 36–38, 110–111, 147–148, 202–207.

Gehrkens, Karl W. *Music in the Grade Schools*. Boston: C. C. Birchard Company, 1936, pp. 12–17.

——. *An Introduction to School Music Teaching*. Boston: C. C. Birchard and Company, 1919, pp. 5–7, 9–10, 16–17, 19–21; Chaps. IV–VI.

Giddings, Thaddeus P. *Grade School Music Teaching*. New York: Casper Publishing Company, 1919, pp. 18, 56–58, 91–92.

——, Will Earhart, *et al.* The Music Education Series *Music Appreciation in the Schoolroom*. Boston: Ginn and Company, 1926, pp. 42–46.

——. The Music Education Series *Teachers' Book*. Boston: Ginn and Company, 1925, pp. 4–5, 8, 22.

Johnstone, Arthur E., and Harvey W. Loomis. The Lyric Music Series *Third Reader*. Chicago: Scott, Foresman and Company, 1913, p. 3.

MacDowell, Edward. *Critical and Historical Essays*. Boston: Arthur P. Schmidt, 1912.

McConathy, Osbourne. "Teaching Music Theory in the Public Schools," Music Teachers National Association *Volume of Proceedings* (1918), pp. 224–228.

McMurry, Frank M. *Elementary School Standards*. New York: World Book Company, 1914, pp. vii, 156.

Parker, Horatio, *et al.* The Progressive Music Series, *Teachers Manual,* Vol. I. New York: Silver Burdett and Company, 1915, pp. 5–7, 19–20; Vol. II. pp. 4–5; Vol. III. pp. 11–12.

Parry, C. Hubert. *The Evolution of the Art of Music*, 2d ed. New York: D. Appleton and Company, 1930, p. xv.

Putt, W. A. "Correlation of Music with Other Branches of the School Curriculum," National Education Association *Journal of Proceedings and Addresses* (1905), pp. 642–644.

Rugg, Harold. *Culture and Education in America*. New York: Harcourt Brace and Company, 1931, pp. 169, 177.

Shaw, Charles Gray. *Trends of Civilization and Culture*. New York: American Book Company, 1932, pp. 76, 83, 87–89.

Smith, Eleanor. The Eleanor Smith Music Course *Music Primer*. New York: The American Book Company, 1908, 1936, pp. iii–iv.

Chapter 10

Baldwin, Ralph L. "The Aims of Music Courses in Grammar Schools," Music Teachers National Association *Volume of Proceedings* (1907), pp. 96–97.

———. "Report of Committee on Public Schools," Music Teachers National Association *Volume of Proceedings* (1908), pp. 165–174.

Birge, Edward B. *History of Public School Music in the United States*. Boston: Oliver Ditson Company, 1928, pp. 162, 175–176, 179–189, 189–197, 207–208.

———. "The Language Method in Teaching Appreciation." Music Teachers National Association *Volume of Proceedings* (1913), pp. 161–168.

———. "Music Appreciation in Public Schools," Music Teachers National Association *Volume of Proceedings* (1909), pp. 142–144.

———. "Music Appreciation—The Education of the Listener," Music Teachers National Association *Volume of Proceedings* (1922), pp. 189–193.

Clarke, Frances E. "Forces at Work for the Betterment of School Music," National Education Association *Journal of Proceedings and Addresses* (1915), pp. 848–851.

———. "Our National Music," National Education Association *Journal of Proceedings and Addresses* (1908), pp. 836–840.

Cole, Lucy K. "Music and the Social Problem," National Education Association *Journal of Proceedings and Addresses* (1913), pp. 604–609.

Courtis, S. A. *"The Courtis-Standard Research Tests—Recognition of Characteristic Rhythms*. Detroit, Michigan.

———. *Recognition of Mood from Melody*. Detroit, Michigan.

Earhart, Will. "The Evolution of High School Music," Music Teachers National Association *Volume of Proceedings* (1922), pp. 184–188.

———. "A Presentation of the High-School Course Which was Adopted by the Music Supervisors' National Conference: What It Is and How to Administer It," National Education Association *Journal of Proceedings and Addresses* (1912), pp. 1004–1005.

Farnsworth, Charles H. "Why Teach Appreciation?" Music Teachers National Association *Volume of Proceedings* (1917), pp. 88–94.

Fernberger, Samuel W. (ed.). *The Psychological Bulletin*, Vol. XXV, 1928, pp. 284–288, 297.

Flemming, Cecile W., and Marion Flagg. *A Descriptive Bibliography of Prognostic and Achievement Tests in Music*. New York: Bureau of Publications, Teachers College Columbia University, 1936.

Gaw, Esther A. "Five Studies of the Music Tests," *Psychological Monographs*, Vol. XXXIX, No. 2 (1928), pp. 146–148.

Kwalwasser, Jacob. "Scientific Testing in Music," Music Teachers National Association *Volume of Proceedings* (1925), pp. 155–164.

———, and Peter W. Dykema. K-D Music Tests *Manual of Directions*. New York: Carl Fischer Inc., 1930.

———, and G. M. Ruch. *Kwalwasser-Ruch Test of Musical Accomplishment*. Iowa City-Extension Division of the State University of Iowa, 1924.

Lutkin, Peter C. "Musical Appreciation—How Is It to Be Developed?" National Education Association *Journal of Proceedings and Addresses*, pp. 1009–1013.

McConathy, Osbourne. "Harmony Courses in High Schools," National Education Association *Journal of Proceedings and Addresses* (1910), pp. 811–815.

Miller, C. H. "Music in the Grade Schools of the United States," Music Teachers National Association *Volume of Proceedings* (1920), p. 52.

Mosher, Raymond M. *A Study of the Group Method of Measurement of Sight-Singing*. New York: Bureau of Publications, Teachers College Columbia University, 1925, No. 194.

Mursell, James L., and Mabelle Glenn. *The Psychology of School Music Teaching*. New York: Silver Burdett Company, 1931, pp. 324–325.

Ream, M. "The Tapping Test; A Measure of Motility," University of Iowa Studies in Psychology, 1922.

Reisner, Edward H. *The Evolution of the Common School*. New York: The Macmillan Company, 1935, pp. 503–504.

Rhetts, Edith M. "The Development of Music Appreciation in America," Music Teachers National Association *Volume of Proceedings* (1921), pp. 112–120.

Russell, John Dale, and Charles H. Judd. *The American Educational System*. New York: Houghton Mifflin Company, 1940, pp. 457–459.

Scott, Walter. "The Movement for the Advancement of Music in Secondary Education," Music Teachers National Association *Volume of Proceedings* (1907), pp. 69–77.

———. "Some Questions Involved in Making Music a Major Study," National Education Association *Journal of Proceedings and Addresses* (1905), pp. 633–637.

Seashore, C. E., Manual of Instructions and Interpretations for the Measures of Musical Talent. New York: Columbia Phonograph Company.

Thwing, Charles F. "The Progress of Education for the Year," National Education Association *Journal of Proceedings and Addresses* (1908), pp. 326–333.

Chapter 11

Bode, Boyd H. *Conflicting Psychologies of Learning.* New York: D. C. Heath and Company, 1929, pp. 180–190.

Butts, R. Freeman. *A Cultural History of Education.* New York: McGraw-Hill Book Company, Inc., 1947, pp. 644–645.

Cole, Lawrence E., and William F. Bruce. *Educational Psychology.* New York: The World Book Company, 1950, pp. 466–479.

Croly, Herbert. *Progressive Democracy.* New York: The Macmillan Company, 1914, pp. 406–409.

Curti, Merle. *The Growth of American Thought*, 2d ed. New York: Harper & Brothers, 1951, pp. 686–709, 717–730, 736–740.

Dewey, John. *Art As Experience.* New York: Minton, Balch and Company, 1934, pp. 3–11, 115, 127, 326–341.

———. *Democracy and Education.* New York: The Macmillan Company, 1916, pp. 1–4, 12–17, 95, 100–102, 115, 176, 179–181, 187–188, 225, 391–395, 400, 414–417; Chaps. IV, IX, X.

———, *et al. Art and Education*, 2d ed. Merion, Pa.: Barnes Foundation, 1947, p. 8.

Gabriel, Ralph H. *The Course of American Democratic Thought.* New York: The Ronald Press Company, 1940, p. 416.

Murphy, Gardner. *Historical Introduction to Modern Psychology*, rev. ed. New York: Harcourt, Brace, and Company, 1949, pp. 209–293, 402–417.

Progressive Education Yearbook, "Progressive Education: Its Philosophy and Challenge," Special Supplement (May 1941), pp. 3, 5.

Rusk, Robert R. *The Philosophical Basis of Education.* London: University of London Press, Ltd., 1928, pp. 54–56.

Chapter 12

Beattie, John W. "Theory and Practice," *Yearbook of the Music Educators National Conference* (1938), p. 66.

Curtis, Louis W. "The Conference and the New Education," *Music Supervisors Journal* (March 1934), p. 17.

Gehrkens, Karl W. "Correlation: Its Philosophy and Practice," *Music Supervisors Journal* (February 1934), pp. 16–17.

Jones, Archie. "The Changing Status of the Music Supervisor," *Music Educators Journal* (February 1936), pp. 18–19.

Kidd, Elizabeth Ayres. "A Practical Program of Integration," Yearbook of the Music Educators National Conference (1937), pp. 141–142.

McConathy, Osbourne. "Music and the Integrated Program," Yearbook of the Music Educators National Conference (1937), p. 129.

Miessner, Otto. "Music As Integrated Experience," *Yearbook of the Music Educators National Conference* (1937), p. 118.

Morgan, Russell V. "Modern Trends in School Music," *Yearbook of the Music Educators National Conference* (1937), p. 45.

Mursell, James L. *Education for Musical Growth.* Boston: Ginn and Company, 1948, Chaps. II, III; pp. v, 3–7, 19–20, 50, 125–127, 152, 155, 167, 176, 178, 180, 192–197, 200–201, 211–212, 215–217, 220–223, 225–240, 244–246.

―――. *Music in American Schools.* Morristown, N.J.: Silver Burdett Company, 1943, pp. 16–22, 29–35, 37–38, 41–42, 56, 132–137, 139–142.

―――. *Psychology for Modern Education.* New York: W. W. Norton and Company, Inc., 1952, Chap. II.

―――. *New Music Horizons*, Teachers' Manual for Primary Grades. Morristown, N.J.: Silver Burdett Company, 1948, Introduction; pp. 2, 9, 12–13, 34, 40, 43, 55, 67.

――― et al. *Music for Living*, Book IV. Morristown, N.J.: Silver Burdett Company, 1956, p. vii.

―――, and Mabelle Glenn. *The Psychology of School Music Teaching.* Morristown, N.J.: Silver Burdett Company, 1938, pp. 13–21, 42–69, 73–75, 86–91.

————. *et al. New Music Horizons*, Teachers' Manual for Intermediate Grades. Morristown, N.J.: Silver Burdett Company, 1948, Introduction; pp. 1–15, 33.

Pierce, Anne. "A Challenge to Commonly Accepted Practices in Elementary Music Education," Yearbook of the Music Educators National Conference (1937), p. 150.

————. "Music in the Modern School," *Music Educators Journal* (May 1940), pp. 13, 65.

Pitts, Lilla Belle, *et al. Our Singing World*, enlarged ed. Manual for *Singing Every Day*, p. v. Manual for *Singing Juniors* and *Singing Teen-Agers*. Boston: Ginn and Company, 1961, pp. 5, 12.

Sur, William, *et al. This Is Music*. Boston: Allyn and Bacon, Inc., 1961.

Wolfe, Irving, *et al. The Together-We-Sing* Music Series. Chicago: Follett Publishing Company, 1961.

Chapter 13

American Association of School Administrators. "Music in the Curriculum," *Curriculum Handbook For School Administrators*. Reprinted by Music Educators National Conference, Washington, D.C., 1967, p. 195.

Behrend, Louise. *Rosin in the Left Hand*. New York: Music School of the Henry Street Settlement, 1967. (Mimeographed.)

Berg, Richard C., *et al. Music For Young Americans*, 2d ed. New York: American Book Company, 1966.

Bergethon, Bjornar, and Eunice Boardman. *Musical Growth in the Elementary School*. New York: Holt, Rinehart and Winston, Inc., 1963, pp. 2–6, 7–8, 10–12, 49.

Bloom, Benjamin (ed.). *Taxonomy of Educational Objectives*. New York: David McKay Company, Inc., 1966, p. 7.

Boardman, Eunice and Beth Landis. *Exploring Music Book IV, Teacher's Edition*. New York: Holt, Rinehart and Winston, Inc., 1966, p. iii.

Bruner, Jerome S. "The Course of Cognitive Growth," *American Psychologist*, Vol. 19 (January 1964), pp. 1–15.

————. *The Process of Education*. New York: (Vintage Books) Alfred A. Knopf, Inc., and Random House, Inc., 1963, pp. vii–x, 1–7, 17, 31–33, 35–56.

————, *et al. Studies in Cognitive Growth*. New York: John Wiley and Sons, Inc., 1966, pp. 1–67.

Burakoff, Gerald, and Lawrence Wheeler. *Music Making in the Elementary School.* New York: Hargail Music Press, 1968.

Choate, Robert. "The Symposium—An Introduction," *Music Educators Journal,* Vol. 54, No. 3 (November 1967), p. 50.

Darazs, Arpad, and Stephen Jay. *Sight and Sound.* Oceanside, N.Y.: Boosey and Hawkes, Inc., 1965.

Dewey, John. *Democracy and Education* New York: The Macmillan Company, 1926, p. 3.

Eösze, Lászlo. *Zoltán Kodály, His Life and Work.* London: Collet's Holdings Ltd., 1962 (published in cooperation with Corvina Press, Budapest), pp. 80–81.

Ford, G. W., and Lawrence Pugno (eds.). *The Structure of Knowledge and the Curriculum.* Chicago: Rand McNally & Company, 1964, pp. 2–3, 12–14, 25–28, 46–48.

Fowler, Charles. "Music Education: Joining the Mainstream," *Music Educators Journal,* Vol. 54, No. 3 (November 1967), pp. 68–70.

Gagné, Robert M. *The Conditions of Learning.* New York: Holt, Rinehart and Winston, Inc., 1965, pp. 25, 139–146, 151, 202, 247.

Gary, Charles L. (ed.). *The Study of Music in the Elementary School— A Conceptual Approach.* Washington, D.C.: Music Educators National Conference, 1967, pp. vii, 2–5, 221–222.

Hall, Doreen. *Music for Children, Teacher's Manual.* Mainz: B. Schott's Söhne, 1960, pp. 6–26.

Holman, H. *Pestalozzi.* London: Longmans Green and Company, 1908, p. 144

Kaplan, Max. *Foundations and Frontiers of Music Education.* New York: Holt, Rinehart and Winston, Inc., 1966, pp. 20, 23, 26.

Keller, Charles R. "The Educational Revolution and Music," *Music Educators Journal,* Vol. 51, No. 5 (April-May 1965), pp. 35–37, 146–148.

Kendall, John D. *Talent Education—The Violin Teaching Methods of Mr. Shinichi Suzuki.* Southern Illinois University, Edwardsville Campus, 1964. (Mimeographed.)

Leonhard, Charles, *et al. Discovering Music Together.* Chicago: Follett Publishing Company, 1967.

Mason, Lowell, and George Webb. *The Primary School Song Book.* New York: Mason Brothers, 1846.

Mason, Luther W. "Time-Names," *The School Music Journal*, Vol. I (June 1886), p. 164.

McMichael, Shirlene. "Talent Education in Pendleton, Oregon," *Orchestra News*, Vol. VII, No. 1, p. 4.

McMurray, Foster. "Pragmatism in Music Education," *Basic Concepts in Music Education*, The Fifty-Seventh Yearbook of the National Society for the Study of Education, edited by Nelson B. Henry. Chicago: The University of Chicago Press, 1958, pp. 41, 47–56.

Ministry of Education. *Curriculum of Singing and Music Tuition with Instructions for Primary Schools with a Special Music Programme.* Budapest: Public Education Department, 1966.

Mueller, John H. "Music and Education: A Sociological Approach," *Basic Concepts in Music Education*, The Fifty-Seventh Yearbook of the National Society for the Study of Education, edited by Nelson B. Henry. Chicago: The University of Chicago Press, 1958, pp. 102–103.

Murray, Margaret (trans.). *Orff-Schulwerk, Music for Children.* London: Schott & Company Ltd., 1958–1966. Five vols.

Mursell, James L. "Growth Processes in Music Education," *Basic Concepts in Music Education*, The Fifty-Seventh Yearbook of the National Society for the Study of Education, edited by Nelson B. Henry. Chicago: The University of Chicago Press, 1958, pp. 157–158.

————. *Music Education: Principles and Programs.* Morristown, N.J.: Silver Burdett Co., 1956, pp. 65–66, 186–194.

————. *Successful Teaching—Its Psychological Principles.* New York: McGraw-Hill Book Co., Inc., 1954, pp. 71–75, 111–117, 125, 211–213, 218–219.

Nash, Grace. *Music with Children.* Scottsdale, Arizona: Swarthout Enterprises, 1965, p. 1.

Palisca, Claude V. *Music in Our Schools: A Search for Improvement* (Report of the Yale Seminar on Music Education) U.S. Department of Health, Education and Welfare, Office of Education, Washington, D.C.: Bulletin 1964, No. 28, OE-33033, pp. iii, 1–17.

Reimer, Bennett. "The Development of Aesthetic Sensitivity," *Music Educators Journal*, Vol. 51, No. 3 (January 1965), pp. 33–36.

Ritter, Sol. "Observations from ASTA-SUZUKI Tour," *Orchestra News*, Vol. VII, No. 1 (December 1967), p. 3.

Richards, Mary Helen. *Threshold to Music Series.* San Francisco: Fearon Publishers, Inc., 1964.

Sandor, Frigyes (ed.). *Musical Education in Hungary*. London: Barrie and Rockliff, 1966, pp. 22, 26–30, 69, 135.

Schwadron, Abraham A. "Aesthetic Values and Music Education," *Perspectives in Music Education, Source Book III*, edited by Bonnie C. Kowal. Washington, D.C.: Music Educators National Conference, 1966, pp. 185–194.

Seward, Theodore. "Teaching and Teaching Reforms—Music in Public Schools," Music Teachers National Association *Volume of Proceedings* (1889), p. 125.

Sur, William, *et al. This is Music*. Boston: Allyn and Bacon, Inc., 1967.

The Tanglewood Symposium—Music in American Society. "Problems and Responsibilities," *Music Educators Journal*. Vol. 54, No. 3 (November 1967), pp. 77–78.

Tufts, John W., and H. E. Holt, *Manual for the Use of Teachers: To Accompany the Readers and Charts of the Normal Music Course*. New York: D. Appleton & Company, 1884.

Watters, Lorrain E., *et al. The Magic of Music*. Boston: Ginn and Company, 1965.

Wilson, Harry R., *et al. Growing with Music*. Englewood Cliffs, N.J.: Prentice-Hall, Inc., 1966.

Woodruff, Asahel D. "Concept Teaching," *Perspectives in Music Education, Source Book III*, edited by Bonnie C. Kowal. Washington, D.C.: Music Educators National Conference, 1966, pp. 219–222.

Youngberg, Harold C., *et al. Making Music Your Own*. Morristown, N.J.: Silver Burdett Company, 1968.

Chapter 14

The American Music Conference. *Report on Amateur Instrumental Music in the United States*. Chicago: The American Music Conference, 1966, p. 5.

Aronoff, Frances W. *Music and Young Children*. New York: Holt, Rinehart and Winston, Inc., 1969, pp. 11–20.

Bloom, Benjamin S. *Stability and Change in Human Characteristics*. New York: John Wiley and Sons, Inc., 1964, pp. 88, 110.

———— (ed.). *Taxonomy of Educational Objectives, Handbook I*. New York: David McKay Company, Inc., 1956, p. 7.

Bruner, Jerome S. "The Course of Cognitive Growth," *American Psychologist*, Vol. 19 (January 1964), pp. 1–15.

————, et al. *Studies in Cognitive Growth.* New York: John Wiley and Sons, Inc., 1966, pp. vi–xv, 1–67, 319–326.

Carabo-Cone, M. "Notes for Disadvantaged Pre-School Children," Reprinted from *Music Journal* 1969 Anthology.

Cohen, Morris, "The Conception of Philosophy in Recent Discussion," *The Journal of Philosophy and Scientific Method*, Vol. VII (July 21, 1910), pp. 401–410.

Conant, James B. *The American High School Today: A First Report to Interested Citizens.* New York: McGraw-Hill Book Company, Inc., 1959, p. 48.

Dello Joio, Norman. "Contemporary Music Project for Creativity in Music Education," *Music Educators Journal*, Vol. 54, No. 7 (March 1968), pp. 41–72.

Dennis, Lawrence E., and Renate M. Jacob (eds.). *The Arts in Higher Education.* San Francisco: Jossey-Bass Inc., 1968, pp. 1–19.

Egbert, Marion S. "Progress in School Music Programs," *Creative Approaches to School Music.* Sponsored and published by American Music Conference. Chicago, January 1967, pp. 31–32.

————. "They're Making Music in School," *Today's Health For the American Family*, published by the American Medical Association and reprinted, January 1963, by the American Music Conference with permission by the American Medical Association.

Gideonse, Harry D. *Against the Running Tide.* New York: Twayne Publishers, Inc., 1967, pp. 32–37, 41.

Goodlad, John I. *School Curriculum Reform in the United States.* New York: The Fund for the Advancement of Education, 1964, pp. 56–59, 77–78.

Gould, Samuel B. "The Arts in Higher Education: Valid or Valueless," *The Arts and Education.* New York: New York State Council on the Arts, 1968.

Hartshorn, William C. *The Study of Music as an Academic Discipline.* Washington, D.C.: Music Educators National Conference, 1963, pp. 23–30.

————, et al. *Music for the Academically Talented Student in the Secondary School.* Washington, D.C.: National Education Association, 1960, pp. 87, 102–104, 107.

Kaplan, Max. *Foundations and Frontiers of Music Education.* New York: Holt, Rinehart and Winston, Inc., 1966, pp. 20, 23.

Kowall, Bonnie C. (ed.). "Music in the Public Schools," Digest of NEA Monograph, *Perspectives in Music Education, Source Book III.* Washington, D.C.: Music Educators National Conference, 1966, pp. 204–205.

"Music and Art in the Public Schools," *Research Monograph 1963–M3.* Washington, D.C.: Research Division, National Education Association, August, 1963.

Joint Statement by the Music Educators National Conference and the American Association of School Administrators. "Music in the School Curriculum," *Music Educators Journal,* Vol. 52, No. 2 (November–December 1965), pp. 37–39, 191–194, 196–197, 200.

Palisca, Claude V. *Music in Our Schools: A Search for Improvement.* (Report of the Yale Seminar on Music Education), U.S. Department of Health, Education and Welfare, Office of Education, Washington, D.C.: Bulletin 1964, No. 28, OE-33033, pp. 26–30.

Reimer, Bennett. "The Curriculum Reform Explosion and the Problem of Secondary General Music," *Music Educators Journal,* Vol. 52, No. 3 (January 1966), pp. 38–41, 117–121.

Rodean, Richard W. "Comparative Music Survey: An Integration of the Arts," *Music Educators Journal,* Vol. 51, No. 3 (January 1965), pp. 55–56.

Sand, Ole. "Schools for the Seventies," *Music Educators Journal,* Vol. 52, No. 6 (June–July 1966), pp. 40–42, 122–128.

Report on the Tanglewood Symposium, *Music Educators Journal,* Vol. 54, No. 3 (November 1967), pp. 75–76.

Taylor, Harold. "Music as a Source of Knowledge," *Music Educators Journal,* Vol. 51, No. 1 (September–October 1964), pp. 35–38, 151–154.

———. "The Spirit of Humanism," *Music Educators Journal,* Vol. 53, No. 1 (September 1966), pp. 51–53, 107–110.

The University of the State of New York. Albany: The State Education Department. *The Cue Do It Yourself Guide,* 1963, pp. 13, 609.

The University of the State of New York. *Re-encounter with the Performing Arts.* Albany: The State Education Department, Division of the Humanities and the Arts, 1968, pp. 4–5.

Wann, Kenneth, *et al. Fostering Intellectual Development in Young Children.* New York: Bureau of Publications, Teachers College, Columbia University, 1962, p. 10.

Wilhelms, Fred T. "The Humanities at the Crossroads," *Music Educators Journal*, Vol. 3, No. 4 (December 1966), pp. 27–29.

Wilson, John S. *Fun With Music*. New York: Birk and Co., Inc., 1965.

Woodworth, G. Wallace. "The Place of Music in the Curriculum," *Music Educators Journal*, Vol. 52, No. 4 (February–March 1966), pp. 48–50.

Youth Music—A Special Report. *Music Educators Journal*, Vol. 56, No. 3 (November 1969), pp. 43–74.

Index

Index

Folios in italics indicate illustrations.

339